THE HAITIAN VODOU HANDBOOK

"Refreshingly original, well-documented, and just plain fun. Kenaz brings just the right combination of insider insights and skeptical observations to this must-read for anyone fascinated by the world of Afro-diasporan religious movements. Highly recommended."

ANNE NEWKIRK NIVEN,
EDITOR IN CHIEF
SAGEWOMAN, PANGAIA, NEWWITCH

"Filan's clear and sensible approach shares the rudiments of Vodou and gives us a fascinating introduction to the history and culture of Haiti. This book will be important to all who feel that religious practice makes a practical difference in our lives."

JUDY HARROW,
AUTHOR OF
DEVOTED TO YOU: HONORING DEITY

THE HAITIAN VODOU HANDBOOK

PROTOCOLS FOR RIDING WITH THE LWA

Kenaz Filan
(Houngan Coquille du Mer)

Destiny Books
Rochester, Vermont

Destiny Books
One Park Street
Rochester, Vermont 05767
www.DestinyBooks.com

Destiny Books is a division of Inner Traditions International

Library of Congress Cataloging-in-Publication Data
Filan, Kenaz.
The Haitian vodou handbook : protocols for riding with the Lwa / Kenaz Filan.
p. cm.
Includes bibliographical references and index.
ISBN-13: 978-1-59477-125-5 (pbk.)
ISBN-10: 1-59477-125-1 (pbk.)
1. Voodooism—Haiti. 2. Haiti—Religion. I. Title.
BL2530.H3F55 2007
299.6'75097294—dc22

2006028676

Printed and bound in the United States by Lake Book Manufacturing

10 9 8 7 6 5 4 3

Text design and layout by Rachel Goldenberg
This book was typeset in Sabon, with Neuland and Agenda as display typefaces

To send correspondence to the author of this book, mail a first-class letter to the author c/o Inner Traditions • Bear & Company, One Park Street, Rochester, VT 05767, and we will forward the communication.

CONTENTS

ACKNOWLEDGMENTS

No person is an island; no tree can grow without roots. Many people have helped me in my studies of the lwa. Thanks are due to Edeline St.-Amand (Mambo Azan Taye) and Hugue Pierre (Houngan Si Gan Temps), my initiatory mother and father. Kathleen Latzoni, my partner, has provided invaluable editorial assistance, organizational advice, and moral support. Anne Newkirk Niven, Dagonet Dewr, and Elizabeth Barrette, the editorial masterminds behind *PanGaia* and *newWitch* magazines, deserve thanks for believing in me and for running earlier versions of some of the material that appears in this book. Thanks are also due to Shannon McRae and Clifford Low for their assistance in proofreading an earlier draft of this manuscript, and to Reverend Samantha Kaye and the readers of her "Spellmaker" mailing list for their feedback and support.

PREFACE

Until recently, Vodou was more often found in pulp fiction and B-movies than in Pagan gatherings. Many Pagans bought into the stereotype and identified Vodou with devil worship, dark curses, and drumbeat-driven orgies performed at midnight. They never stopped to think that many of these charges had been leveled against medieval and Renaissance "witches"—and, earlier, against Jews and Christians. Some Pagans saw the saint images and the Catholic influences and wrote Vodou off as a "Christian aberration"; others were appalled by the animal sacrifices and by the fact that *houngans* and *mambos* (priests and priestesses) charged money for their services. Those who didn't run screaming were likely to follow the lead of Haiti's Catholic clergy and dismiss Vodou as "superstition and folly."

Others sought Vodou because they believed it was "evil." Most were disappointed at their efforts to gain Fame, Fortune, and Endless Sex Partners and wound up trading in their "voodoo fetishes" for speed-metal CDs and Hammer films. A few managed to get the attention of the *lwa,* the spirits served in Haitian Vodou. Alas, said spirits generally were none too pleased at being treated like attack dogs or genies in a bottle, and they sometimes responded by applying the Cosmic Boot to Yon Errant Backside. This only served to cement Vodou's reputation as "dangerous" . . . and to attract still more "Dark Mages" seeking a Vodou that never existed save in the fevered imaginations of yellow journalists and movie producers.

Today, we have come to understand that many of those earlier attitudes about Vodou were rooted in racism and ignorance. We've begun to appreciate the complexity, depth, and beauty of African and African diaspora spirituality, and many Pagans have heard and responded to the call of the lwa. It is no longer uncommon to see Ezili Freda, the beautiful lwa of love and luxury, honored alongside Aphrodite in Pagan ceremonies. Some even start their ceremonies with a small offering to Papa Legba—the lwa of the gateway who facilitates communication with the spirit world—asking him to "open the door" for them. Most of these people are coming to the African and Afro-Caribbean spirits with open hearts, and they are showing the lwa the love and respect they deserve. In return, they have found that the lwa have blessed them and enriched their practices and their lives.

Unfortunately, Pagans who have sought to serve the lwa on their own have been forced to deal with a scarcity of resources. Most of the literature on Haitian Vodou has been written by anthropologists and scholars, not by *Vodouisants* (practitioners of Vodou). Some of these books are excellent resources for cataloging the major lwa and listing some of the ways they are served in Haiti, but they don't have much information on how an individual can honor the lwa. Other books promise to teach you the "ancient secrets of Voodoo power." They won't show you how to serve the spirits or tell you anything about Haiti, but they will teach you everything you (n)ever wanted to know about sticking pins in dolls, burning candles to destroy your enemies, and finding your lucky lottery numbers.

Today, many practitioners of Vodou have "come aboveground." Houngans and mambos have Web sites and mailing lists, hold public ceremonies, and offer as much information as they can without violating their initiatory oaths. Unfortunately, many of these houngans and mambos speak disparagingly of "Wicca-Doo" and believe that one can only serve the lwa in the "time-honored traditional way"—meaning, of course, their way. Others will happily take you into the *djevo* (the initiatory chamber) and teach you their secrets for "one low fee," airfare and lodging not included. A person who is an interested outsider this week can be *asogwe* (the highest rank in Haitian Vodou) by Sunday, if the check clears. We don't assume that everyone who does a few Yogic stretches is called to join an ashram. We don't believe that everyone who attends Mass should take Holy Orders and join a monastery. And yet many seem to think that the priesthood should be an introduction to Vodou, and not the culmination of years of involvement with the tradition; or they believe that everyone who serves the lwa must do so in a priestly capacity.

There is a Vodou priesthood, but there are also many believers and practitioners who have never been initiated but who are dedicated servants of the lwa. Some of these believers have powerful lwa who assist them in performing *wanga* (magic) and are well regarded as healers and magicians. Although many choose to honor the lwa at *fets* (public parties), there are also many who serve their spirits in the privacy of their homes. They seek counsel from the lwa, make offerings to them, and prepare shrines on their behalf without the guidance or aid of priests or initiates. If you choose to honor the lwa as a solitary practitioner, you are following in the footsteps of many Haitians.

Vodou has always incorporated material from other sources. When the slaves were brought to St. Domingue (the old French name for Haiti), they were forced to re-create their ancestral religious practices from scratch. Many of the materials they used to honor the spirits in Africa were not available in St. Domingue; often they had no access to the priests and priestesses who had led the ceremonies in their homeland. They made do with what was available and served the spirits of the native Carib and Arawak peoples alongside Catholic saints and ancestral lwa. Today, Vodouisants have incorporated some of the symbolism and practices of Freemasonry into Haitian Vodou. They have been influenced by Martinism (a French Catholic mystical/magical tradition that originated in eighteenth-century Port-au-Prince) and by the writings of the ceremonial magician Eliphas Levi. There is no reason why you cannot incorporate your own spiritual practices into your service of the lwa.

Indeed, Vodou has always demanded direct and personal involvement. Every Vodouisant puts his or her unique spin on *sevis lwa* (service to the lwa). Frank Sinatra, Elvis Presley, and Sid Vicious each sang "My

Way," and each added his own personal touch to the song so that no one would mistake one version for the other. Vodou isn't a religion where you sit back and listen to someone else talk about divinity. It's a faith where divinity comes down and talks to you. The lwa are quite happy to make their needs and their wants known to you, and to offer counsel and protection in exchange. You may not be honoring them the way they are honored in Haiti, but so long as you are honoring them, they will notice and will show their appreciation.

Vodou is a religion where the sacred and the secular are intertwined. Many Western traditions draw a distinction between the sacred and the profane. People go to church to commune with the divine, and then they go about their daily business without thinking much about God. This is not so in Vodou. The lwa and the saints are a tangible presence in every Vodouisant's life. They are present in wind and storm, river and ocean, marketplace and brothel . . . and, once you get to know them, you will find them present in your daily life as well.

Which Brings Us to This Book

This book is intended to teach you a bit about how the lwa are served in Haitian Vodou. It incorporates much of the knowledge I have gained as a houngan in Société la Belle Venus #2, a *peristyle* (Vodou temple) located in Canarsie, Brooklyn, New York. In this book, I discuss Haitian Vodou and Haitian culture, and the ways they interact. I have also provided a list of things that are commonly offered to the various lwa, and I've offered some suggestions as to how you can honor and serve the lwa as a solitary practitioner. I have not included any "blinds" or deliberate misinformation. Where I could, I have provided accurate information. When my initiatory vows required my silence, I have said as much; and, where possible, I have provided some alternative techniques that can substitute for the oathbound secrets.

I have written this book for interested newcomers who have not previously studied Vodou. With this book, you can begin your journey toward Gineh (ancestral Africa). Those who are further along on that path may also find useful material herein; and those who have already been through the djevo may find it interesting to compare my house's teachings to theirs. I also have provided a list of resources for further study. This book is a beginning, not an end. The road to Gineh is a long and winding one.

Wicca, the religious system revealed—or created—by Gerald Gardner, has become the model for much modern Neopaganism. Although I am not an initiate of any Wiccan lineage, I am familiar with much of the literature and my own practices have been influenced by the work of Gerald Gardner, Alex Saunders, Scott Cunningham, and other Wiccan and Neopagan authors. Like Cunningham in his excellent book *Wicca: A Guide for the Solitary Practitioner,* I hope to introduce some of the basic ideas of my faith to those who are not initiates. Many of the substitute practices I have described where my oaths have commanded my silence have come from modern witchcraft.

I have not tried to teach all the specific ways an initiate of Haitian Vodou would serve the lwa. (My oaths—and my publisher's desire to keep this book smaller than the Manhattan yellow pages—would make that impossible.) What I would like to do is show something of the mindset of an average Vodouisant. To that end, I've given a brief synopsis of Haitian history and contemporary Haitian society. It is impossible to understand Vodou without understanding the Haitian people who have shaped, and who have been shaped by, Vodou. Appreciating their struggles, failures, and triumphs can help to keep us from being "culture vultures" who appropriate the symbols of various systems without respect for their originators or understanding their original meaning.

Vodou's ethical precepts differ from our own. There are no proscriptions in Vodou against using wanga to gain a lover or to better your health or your financial well-being, or even to destroy an enemy. Accordingly, I have included some spells you can use to improve your finances or your love life. I have not included any "super Vodou death curses," but I have provided a number of defensive measures you can use to stop someone from injuring you. Vodou is a practical tradition: people who petition the saints and the lwa are typically asking not for "peace of mind" or "spiritual enlightenment" but for real-world, real-time assistance. (We should remember Abraham Maslow's "hierarchy of needs." People who are worried about where their next meal is coming from—that is, most Vodouisants in Haiti—are going to be far more concerned with material things than those who are assured of three meals a day—that is, me, and most of the people reading this book.)

These spells are not intended to be a substitute for legal or medical advice; nor will they cause your desire to materialize in your lap as you sit watching TV. Wanga to get a new job will only work if you read the want ads, send out resumes, and put in the other required legwork. You can sit at home all day casting spells to make yourself more attractive, but if you never make an effort to meet that certain somebody, it will all be for naught. Vodou demands your personal attention and efforts. It's an active faith, not a passive one. As you do for the lwa—and for yourself—so they will do for you.

Although I have included spells, I have focused more on the culture and religion of Vodou. If you are just looking for spirits who will jump through hoops at your command, this is not the book for you. Vodouisants practice magic, yes; but in the end, Vodou is a religion, a way of dealing with the divine and of finding meaning in our lives. If you treat the lwa with respect, reverence, and love, you will find that the magic follows soon enough. There is real power in this tradition—but in our quest for power, we should not ignore its beauty or its wisdom.

If you wish to incorporate service of the lwa into your present spiritual practices, this book may be all that you need. If you wish to study Vodou more seriously, or to become a priest or priestess of the lwa, you will need to study with a *société,* and, ultimately, you may need to pass the djevo and become an initiate. Haitian Vodou is a hands-on tradition. No book can make you a houngan or mambo, just as no book could make you a concert pianist or champion gymnast. I have provided some suggestions in the conclusion as to where you might meet other Vodouisants and how you might find a teacher. Let the lwa guide you where they want you to be, and you will get there when you are ready.

The gateway is open. Papa Legba stands at the entrance, smiling as he leans on his cane. In the distance, Papa Ogou wields his machete as the Ghede trade dirty jokes with one another. You are about to meet the lwa and they are about to meet you. May your journey be as interesting, and as blessed, as mine has been—and may God, the ancestors, and the lwa lead us both to Gineh.

Part One

WHERE ARE WE GOING, WHERE HAVE WE BEEN?

Before you begin any journey, it's best to be prepared. Much as you would make sure you had all the appropriate tickets, visas, and inoculations before you traveled to a far-off land, you should prepare yourself for a journey into Vodou. Knowing what to expect, and what to avoid, can help make your trip much more pleasant. Thus, I have begun with a few cautionary words—travel advisories, if you will.

When visiting a new destination, it often helps to know a bit about its history. To that end, I've also provided a brief analysis of the interplay between Haitian Vodou and Haitian history. By understanding the forces that shaped Vodou, we can better understand the faith as it is practiced today.

1

SOME WORDS OF CAUTION: THE DANGERS OF HAITIAN VODOU

With the increased interest in Haitian spirituality has come increased concern over those who would incorporate elements of Vodou into their own practices. Critics have raised a number of questions, ranging from "isn't that dangerous?" to "what gives you the right to co-opt the spirituality of oppressed people?" As you continue serving the lwa, you are likely to be confronted with some of these questions, if you haven't heard them, or thought about them, already.

We might be tempted to dismiss these challenges out of hand, but we may be wise to give them careful consideration. Some critics may be misguided, and others may have ulterior motives—but others have raised valid questions that deserve honest replies. In answering these queries, we can help to deepen our own understanding of Vodou, and avoid stumbling into some ugly pitfalls.

The "Dangers" of Vodou

Some will caution you at great length about the dangers of Vodou. They will tell you that the lwa are jealous, thin-skinned, and hot-tempered. Only those with years of training can serve them properly, they claim—

and if you miss one minute detail, you run the risk of being ruined body and soul. Others will tell you there is no danger at all in serving the lwa; the spirits love their children and would never do anything to hurt them.

The truth, as is often the case, lies somewhere in the middle. Many of the horror stories are based on the old chestnuts about "blood-soaked devil worship" and "drum-driven Negro orgies." Dire warnings about human sacrifice owe more to the *Late Night Creature Feature* than to anything taking place in Haiti or the Haitian diaspora. Still, not all the horror stories are apocryphal. When they are offended, the lwa can wreak a frightening vengeance. If you are used to more sedate spiritual paths, you may be a bit intimidated by how forceful and direct the lwa can be. After seeing your first possession, you may be scared silly.

I will not tell you that the lwa are incapable of doing you harm, but I will tell you that you can avoid most lwa troubles with a little common sense, a dollop of understanding, and a healthy dose of caution. Every day people are injured in electrical accidents. We can say "electricity is bad"—or we can teach people how to use electricity safely and responsibly, while acknowledging that stupidity and carelessness can be hazardous and even fatal. If you take the same approach to serving the lwa, you'll have no problems.

You must realize that the lwa come from a hierarchical society, where respect for the elders is expected and disrespect is seen as a major offense. If you try treating the lwa like trained animals jumping through hoops—ordering them around when you want something, then ignoring them until the next time you're in need—they will (rightly) get annoyed. If, on the other hand, you treat them with as much consideration as you would show for a parent or a dear friend, you'll do just fine. You don't have to approach them with trembling fear—but you must approach them with reverence and respect.

There are taboos and "thou shalt nots" that you must observe when serving the lwa. I list some of these in part 3, and I strongly encourage you to take them seriously. If you take something you previously gave to Zaka, or if you place Freda's things next to your Ghede shrine, you will likely regret it. These taboos are serious—but they are not particularly rigorous or difficult to understand. If you can remember "look both ways before crossing a street," you should be able to remember "make sure you are clean before giving an offering to Damballah."

Some lwa are "hotter" than others—that is to say, more forceful and more inclined toward violence. They should not be approached without guidance from a skilled teacher. The lwa I have included in this book are among the most frequently served, and they can be approached by a respectful beginner. I have not included instructions on how to serve or contact others who may not be so forgiving of honest mistakes. There is no reason for a solitary practitioner to call upon the services of Jan Zombi, Bawon Kriminel, Linglessou Basin-Sang (aka Linglessou Bucket-of-Blood), Bakalou Baka, or other fierce lwa. These spirits serve an important role in the Vodou pantheon, and they are widely served in Haiti; but those who serve them are skilled practitioners who grew up in a Vodou culture. Until you have some training and experience under your belt, you should confine your attention to cooler lwa.

To further complicate matters, there are also trickster spirits—malevolent entities that will masquerade as lwa, ancestors, or other beings, and then wreak havoc once you let them into your lives. Houngans and mambos aren't just wasting time when they spend hours cleansing their workspace or purifying a room before a fet lwa. If you want to contact the lwa, you should make sure to purify and cleanse yourself and your space first. Doing so will greatly reduce the chance of a trickster spirit bothering you. I have included a few suggested methods for cleansing and purification in chapter 4. Taking a little time beforehand to banish negativity will save you the trouble of extensive cleansings later on.

In Vodou, bad luck is often seen as a sign that the lwa are displeased with you—or, more precisely, with what you are doing. Vodouisants believe that if the lwa are pleased with your actions, they will reward you with health, financial success, and all-around good luck. If you are having a lot of problems, it could be that the lwa want something from you. You may need to have a *maryaj lwa* (marriage ceremony uniting a Vodouisant and one or more lwa) or a *lave tet* (head-washing ceremony), you may need to *kanzo* (become an initiate), or you may just need to give some attention to a lwa or a forgotten ancestor you've been neglecting. But the problems don't arise because you are involved with the lwa. They start because you are not.

In the Western world, we tend to think of religion as a choice. On the contrary, among many Vodouisants, there is a belief that the lwa choose you. This may seem like coercion to someone who is coming to Vodou from another paradigm, but Vodouisants see it as an inevitable law of nature. Eating the wrong foods or avoiding exercise is bad for your health; forgetting to balance your checkbook can cause financial problems; saving money by skipping a tune-up and an oil change can cost you much more later on when your car breaks down. As with the material world, there are things you must do in the spiritual realm. Neglecting your spiritual needs can be just as bad as avoiding material responsibilities.

You should also remember that our ideas of free will are comparatively modern and come from a culture that has far more social mobility than Haiti. Poor Americans definitely face many disadvantages, but they still have far more opportunity for advancement than poor Haitians, who have limited if any access to education and vocational training. When you have been raised in a country where the rich stay rich, the poor stay poor, and those who question the status quo frequently end up dead, the idea of free will may not seem all that convincing.

"Of course he's not safe," C. S. Lewis said of the great lion Aslan, "but he's good."[1] The same could be said of the lwa. If you are careless or flippant, you will find yourself called on the carpet. If you approach them respectfully and with a pure heart, you will find they are great protectors, companions, and friends.

Doing Vodou "Right"—and Doing It "Wrong"

Some will tell you that do-it-yourself Vodou is dangerous. Others will tell you it is ineffective. For both, Vodou is not an art but a science. They claim that the lwa will only respond to those who have been properly introduced and who approach them in strict accordance with the *reglamen* ("regimen" in English—the ceremonial order in which the lwa are saluted). Anyone else who tries to call on the lwa will be ignored. These people say that those who practice "Wicca-doo" are only kidding themselves. They claim that because they haven't been introduced to the lwa, and don't have "real roots," they can't be getting real results.

There are certain things you can only learn from a teacher, and things you will only be taught after taking an oath of secrecy. Being initiated can help you become closer to the lwa; and working within an established paradigm can provide structure and help you make sense of an intricate and complicated religion. That being said, there is a difference between "helpful" and "necessary." You *can* contact and serve the lwa without a teacher—and without encyclopedic knowledge of Haitian Vodou.

The lwa may not respond to a random call from a perfect stranger, but they may well decide to introduce themselves on their own. I have found that the lwa are quite willing to do things independently, even when you don't expect them. If Legba decides that he wants to "open the door" for Joe Wiccan or Jane Asatruar, he isn't likely to check in first with the authenticity police. Based on everything I've seen, I've come to believe that the lwa want to reach out to those who can benefit from their wisdom and their love. If you are feeling called to serve the lwa, it could well be that they have decided to reach out to you. Instead of trusting those who will swear you aren't worthy, it may be wiser to trust the spirits.

It is worthwhile to reflect on the phrase "serve the lwa." What does that involve? Just what it says: serving the lwa. If you are lighting a candle for Legba, if you are giving Freda perfume, if you are honoring your ancestors, you are serving the lwa. You may not be doing it the way Vodouisants do it in Port-au-Prince or Jacmel . . . but then, they aren't doing it the way Vodouisants do it in Cap Haitien or Gonaïves. (Although there is a regleman that's followed in many houses, and although the basic structure of the *priye Gineh* [prayer of Gineh] is more or less consistent, there are any number of variations. You'll often find Houngan X telling you "Mambo Y don't know nothing" while Mambo Y tells you "Houngan X does everything wrong." This is particularly true if they are competing for your business, or if they have a personal grudge.)

If we wish to practice "authentic Haitian Vodou," we may well be on a fool's quest, searching for the Holy Grail. If, on the other hand, we say "we serve the lwa," then we can rest assured that we are serving the lwa. We can try to learn the way they are served in Haiti, and in the Haitian diaspora; we can learn their likes and dislikes from people who know them intimately. And we can try to make our spirits happy and give them our best, in return for their care and support. If we do that, they will lead us to the place where we need to be. If our société of Haitians (or of people trained by Haitians) accepts us as initiates, and our lwa accept us as initiates, then we are practicing "authentic Haitian Vodou" for any reasonable value of that term.

It is difficult to judge whether other people are "getting something" out of their spiritual practices. Any spiritual practice may appear silly or incomprehensible to nonbelievers. Many Christians laugh at those wacky crystal polishers who dance about naked in the woods and honor "Mother Earth." Many Jews can't fathom how otherwise rational people could believe that a man was born of a virgin and came back from the dead. And yet Christianity, Neopaganism, and Judaism have each brought many people inner peace, spiritual equilibrium, and a sense of purpose. Before we belittle another person's spirituality, we may want to consider how we look to outsiders.

We may also want to ask ourselves why we must mock or dismiss those who do things differently, or why they mock us. Is it to "preserve the religion" or to feel superior? Far too often we find ourselves back in the pecking order of our elementary school playgrounds. We laugh at others in the hopes that by doing so no one will laugh at us. Many non-Haitians who come to Vodou are painfully aware of the cultural differences that separate them from most Vodouisants. By finding the "right way" of doing things, they hope to distance themselves from Those Other Non-Haitians Who Do It Wrong, and prove they are Authentic Enough for the Haitians.

Instead of asking, "Are they doing *real* Vodou?" perhaps we should ask, "Are they hurting anyone?" Any group that practices (or tolerates) sexual abuse, financial exploitation, or other negative behaviors should be avoided, regardless of how impressive their credentials may appear. On the other hand, those groups whose members appear happy and well adjusted may well benefit you spiritually, even if they are not "authentic" enough for some. Those "Wicca-doans" may not know the reglamen—but the lwa may appreciate their sincerity and bestow their blessings upon them. Ultimately, houngans and mambos are *servants* of the lwa; they are not empowered to speak for them. I have found that the lwa are quite capable of making their feelings known. Vodouisants who are behaving badly will find out quickly enough without my input.

The information I have given here is what I learned from my mama and papa and other Vodouisants. You may find that others disagree with things I have written. That does not necessarily mean I am wrong, or even that they are wrong. Vodou in Haiti was synthesized from many different traditions and cultures, and it has many different roots. Some houses will favor spirits from the Kongo region of central and southern Africa, others will work almost exclusively with Rada lwa, such as Legba and Freda, and still others will honor Ti-Miste ("little mysteries")—spirits served only by a few people. They may use different saint images, or they may use no saint images at all. Orthodox Christians and Roman Catholics have fought wars over whether the Holy Ghost proceeds from the Father or from the Father and the Son; Sunni and Shia Muslims continue to quarrel over who should have been chosen as successor after Muhammed's death. I see nothing to be gained—and a great deal to be lost—in endless arguments about how many lwa can dance on the head of a pin.

This may be disconcerting to those who expect to find the One True Way of Serving the Lwa and thereby avoid the danger of Blundering Forward on Their Own. There is no One True Way in Vodou: it is a direct and experiential path. You do not become closer to the lwa by memorizing passages in a book, by learning to speak fluent Kreyol, or by mastering the nuances of every ceremony. Rather, you become closer to the lwa by serving them, listening to them, and working with them. Knowledge can help you, but in the end direct experience is going to be far more important than rote recitation. In your Vodou journey, you must create your own map, because the terrain will differ for every person. Although you can learn from the success and failure of others, you ultimately will have to stop studying and start doing. This may be frightening to those of a more cerebral bent (it scared the hell out of me!), but it's an unavoidable truth.

Cultural Appropriation and Vodou

Other critics attack "cultural appropriation." They scorn those who use other traditions as window dressing; they claim that non-Haitians who honor the lwa in their own fashion do so out of a sense of entitlement and from a position of privilege. It would be easy enough to dismiss this criticism as politically correct nonsense—but we would be wise to take a closer look.

Most Wiccan and Neopagan traditions work with cultures that have long since vanished. There are no Lugh worshippers left to say, "Our religion had nothing to do with listening to Enya, eating potatoes, and dressing up in Renaissance Faire garb!" You can do whatever you like and call it Norse spirituality without fearing the fury of sword-wielding Norsemen. You can use the images of these departed cultures as you like. At worst, you may incur the wrath of a few scholars. Living traditions like Vodou are another story. There are approximately 10 million people who still serve the lwa as their ancestors served them.

Haitian Vodouisants did not create the lwa. The spirits are not something we can own or copyright; they come and go as they deem fit. Are Pagans who honor the lwa guilty of "cultural appropriation"—or have the lwa decided that they want to be served outside Haiti? If you accept that the lwa are independent beings, not just symbols or archetypes, then you should also realize that the lwa are capable of independent action. They do not need to be protected; they are quite capable of taking care of themselves, and of making their likes and dislikes abundantly clear.

Still, we should remember that racism can be more than just simple-minded race hatred. The flip side of the "bloodthirsty savage" is the "noble savage." This concept originated with the French Enlightenment philosopher Rousseau. He believed that people in a "state of nature" did not know good and evil, but that "the peacefulness of their passions, and their ignorance of vice," kept them from doing wrong.[2] The image of the noble savage became particularly popular during the Industrial Revolution. Looking around their polluted cities, poets and philosophers yearned for a simpler way of living. They claimed primitive people led peaceful, harmonious lives before they were exposed to civilization's corrupting taint, and they sought to emulate them instead of cruel and selfish "civilized" people.

This romanticized view is less offensive at first glance than the "brutal darkies" imagery so beloved by 1930s pulp authors, such as Robert E. Howard *(Conan the Barbarian)* and Sax Rohmer *(Fu Manchu)*. And yet it can be equally dehumanizing. According to this line of thought, we don't need to civilize noble savages. We don't need to bring them things like medicine, electricity, and education, because that would only "corrupt" them. This provides us with a convenient way to assuage our own guilt. ("Sure, they're hungry, poor, and disease ridden . . . but their simple lives are so much happier than ours!") It also reduces human beings, in all their complexity, to caricatures—sweet-natured and lovable caricatures, maybe, but caricatures for all that.

Whether we like it or not, we have already corrupted the innocents. The Haitian people have reaped few of the benefits of modern civilization. Medical care, educational resources, opportunities for advancement—for most Haitians these things are scarce to nonexistent. But we have made them victims of many of our worst excesses. Drug smuggling enriches small cartels of armed thugs who ensure that Haiti's poor and powerless stay that way. The U.S. government funds coups and countercoups in the name of fighting communism (only to create hordes of starving emigrants). There is nothing happy or innocent about poverty and oppression.

As with all religions, Vodou encompasses humanity at its best and its worst. The healer who saves a sick child with herbal medicine is part of Vodou; so too are the Tonton Macoutes terrorizing the populace. At its best, Vodou has served to preserve a community and its history in the face of oppression and privation. At its worst, Vodou has become an instrument of oppression and privation. You cannot understand Catholicism without engaging with both the Inquisition and Mother Teresa . . . and you cannot understand Vodou until you study its uses and abuses, its highs and lows.

Working with the lwa may not, in and of itself, be cultural appropriation. That being said, it behooves servants of the lwa to show respect to Vodou's homeland, and to the people who have been honoring the lwa for centuries. Like it or not, we *do* come to Haitian Vodou from a position of privilege. Over half of Haiti's children suffer from malnutrition; 15 percent die before their fifth birthday; only thirty-eight out of a thousand will ever complete high school. The average yearly income in Haiti is lower than the average weekly income in the United States and Great Britain. We may want to paint Haitian life as "joyful despite poverty," but we shouldn't forget that most Haitians would be a lot more joyful if they had access to health care, job opportunities, education, and regular meals. If we wish to incorporate Haitian concepts into our worldview, we should consider giving something back to Haiti. There are numerous charities that are working to improve the Haitian standard of living. A few are listed in the resources section of this book.

Even if you're short on financial resources, you can help by becoming informed about Haitian affairs and writing to your elected officials. Amnesty International, Human Rights Watch, and other grassroots advocacy groups have saved many lives and educated many about atrocities that might otherwise have remained unknown. They have proven that a few informed people can make a difference. When you protest foreign support of Haitian dictators and prejudice against Haitian immigrants in your country, you raise awareness and help change things for the better.

2

THE ROOTS OF HAITIAN VODOU

In Vodou, as in all African-derived religions, roots are important. You cannot understand Haitian Vodou as it is practiced today without first knowing something about the culture from which it sprang, and the ways history has shaped religion, and vice versa.

The Beginnings: Hispaniola and St. Domingue

Soon after landing on the island he called Hispaniola, Christopher Columbus realized that the Arawak and Taino Indians had golden ornaments but no iron weapons. Further exploration revealed less gold than he had imagined—and had promised to Spain's king and queen. In its place, the new colonists had to content themselves with an *encomienda*—a system of serfdom that treated natives and land alike as property. By the mid-sixteenth century, less than fifty years after Columbus's 1492 encounter with the island, there was no more gold . . . and no more Indians. Overwork, combined with smallpox and other diseases, had destroyed almost the entire population.

After the Europeans discovered the great silver mines of Mexico, the island of Hispaniola became comparatively unimportant. The few thousand Spanish settlers who remained mostly occupied themselves with raising livestock and growing provisions for ships stopping along their way to resupply. Pirates also found their way to this place, and the island of Tortuga, off the coast of what is today Cap Haitien, became a notorious home for smugglers, escaped slaves, and French privateers. When the Spanish finally ceded the western half of Hispaniola to the French with the 1697 Treaty of Ryswick, they must have breathed a sigh of relief that now this wretched hive of scum and debauchery was France's problem.

Although the gold reserves were gone, the French soon realized there were other possibilities for this untamed island. The fertile land and mild climate were ideal for growing sugar, coffee, sisal, and indigo plants—lucrative, but labor-intensive, crops. To replace the Indians, the French took to importing African slaves en masse. A "triangular trade" developed. French ships would travel to Africa carrying European goods, which they exchanged for slaves. From there they sailed to the newly-renamed St. Domingue, selling the slaves and returning to France with sugar and other items from the New World. Before long, the new French colony of St. Domingue was the richest in the West Indies—but all this wealth came at a terrible price.

Outnumbered ten to one, the white plantation owners tried to maintain order through terror. Floggings and brandings were commonplace, with more brutal tortures like the rack, castration, hanging by a meat hook through the ribs, and burning at the stake reserved for any slaves who dared assert their humanity. Slavery was rarely pleasant, but the conditions on St. Domingue were notoriously bad. Forced to labor in the hot sun from dawn to dusk, ill fed and lacking even the most primitive medical treatment, most slaves who landed on St. Domingue were dead of overwork within ten years after their arrival.

Under this brutal system, revolts were common. Escaped slaves found refuge in the rugged Haitian hills. Joining others who had escaped before them, they formed communities of Maroons in which many traditional African customs and social mores were preserved. Others who were not fortunate enough to escape were still able to preserve many of their homeland beliefs. Most of these slaves came from animist tribes that practiced traditional African religions. The Muslims who controlled the slave trade in Africa were not allowed to enslave "people of the book" like Christians or Muslims, but they had no qualms about capturing "pagans" and "infidels." The slaves used their rare days off—typically feast days and Sundays—to remember the songs and dances of their African homes, and to honor the spirits they had served in Africa.

All these communities, slave and Maroon alike, were composed of people from disparate regions. Coming from different tribes and speaking different languages, they were forced to coexist in the New World under the heel of a common enemy. As time went on, a reglamen developed, by which the spirits from each tribe could be honored in order. The Kongo deities of southeastern Africa were praised along with the Rada lwa of the Fon and Ewe tribes of Dahomey (modern-day Benin) and the Nago spirits of Yorubaland (modern-day Nigeria). This reglamen survives to this day, a memorial to the dedication by which slaves preserved their native beliefs despite overwhelming odds, and to the cooperation that allowed them to survive.

Other, non-African spirits joined the ranks. Since the days of Spanish occupation, the surviving Indians had mingled with the Africans who escaped their Spanish captors. The indigenous practice of sand painting was preserved in the practice of creating *vévés,* intricate drawings in cornmeal that were used to call various spirits. Ghede's propensity for dirty jokes mirrors the foul-mouthed dead spirits of Arawak and Taino culture. Indeed, the Taino word for "mountainous," *ayiti,* became the name by which the Africans knew their new home—and the name by which we know Haiti today.

Roman Catholicism also had a substantial impact on this new religion. Under the Code Noir, slave owners were required to baptize their slaves and provide them with religious instruction. For the most part, this "baptism" consisted of sprinkling them with holy water as they were unloaded from the slave ships, while "instruction" consisted of house slaves accompanying their masters and mistresses to church on Sundays and holy days. Still, the iconography of Catholicism had a powerful impact on the slaves. Saints were used to represent various lwa: St. Patrick with his staff and his snakes became a stand-in for Damballah, the great serpent, and the bejewelled and sorrowing Mater Dolorosa became Ezili Freda, lwa of love and luxury. In still other cases, the saints were honored as powerful intercessors. St. John the Baptist was not only used as a representation for Ti-Jan Danto, but also venerated in his own right as a powerful spirit who could grant favors to those who honored him.

In many African tribes, secret societies played a major role. Despite sensational reports of shadowy "African cannibal cults," it is likely that most of these secret practices were more similar to the Mithraic or Eleusinian mysteries: initiatory rites that marked the passage between adolescence and adulthood, or that served as a recognition of an individual's leadership abilities or status in the community. When much of this secret knowledge was lost to the slaves of the New World, they found a substitute in Freemasonry. This European mystery tradition influenced the development of Vodou and of Haitian secret societies like the Sanpwel, which came to serve as a police force, for good and ill, in the near anarchy that has characterized too much of Haitian history.

The Revolution(s)

The slave owners did everything in their power to suppress these traditional survivals. Slaves were prohibited from attending dances under pain of flogging, and prominent houngans and mambos were often put to death in the most hair-raising ways to discourage participation in Vodou ceremonies. The colonists feared the power of Vodou—not least its power to unite the slaves. History suggests those fears were not misplaced. From 1751 to 1758, Makandal, a one-armed former slave and houngan, staged a rebellion that claimed some six thousand lives. A skilled herbalist, Makandal had an ability with poison that was as lethal as his skill at commanding guerrilla troops. Throughout the island, overseers and owners died horribly, vomiting blood as they fell writhing. Even after his capture, torture, and execution, Makandal remained an inspiration to the slaves, who claimed he had transformed himself into a fly and fled the stake before the flames could reach him.

Forty years after Makandal began his rebellion, another houngan sought to lead the Haitian slaves to freedom. On the night of August 14, 1791, Dutty Boukman led a ceremony at Bwa Kayman (Alligator Forest). One week later, slaves working in the cane fields turned their machetes on the overseers, then on the plantation owners. By the end of the first day, over two thousand whites were dead and over one thousand plantations had been put to the torch. The slaves sustained heavy losses (among the dead was Boukman, killed shortly after the battle began), but the dye had been cast and the Haitian War of Independence was under way.

L'Overture and Dessalines

As in the United States, there was a division between "house hands" and "field hands." Slaves who worked in the kitchens and houses had more access to education than their brothers who worked the farms, and they were frequently spared from the worst excesses of the overseers. Toussaint L'Overture, one of the first leaders of the revolution, had been educated by a relatively humane master. When the revolution began in 1791, he helped his former owner to escape. He repeatedly made efforts to negotiate with the French, and on several occasions he punished his lieutenants for excessive cruelty.

In 1803, the French invited Toussaint to come to a negotiating meeting with full safe conduct. When he arrived, the French (at Napoleon's orders) betrayed the safe conduct and arrested him, putting him on a ship headed for France. Napoleon ordered that Toussaint be placed in a prison dungeon in the mountains and murdered by means of cold, starvation, and neglect. Control now passed to Toussaint's most trusted general, Jean-Jacques Dessalines. Raised as a farmhand, Dessalines had not had the comparative advantages afforded to Toussaint, and he answered pleas for tolerance by showing his whip-scarred back.

Dessalines managed to rid the island of the white slaveholders, but he proved to be a more effective military commander than a ruler. The *affranchis* (mulattoes and free blacks) despised Dessalines and considered him an illiterate thug, and the newly freed slaves found themselves back on the plantations, forced to labor in the name of "the Black Republic" as they had once labored for their masters. Having been raised in the harshest brutality, Dessalines had never experienced negotiation or consensus. As a result, he ruled as a despot.

Toussaint L'Overture had looked upon Vodou with horror, and he forbade it in the areas he controlled. By most accounts, Jean-Jacques Dessalines was a houngan, yet upon coming to power he too issued decrees against the practice of Vodou. Like the whites who had ruled before him, Dessalines recognized Vodou's power to organize the masses and feared the challenge to his authority that a popular houngan or mambo could provide. Most of Haiti's rulers to come would follow this lead. Thus Vodou was forced underground, which led to much of the secrecy that still surrounds Vodou today.

In 1806, Dessalines was assassinated, most likely at the request of Alexandre Pétion, an affranchi general who had at various times during the revolution fought for and against the French. Pétion envisioned a system of *politique de doublure* (politics by understudies), with the black general Henri Christophe serving as a figurehead president while Pétion, as president of the mulatto-controlled legislature, retained real power. Unfortunately, Christophe had other plans. After a struggle, Haiti was divided into a northern territory ruled by King Henry I from his massive citadel in Cap Haitien, and a southern "republic" ruled by Pétion with its capital in Port-au-Prince.

The Long Descent into Chaos—and the American Intervention

After Christophe's death in 1820, and Haiti's reunification under Pétion's successor, the mulatto Jean Pierre Boyer, the rule of the mulatto elite over the black peasants became firmly entrenched. With Boyer's ouster in 1843, another Haitian tradition became entrenched: the coup. Between 1843 and 1915, Haiti was ruled by twenty-two different leaders, only one of whom served out his term of office. The period between 1912 and

1915 saw five different presidents, the last of whom, Guillaume Sam, was torn to pieces by an angry mob that then paraded his dismembered corpse through the streets of Port-au-Prince. This last spectacle was the excuse for the United States to step in, in 1915, and make sure that no other foreign power took control of Haiti's strategically important ports. Robert Lansing, the secretary of state, justified the occupation by saying "the African race are devoid of any capacity for political organization and lack genius for government."[1]

To their credit, the U.S. Marines helped build roads and bridges; to their shame, they did so largely through "press gangs" of forced labor that evoked the bad old days of slavery. This was the period when Americans first became aware of Vodou—if "aware" is the right word. During this time, the stereotypes first arose: images of cannibalism, shuffling zombies, and drumbeat-driven orgies that provided decades of fodder for monster movies. The American soldiers treated Vodou with a mixture of contempt and terror, and American Protestant missionaries saw these African customs as "devil worship" and "idolatry." The Catholic Church had launched "antisuperstition campaigns" seeking to eradicate Vodou from Haiti, which had led to the destruction of many irreplaceable Vodou artifacts and peristyles. Now Protestant missionaries came to this impoverished country seeking to "save the souls" of the poor benighted Haitians from what they considered idolatry—and in this they included both Vodou and Roman Catholicism.

This was also a time when scholars became interested in Vodou. Drawing on his work in Haiti, Suriname, Trinidad, and Dahomey (modern-day Benin), anthropologist Melville J. Herskovits's 1941 work *The Myth of the Negro Past* showed that slavery had not wiped out African cultural influences in the New World. Zora Neale Hurston, a leading figure in the Harlem Renaissance, went to Haiti and in 1937 described her experiences of Haitian culture and Vodou in *Tell My Horse: Voodoo and Life in Haiti and Jamaica*. In 1940, the African American choreographer and Vodou initiate Katherine Dunham drew upon her time in Haiti to produce the groundbreaking dance production "Tropics and Le Jazz Hot: From Haiti to Harlem." Later her secretary, Maya Deren, went on to become an initiate herself and to write the classic *Divine Horsemen: The Living Gods of Haiti*. Unfortunately, these few diamonds were buried in a dungheap of sensationalist nonsense like *Cannibal Cousins* and *I Walked with a Zombie*.

This was also a time when Haiti's elite began taking a closer look at Vodou. Haiti's ruling classes had long considered themselves superior to the superstitious masses and their "African" customs. They were shocked to discover that the occupying Americans did not honor their distinctions between black and mulatto. Hotels that catered to American officials and their families instituted the same Jim Crow rules found in the United States. Even wealthy light-skinned Haitians were forced to enter through the back door and were barred from eating at "white" restaurants. Stung by these insults, many Haitian intellectuals responded to this new white occupation with "Haitian pride." Instead of trying to live up to American and European ideals, they instead took pride in their Haitian roots and in Haitian folklore, culture, and customs.

The Rise of Papa Doc

These ideas continued even after the Americans left in 1934 and the mulatto elite once again assumed the reins of power. In Port-au-Prince, a young doctor named François Duvalier led a collective of artists, writers and Haitian intellectuals known as Les Griots, which glorified Haiti's African heritage—including its Vodou religion. Up to this time, educated Haitians had sought to distance themselves from Vodou. The Griots looked with pride upon this uniquely Haitian survival of African religious practices, and many openly proclaimed their adherence to the religion. By 1957, Duvalier had become one of the most powerful men in Haiti. His work in ending the tropical disease yaws made him famous as a humanitarian, and his promises to break the power of the mulatto elite and empower the black majority made him wildly popular. On September 22, 1957, Duvalier was elected to Haiti's presidency with 69 percent of the vote. Unfortunately, it was to be the last free election Haiti would see for over thirty years.

As had become customary, Duvalier cemented his hold on power by intimidating, executing, or driving into exile his opposition. In a break with tradition, he openly proclaimed his adherence to Vodou. His private militia used many of the trappings of Vodou, like Zaka's denim clothing and Papa Ogou's machete. Even the militia's name, the Tonton Macoutes, came from Haitian folklore and signified a bogeyman who carried children away in his *makoute* (sack). Drawing troops from the rural peasantry and from Haiti's slums, the Tonton Macoutes were accountable only to Duvalier. Ostensibly, they were put in power to protect the peasants and the president from excesses by the Haitian military. Unfortunately, the cure quickly became worse than the disease, as the Macoutes used their privileged status as a license for rape, extortion, and murder.

As his reign continued, Duvalier, who went by the nickname Papa Doc, grew increasingly paranoid and megalomaniacal. He was rarely seen in public without his trademark black undertaker's suit, heavy glasses, and hat—symbols of Bawon Samedi, the lwa of death and the cemetery. From the early days, Duvalier had regularly compared himself to Lenin and de Gaulle; by the end, he was presenting himself as a Christ figure. Schoolchildren began their day with a prayer to "Our Doc, who art in the National Palace for life," and they were taught that former leaders like Dessalines and Toussaint were "distinct Chiefs of State who are substantiated in and form only one and the same President in the person of François Duvalier."[2] This was conjoined with rampant corruption, as Duvalier transferred most of the country's wealth to himself and his cronies, including the Tonton Macoutes.

For their part, the Macoutes kept Duvalier in office through terror. Dissidents, opponents, and innocents disappeared in the night; in the morning their tortured and mutilated bodies would be found hanging from trees as a warning and as a sign that Duvalier—and the Macoutes—held power over life and death in Haiti. Whole families were murdered when one member was suspected of holding dissident views. By the time Papa Doc went to meet Bawon (i.e., passed away) in 1971, between twenty thousand and fifty thousand Haitians had been murdered by the

Macoutes, and many of the country's middle-class citizens and educated professionals had been driven into exile.

Vodou in Exile: Haitians in the Diaspora

For centuries, Haitians have left their country in search of a better life. In the sugarcane fields of Cuba and the Dominican Republic, Haitian immigrants worked long hours in horrendous conditions. As it did in St. Domingue, Vodou provided them with a way to maintain their culture and their heritage against the forces of racism and economic oppression. Vodu Dominicano and Vodu Cubano were the result: an integration of Haitian beliefs with Espiritismo (Spiritualism) and Santería. Although these traditions have not been as closely studied as Haitian Vodou, they have left an indelible mark on Cuban and Dominican culture.

The United States also beckoned to many Haitians, despite the efforts by authorities to close the "golden door." New York, Boston, and Miami soon became home to a thriving Haitian community of legal and illegal immigrants. Faced with anti-Vodou prejudice, many Haitian Americans chose to distance themselves from Vodou, seeing evangelical Christianity as a way to blend in and become accepted members of the community. Others still practiced Vodou in secret. Peristyles can be found in many Haitian American neighborhoods, if you know where to look or if you receive an invitation . . . and ceremonies like maryajs, fets, and initiations have been held in the United States for decades. As they do in Haiti, these ceremonies, by allowing Haitian Americans to honor their lwa and their history, serve both a religious and a social function.

The Dechoukaj: Haiti after Duvalier

After Papa Doc's death, the Presidency for Life passed to his nineteen-year-old son, Jean-Claude "Baby Doc" Duvalier. Although he implemented some limited judicial and social reforms, most were cosmetic at best, and his regime became famous as one of the most corrupt in the world. Baby Doc lacked the political skill and charisma of his father, and he quickly found himself losing support both among the population and the Tonton Macoutes. By 1986, he was forced into exile, taking with him a fortune pilfered from Haiti's treasury and leaving behind a country in ruins.

The end of the Duvalier dynasty was greeted with joy—and anger. Throughout Haiti, the populace rose up in a *dechoukaj* (uprooting) designed to remove all traces of the hated Duvalier regime. In Port-au-Prince, Papa Doc's ornate tombstone was smashed to pieces, and throughout the countryside, Macoute peristyles were ransacked and Macoutes "necklaced": gasoline-soaked tires were placed around their necks and then set on fire. The Macoutes responded by murdering some of their more public opponents, but it was obvious they were no longer the invulnerable force they had been under Papa Doc.

Against the Macoutes and the Duvalierists stood a popular Salesian priest, Father Jean-Bertrand Aristide. The director of programming for Radio Cacique, he contributed Bible commentaries and dramatizations influenced by liberation theology, a heady blend of Catholicism and Marxism that saw the Gospel not as an injunction for slaves to obey their masters but as a blueprint for social revolution. Aristide's strident condemnation of corruption and government malfeasance attracted growing alarm from his superiors in the church, but he was not to be silenced. In a country where 60 percent of the population was illiterate, radio programs were important, and Aristide was becoming increasingly influential. The Salesian Order tried to silence him, ultimately expelling him for, among other things, "promoting class struggle." All their efforts proved unsuccessful, and Aristide remained popular with his supporters, whom he dubbed "the Flood," or Lavalas.

By 1987, Haiti had another constitution; but, as a Haitian proverb says, "*Konstitisyon se papie, bayonet se fe*" ("the Constitution is paper, bayonets are steel"). Although the constitution gave the judiciary the power to investigate human rights abuses, the military remained in charge and abuses were rampant. After several years of instability, Haiti finally held democratic elections in 1990. Aristide won with 67 percent of the vote and was inaugurated in February 1991—only to be ousted that September and replaced by a military junta. Not until 1994, after a long and economically devastating blockade, would Aristide be able to return to Haiti and to his position as president.

Unfortunately, Aristide's return did not mark an end to Haiti's struggles. Allegations of corruption were aimed at high-ranking Lavalas officials, and the *chimes* (literally "monsters"), independent militiamen with Lavalas ties, followed in the footsteps of the Tonton Macoutes with repeated incidents of thuggery and intimidation. After charges of voter fraud and irregularities in the 2000 election, Haiti found itself on the receiving end of yet another boycott. In another arena, World Bank–sponsored "globalization" led to Haiti's markets being flooded with cheap American rice, thereby causing hardship for the rice farmers of Haiti's Artibonite region. By 2003, tensions had come to a head, and Aristide was driven from power and into exile. As of this writing (October 2004), U.S. troops were once again patrolling the streets of Haiti and America is once again using its military might to bring "freedom" to the Haitian people.

Whatever the future holds for Haiti, it is likely that the days of anti-Vodou campaigns are over. Aristide welcomed prominent houngans and mambos to his inauguration, and Haiti has begun to attract people coming to learn about Vodou, or to be initiated. You can still find the spectacular "Voodoo Show" tourist attractions of the past—but there are also a small but growing number of Haitian peristyles willing to instruct and initiate foreigners. Given Haiti's desperate need for foreign currency, it is unlikely that any administration that succeeds Aristide's will cut off one of its major sources of tourism revenue.

This may prove to be a mixed blessing. Many Vodouisants fear that the reglamen and the historical traditions will become corrupted by being sanitized or "whitewashed" for a foreign audience. Others are more optimistic, pointing out that Vodou is a living tradition, one that simultaneously preserves history, interacts with the present, and prepares its devotees for an uncertain future. Whatever happens, it is likely that Vodou will play an important role in the lives of its followers, both Haitian and non-Haitian.

Part Two

VODOU TODAY

It's easy to feel overwhelmed upon visiting your first Vodou ceremony. There's a great deal of action, lots of color, and plenty of sound (all in a foreign language). At first glance, it all may look chaotic—but there is a method behind the apparent madness. Before diving in, it's best to learn a bit about the key players, corporeal (the *hounsis,* or assistants, houngans, mambos, and other participants) and noncorporeal (God, the ancestors, and the lwa), and about the stages and props that are used. Like a playbill, this section will explain the drama that is Vodou . . . as well as tell you how to join the cast.

3

THE MYSTERIES: BONDYE AND THE LWA

Some commentators refer to the lwa as gods and goddesses of various domains: Freda becomes the goddess of love, Legba the god of the crossroads, and so on. Most Vodouisants would consider this blasphemy. They hold that Bondye (literally, Bon Dieu or Good God) is the only God, and they consider the lwa, angels, and saints to be his servants. According to the Vodou worldview, Bondye created the world—and then, after finishing with his labors, he turned things over to the angels, saints, and lwa. God is distant and unapproachable, but the saints and the spirits are ever-present as they watch over and protect us.

Some have claimed that this is a Christian corruption of the original African beliefs. However, many African tribes have legends of a creator god or goddess who made the world, and then left the day-to-day running of affairs to lesser spirits—spirits that were far more powerful and knowledgeable than humans, but who were still in the service of the Creator. This Creator was recognized and honored but received far less attention than those spirits who were closer to the living world—the tribal ancestors, deceased heroes, totem animals, and plant spirits who rewarded and punished their followers. It was easy for Africans to understand Catholic concepts of saints and angels who acted as "intercessors" between God and humans and to incorporate those ideas into their own religious beliefs.

Vodouisants refer to the lwa as the *misté* or "mysteries." They are mysteries because we do not and cannot understand them in a strictly logical manner: we cannot categorize them into neat little boxes. If the lwa are beyond our comprehension, then we certainly can't hope to say anything definitive about the Great Divinity. You may see Bondye as the Universal Mother, as the Horned God and Mother Goddess, or as the Eternal and Absolute. All these terms are only ways we try to understand that which surpasses understanding. When we argue over whether or not one of these ways is "better" than another, we become like two children sitting on the beach and arguing over whose little plastic bucket really contains the ocean.

In practice, I've found that most Vodouisants don't spend a lot of time worrying about the metaphysics of their tradition. They know, based on practical experience, that serving the lwa provides them with real benefits. Vodou was forged in harsh conditions. Few houngans or mambos have had the time to engage in theoretical debates about the number of hairs in God's beard. They have been more concerned with questions like, "How do I make sure that my wanga works?" or, "Since this sick child's parents can't afford a doctor, what herbs should I use to alleviate his suffering?"

Most Haitian Vodouisants also identify themselves as Roman Catholics. However, I have encountered Jews, Protestants, Ifá practitioners, Wiccans, and others who are not Catholic but who serve the lwa faithfully and who get real rewards from their service. You certainly can serve the lwa without being Catholic, despite the plethora of Catholic imagery you may see at a typical Haitian Vodou service. Islam has djinns, spiritual beings who were created by Allah and who may be of good or evil disposition; there are numerous schools of Islamic folk magic that teach how to approach these djinn and gain their service. Tibetan Buddhists and Japanese Shintoists each have rites by which local spirits and powerful ancestors may be honored and asked for assistance, and pre-Christian Europe had many "sacred woods" that were home to "little people" and to earthbound spirits that could heal or harm. The idea of spirits who intercede on our behalf is not unique to Christianity or to the African traditions.

Some say that all Zakas are Zaka; others say they are individual spirits and that Zaka is a family name. They may behave differently when they manifest, but they all have certain similarities. Vodouisants will frequently use "Ogou" for all Ogous. When a Vodouisant marries Ogou, she marries all the Ogous—yet one Ogou will stand in for all of them at the ceremony. This question is reminiscent of the old "is light a wave or a particle?" debate. Theoreticians write textbooks on the subject; Vodouisants turn on a switch and don't worry about the particulars. In keeping with this tradition, I generally refer to lwa in the singular, but I note different aspects, or ways these lwa can manifest.

That being said, I recommend against the mind-set that treats the lwa as masks, or archetypal symbols. Freda is not just another name for Venus, which is just another name for Lakshmi, which is just another name for Hathor, and so on. Damballah is not just the Fon/Ewe name for Obatala; Gran Bwa is more than just a "symbol that represents the forest." I have found that the lwa are distinct and individual spirits—not masks or aspects, but fully developed and complex personalities. There may be similarities between a particular lwa and its counterpart in another tradition, but that has more to do with their office than their essential nature. We would expect certain similarities between Constable Roberts from London, Police Officer Yukimoto from Tokyo, and Desk Sergeant O'Reilly from New York—but we wouldn't say that they were all "aspects of the one policeman" or "symbols of law enforcement." Instead, we'd treat them as separate individuals, with their own likes and dislikes.

The lwa are not seen as gods, but as servants of God. Hence, Vodouisants have no compunctions about bargaining with the lwa. They serve the spirits, and in return they expect that the spirits will serve them. They do not shrink from telling a demanding lwa, "I'm sorry, I can't give you that big ceremony right now. I can make a smaller offering for you and will give you something bigger if you help me get the money for it." Nor are they afraid to say, "If my luck doesn't change I'm going to have to stop serving you altogether." They treat the lwa with respect—but they're also willing to set boundaries, and to make their needs and wants known. If you want to work with the lwa, you should keep this in mind. You don't have to approach them with fear and trembling; nor does serving the lwa mean you must become their slave. You have every right to expect their assistance in exchange for your service.

The lwa have strongly differentiated personalities, and they may sometimes give their devotees conflicting advice. In her book *Mama Lola: A Vodou Priestess in Brooklyn,* Karen McCarthy Brown describes a situation where Mama Lola chose to follow the advice of the warrior lwa Ogou St. Jacques and terminate a pregnancy during a time when she was impoverished and could not support another child. Later, Ezili Danto forbade her from seeking another abortion since Danto "don't like abortion because she really love children."[1] Those who have worked with the Sephiroth or with planetary energies will be familiar with this. Much as "good" means different things to Venus and Mars, it may mean different things to various lwa. There are even lwa who look after thieves and lawbreakers. Gran Ezili is frequently invoked by prostitutes for protection and financial success, and criminals may ask Ogou Kriminel or Bawon Kriminel to keep them safe from the law and from their fellow thugs. Before a court case, or when they feel the police are getting uncomfortably close, many lawbreakers, drug dealers, and ne'er do wells seek the services of a houngan or mambo. Although this may raise a few eyebrows, we should remember that poor people often interact with the police differently than wealthier people. The latter see the police as protection; the poor frequently see them as an occupying army. Anatole France's line about the infinite justice of the law, which prohibits poor and rich alike from stealing bread and sleeping beneath bridges, should come to mind here.

The Different Types of Lwa

The first spirits honored after the priye Gineh are the Rada lwa. They are generally Fon/Ewe spirits of Dahomey, and they are seen as "cool" and "sweet." They are often given white animals as sacrificial offerings, or feted with cane syrup, *sirop d'orgeat* (almond syrup), or other sweet items. They are generally seen as benevolent; the rhythms played at their ceremonies are slower and more stately, and the songs in their honor are almost prayerful. Most books on Vodou have concentrated largely on the Rada pantheon. Because the Rada lwa are generally cooler and easier to handle, this book has also concentrated on them.

The next part of the ceremony deals with the Nago lwa. These spirits originated in Nagoland—the home of the Yoruba peoples whose ancestral religions were the root of Cuban Lucumí and Brazilian Candomblé. In these traditions, Oggun is just one of many orisha—or Ogum is just one of many orixa, if you are in São Paulo or Bahia. In Haiti, all of the Nago are given the surname Ogou. Some, like Ogou Shango and Ogou Batala, will be familiar to those who know something of the Cuban or Brazilian traditions. Alongside them are honored ancestors like Ogou Dessalines (Jean-Jacques Dessalines, hero of the Haitian Revolution) and others who are not so well known outside Haiti.

After the Nago lwa, the Petwo are honored. There are several theories regarding the origin of the Petwo lwa. Some say they originated in Haiti, under the harsh conditions of plantation slavery. Others claim they come from the Kongo, among people whose culture was torn apart by tribal warfare before the slavers came. The Petwo rhythms are faster and more syncopated than the Rada rhythms; they are accompanied by whip cracking, whistles, and ignited gunpowder. One school of thought attributes the name of this family to a Spanish slave named Don Pedro. Another suggests the name comes from the Portuguese king Dom Pedwo, ruler over the Kongo during slavery's heyday. The Petwo lwa are powerful sorcerers, but they are also known to be fierce and are generally approached with some caution.

Last, but certainly not least, come the salutes to the Ghede lwa. As life ends in death, so does a fet end with homage to the Bawon and Brigitte, the king and queen of the graveyard, and their servants, the Ghede. These black-clad, sunglass-wearing, raucous jesters from the underworld are among the most beloved spirits in Haiti . . . and they have become increasingly popular here as well. They are particularly loved in New Orleans Voodoo, the spicy gumbo of folk Catholicism, hoodoo, and Haitian Vodou that has become such an important part of the Big Easy.

Within these basic divisions, there are numerous *nachons* (nations). The Ibo, the Moudong, the Zandor, and other nations are generally served within the Petwo rites; the Djouba nachon (Zaka and his kinfolk) are served with the Rada, although some Zakas are saluted in the Petwo fashion. The exact details of these various divisions and subdivisions are beyond the scope of this book. Many of these spirits are served only by initiates; others are served only by those who have them "in the blood": those who have received them, and the secrets of serving them, from blood relatives. As a solitary practitioner and servant of the spirits, you need not concern yourself with them for now. Should they feel the need to serve you, they will make their desires known and will lead you to those who can teach you their secrets.

If you have been serving a particular spirit for some time and you are not seeing results, it could be that you do not "have" that lwa. Different people have different spirits. If Freda is not part of your retinue, your services to her will yield no fruit. If you do not have Zaka, you can cook gallons of *chaka* (one of his favorite dishes) and he will not arrive to eat it. You can be introduced to them at a fet—but if you are working as a solitary and do not live near a Vodou community, this may not be an option for you. Lwa can also choose to introduce themselves to you, but it will be their choice.

Everyone has a lwa *met tet*—the "master of their head." In Haiti, this is typically the first spirit that possesses you. Outside Haiti, where Vodou ceremonies are held less frequently and possession is an aberration, not a commonplace, it is more difficult to determine which lwa is your met tet. Some houngans and mambos will do divinations to determine who rules your head; others will tell you there is no need to determine this unless and until you become an initiate. In my house, we take the latter approach. Instead of determining which particular lwa "owns your head," we recommend concentrating on the spirits who have presented themselves to you. Compare the visions you encounter frequently in dreams with the information contained in this and other books. This will help you to determine which spirits do and do not "walk with you." However, one caveat: You should also make regular small offerings to Legba, lwa of the crossroads and guardian of the gate. If Legba does not open the door for you, you will be unable to accomplish anything in Vodou.

4

THE PERISTYLE: SACRED SPACE IN VODOU

In Haiti, most Vodou activities will take place in or around the peristyle (also known as a *hounfo* or *houmfour*). The peristyle is typically a low building that's whitewashed and decorated with images connected with the lwa. There will typically be a vévé (ceremonial drawing) for Legba on the right-hand side, and Carrefour's vévé will be placed on the left; these will be accompanied by other images, which vary from house to house. A houngan who favors Ogou San Jak might decorate his peristyle wall with a large painting of St. Jacques le Majeur on his horse; a mambo who's partial to La Sirene might have an enormous painting of a mermaid on hers. The right-hand side of the peristyle will feature the images of Rada lwa, and the left will feature the Petwo.

Inside the peristyle one will often find still more images on the walls. Typically the space will be divided into two or more rooms. One room will be dedicated to the Rada and will be used during kanzo ceremonies (initiation ceremonies). This room is sometimes called the *badji* or the djevo; those who are initiated are said to have "passed the djevo." There will be a table here on which statues and offerings connected to the Rada lwa are kept. On that table, you may find things like the Pompeii lotion (a kind of cologne) offered to Freda, Ogou's rum and cigars, Papa Legba's St. Lazarus statue, and other items. The other room is dedicated to the Petwo lwa. Here you will find *pakets,* feathered packets that have been tied in a special way and that are believed to be *pwens* ("points"—sites where the divine and human intersect) for spiritual power. You will also find statues, images, and offerings connected with the various Petwo lwa. The lithograph of St. Andrew that represents Simbi and the Florida water (another kind of cologne) that's offered to Ezili Danto will also be stored here for usage during ceremonies.

In cases where space does not allow, one room may be divided in half, with the right-hand side dedicated to the Rada and the left to the Petwo spirits. It is not uncommon for Haitians who live in cramped apartments in America to dedicate a walk-in closet to their spirits and divide the shelves accordingly. When their spirits complain about the cramped conditions, they are often told, "If you want more room, help us to buy a new house and we'll give you more space."

In rural Haiti, one will often find graves near the peristyle where ancestors are buried. The tombs of wealthy or influential people may have tiny sitting rooms built above them, where their descendants can come to meditate and gain insight into problems. Whatever the status of the deceased, the tombs will usually be well maintained, with iron crosses above them. Peristyles in urban Haiti (or in the United States) generally cannot accommodate any dead on the family land, and so Vodouisants must take them to a churchyard that has been set aside for funerals. Nevertheless, they keep the dead around to watch over them. In any peristyle, you will find *govis*—clay pots—into which spirits have been called by the ceremony called *desounin* or *retire nan mo dlo* (drawing out of the water). The govi functions like a telephone, creating a link through which the deceased ancestor can speak and watch over the house. In addition, there will often be a Ghede room where face powder, sunglasses, hats, and other accessories connected to the Ghede will be kept away from both the Rada and Petwo items.

Most peristyles in Haiti have hard-packed dirt floors that can soak up libations when they're poured on the ground in honor of the spirits. Earthen floors are seen as the ideal surface for ceremonies: it's believed that direct contact with the earth eases possession and is favored by the lwa. In the Haitian diaspora, it is not always possible to hold fets on dirt floors. Houngans and mambos sometimes have to rent halls or hold their fets in parking lots or elsewhere. At these ceremonies, libations will usually be poured in an enamelware basin, which will later be dumped onto the earth. During ceremonies, the spirits are offered these libations. Their vévés are also drawn on the floor, using cornmeal, wood ash, or other powdery substances.

The centerpiece of the peristyle is the *poteau-mitan*—a central pole between the ceiling and the floor. The poteau-mitan is a ladder between Heaven and Earth, a pathway by which the ancestors can rise from below and the spirits descend from above. This pole will typically be brightly painted and decorated with glyphs and images, including a vévé of Damballah, the enormous serpent who spans the distance between the sky and the underworld. When Vodouisants are forced to hold a ceremony in a space without a central pillar or support beam, they will sometimes erect a pole and decorate it with crepe paper or other decorations.

Because this space is a focal point for spiritual activity, it gains an enormous "charge." This makes magical workings more effective, makes it easier to attract the attention of the spirits, and facilitates possessions. Negative and unwanted influences are discouraged by repeated purifications. Every ceremony begins with prayer and meditation, most often with the priye Gineh—an invocation of God, the Virgin Mary, various saints, and the lwa—which can last as long as two hours. This helps to keep away trickster or malevolent entities and ensures that possessions are limited to benevolent spirits.

Creating Sacred Space

When you are working with the lwa, you should take pains to cleanse your workspace. Spending several hours performing purification rituals before you light a candle may be overkill—but a little bit of cleansing can go a long way. Make sure that your space is clean and uncluttered. You may want to dust any surfaces, remove any dirty clothes, put all your books and things in neat piles, and otherwise make the area presentable. You should take special care to remove any open containers of water or liquid and any uneaten food. Negative spirits will frequently be drawn to stagnant water and decaying food, and they can sometimes siphon energy from a ritual and even impersonate the spirit you seek to contact.

You can burn some sage, some frankincense, or some other incense or smudge stick intended for purification and cleansing. Perfumes may also help cleanse your area. Many of the spirits have particular perfumes they favor. Generally the Rada lwa can be honored with Pompeii lotion or rose water, whereas the Petwo lwa prefer Florida water. Putting a few drops of these (or some other scent the spirits like) about the place can attract positive forces and repel negative ones. They will also help to increase the "vibrations" in your working area and make it more conducive to spiritual activity.

Vodouisants will often make use of holy water—water that has been blessed by a Catholic priest. You may find that this water has a potent ability to repel negative energy; many psychics can feel a difference between consecrated water and plain tap water. If you feel uncomfortable using this, you can bless your own water by adding a pinch of salt to a chalice full of water and saying, "I dedicate this water to the Most High Power. May it be cleansed of all negativity, and may it serve to drive away all that is evil and impure." If you do not have a chalice, you can use a simple cup or glass. However, if you do this, make sure you use the glass for no other purpose. Dedicating it to magical uses alone will make it a powerful tool. When you pick it up, you will find yourself falling into an appropriately "magical" frame of mind.

As you are saying this, imagine bright light—so bright that it is beyond white, so bright that it burns away all foul things, like a laser burning wax—flowing from the heavens and filling the chalice, until the water is filled with this light and until the water in the chalice vibrates with energy. Now sprinkle a few drops of this consecrated water about the room, and imagine it driving away everything negative.

Before doing anything else, you should first light a small white candle. Most Vodouisants in America use Sabbath candles, also known as emergency candles. They are inexpensive and readily available in most grocery stores. Before you light it, run the lighter or candle flame over the base, and then stick it on a saucer or other fireproof surface. I frequently use Teflon cookie sheets for this purpose. (Of course, you should also be sure to keep lit candles away from all flammable items.) Now light the candle, saying a prayer of your choice. You don't need anything fancy or elaborate. A simple saying will suffice, such as: "I light this candle so that the Light of the Universe may shine in this place and dispel all darkness."

Now do a basic grounding, centering, and banishing ritual. Witches use various means to "cast a circle" and otherwise "declare" sacred space. You can do this by taking a knife that you use for no other purpose. It doesn't have to be a fancy or an elaborate knife, and it doesn't even have to be sharp; a plain, unadorned knife will work just fine. When you pick it up, imagine the same brilliant light that flowed into the chalice flowing into the blade until it glows like a Jedi lightsaber or an enchanted sword. Now use that glowing sword to carve a circle as you turn, saying, "I cast this circle between the worlds. This circle marks the place between the worlds, between the sacred and the profane. There is nothing within this circle that is not sacred." Continue until you, and the items you are going to use to work with the lwa, are within the circle and the mundane world is outside. You may also use other cleansing methods of your choice. Many Vodouisants will pray the rosary; people trained in ceremonial or hermetic magic may use the lesser banishing ritual of the pentagram to prepare themselves and their space. The specific nature of your cleansing is not so important. What is important is that you cleanse and prepare the area.

You should also make sure that you are properly cleansed before you do any work with the lwa. You don't need to wear fancy robes, nor do I recommend that you work "skyclad" with the African spirits, because they come from a culture where nudity before your spirits is seen as disrespectful. However, I would recommend that you bathe or shower before beginning any ritual with the lwa, and that you wear clean clothing. When you are washing yourself, imagine all your problems, and all your negativity, flowing away from you and down the drain. You may want to use the cleansing bath I've explained in chapter 28, or you may just want to clean up with soap and water. The important thing is that you are clean when you begin. If you are pure, and your workspace is pure, you will be far more likely to make actual contact with the lwa instead of trickster spirits, wandering *morts* (malevolent dead), or other beings who will harm rather than help you.

5

IMPLEMENTS: THE TOOLS OF VODOU

The Africans brought only memories with them to St. Domingue; chained naked in the holds of the slave ships, they had none of the items with which they had served the spirits in the motherland. When they arrived in the New World, they had to make do with the scraps they could glean from their masters and what they could wrest from the soil of their new home. The religion they created was flexible, one that could work with limited resources and one that allowed considerable leeway for substitution and improvisation. This flexibility has continued to this day, as Vodouisants in contemporary Haiti and in the diaspora pay homage to their ancestors with what they have available.

Vévés

The vévés are among the most beautiful—and transient—artworks of Haitian Vodou. These elaborate figures are typically drawn on the ground before fets, and then destroyed by the dancers as the ceremony commences. Using cornmeal, wood ash, cayenne pepper, or other powdery substances, initiates trace the vévé by taking the powder between their fingers, and then pouring it onto the ground in straight and curved lines. Each lwa is honored with a specific vévé: the markings form a glyph that expresses the spirit's nature and forms a doorway by which the lwa can be brought to Earth.

Some scholars believe the practice of drawing vévés originated with the Arawak and Carib peoples who lived in pre-Colombian Hispaniola; others trace their origins to Africa, where even today, "cosmograms" describing the various spirits and their relationships to one another and their followers can be found throughout the Kongo. It is difficult to say for certain, because traditions of ceremonial ground markings appear throughout the world. In India, devout Hindus trace *kolams* to bring prosperity and honor the gods; in southwestern America, Hopi and Diné (Navajo) shamans trace sand paintings to draw down the spirits in ceremonies designed to restore healing and balance. (The Diné word for sand painting, *iikaah,* can be translated as "the place where gods come and go.")[1]

Once the vévé has been traced, it is sprinkled with rum or another appropriate libation, and a candle is placed in the center. A houngan or mambo then shakes an *asson* (sacred rattle) or *cha-cha* (painted rattle) over the vévé and "activates" it by calling the spirit with the appropriate *langaj* (ceremonial language). Often a fet will feature the vévé for several lwa drawn together (a party for Freda might have her vévé beside the vévés for her husbands Damballah and Ogou, for example); at other times a single vévé is drawn.

When you see a skilled houngan or mambo drawing a vévé, you may think it's simple. When you try it yourself, you'll quickly discover how difficult it is to create even, unbroken lines and to keep the intricate patterns symmetrical. The langaj used for activation and the specific combinations required for a ceremony are initiatory secrets. However, a solitary practitioner can definitely use the vévés as a tool to work with and contact the lwa.

In Haiti, vévés are painted on the walls of peristyles. You can also use the vévé as the focal point for a shrine, or as the doorway to a creative visualization. If you do this, be sure to draw the vévé yourself, using tools you have purchased specially for the occasion and that you will use for no other purpose. As Sallie Ann Glassman says in her book *Vodou Visions,* "The act of drawing the vévé is magical. It holds the quintessential force, and is the essential signature of the lwa. Drawn with power and focus, the vévé itself can be enough to call the Lwa."[2]

In my descriptions of the lwa, I have included pictures of the vévés that can be used to call upon them. I have not included vévés for the ancestors or the Djabs (personal spirits). You call upon your ancestors by giving them things that were important to them in life; you call upon Djabs or "work spirits" by using their individual symbols. Because I do not know your ancestors or your personal spirits, I cannot give you those symbols.

As with many things in Vodou, you will find variations in the vévés used from house to house. Skilled vévé artists will add touches of their own: extra curlicues around Freda's heart, or an extra sail on Agwe's boat. If you want to experiment with the vévés I have given you here, feel free to do so. And if your efforts look a bit awkward, don't worry. The act of drawing the vévés is what's important. You'll get better results with a clumsy sketch you do yourself than you will with a sharp, clean photocopy.

The Asson and Cha-Cha

The asson, a calabash gourd decorated with glass beads and snake vertebrae, has become one of the most famous emblems of Haitian Vodou. It is used by houngans and mambos when they salute the four directions. Its distinctive rattle can be used to induce possessions in the bearer and in those nearby. Those who have been initiated can "talk asson." By exchanging ceremonial gestures with one another, they can ascertain the other person's rank and initiatory status. The asson comes from the royal line of priests of Dahomey, where it was called an asogwe, which is the term for the highest rank of priesthood. The asson is given to houngans and mambos asogwe (houngans and mambos of asogwe rank) by Papa Loko at the *demambwe* (an untilled patch of sacred "wild ground"), and it confers upon them all the rights and responsibilities attendant upon being a senior member of the Vodou clergy. It also gives them access to all of the spirits of the house, and allows them to "work" with these spirits and to call upon them.

Although the asson is a well-known tool of Vodou, its use was not always so widespread. Even today, many priests in Haiti work using a cha-cha (a painted rattle that has its origins with the indigenous Arawak and Carib peoples of Hispaniola and that resembles the Central American maraca). Originally the asson was given only by blood, the way it was in Africa. There was no kanzo ceremony per se; rather, a descendant of one of the royal priests would pass the asson to his sons and daughters.

According to Houngan Aboudja (Mark Mollendorf), a hougan asogwe and scholar of Vodou, this changed at some point between 1840 and 1860, when priests in some asson lineages began initiating those outside their bloodlines. At first this new lineage grew slowly. Most Haitians continued to serve their ancestral lwa on their ancestral lands, and they saw nothing to be gained by an elaborate and expensive ceremony that would give them an asson. It wasn't until some sixty years later that the asson lineage became widespread. In the 1920s (and today), Port-au-Prince had many people who were forced off their ancestral land and had lost touch with their ancestral roots. By taking the asson, they were able to connect with a lineage and use the authority this conferred to work with the spirits. By 1950, the asson lineage was dominant in Port-au-Prince—as it was later in the Haitian diaspora.[3]

Most of the anthropologists and scholars who studied Vodou during the American occupation concentrated on Port-au-Prince instead of the more inaccessible highlands to the north. As a result, they came to identify the asson with Vodou, and vice versa.* And so a lineage that was little known in 1900 became the most well-known and popular form of Haitian Vodou—so much so that today some refer to the asson lineage as orthodox Vodou and claim that it is the only form of "real"

*Katherine Dunham is a notable exception. Her book *Island Possessed* (Chicago: University of Chicago Press, 1994) describes her initiation into a nonasson lineage.

Vodou. This would come as a surprise to many Vodouisants in the north of Haiti, where the asson is still rarely seen and where spirits are more commonly given by ancestry rather than initiation.

Only the Rada and Nago spirits are honored with the asson. The Rada and Nago spirits generally originated in and around Dahomey; as such, they are familiar with the asson and recognize it. The Petwo and Ghede lwa are mostly Kreyol spirits, first recognized and served in St. Domingue and Haiti. They do not recognize the asson and so are saluted instead with a cha-cha. Paradoxically, the comparatively new "asson lineage" focuses much of its attention on the ancient "root lwa" of western Africa—whereas the "older" lineages are often more concerned with the spirits who first appeared during the days of slavery.

You can purchase beaded calabash gourds at some Haitian botanicas—but there's only one way to get an asson, and that's to go into the djevo and be initiated. Trying to use the tool without the proper training will be fruitless at best and dangerous at worst. If a spirit sees you with an asson, it may well expect you to give the proper signs and gestures of your rank and interpret your ignorance as disrespect. Serving them with a cha-cha or maraca will be more appropriate. You can shake this to announce yourself to the spirits, or you can use it to open your conversations with the lwa, much as many churches begin services with an opening hymn. With continued work, the cha-cha will assist you in attaining the appropriate mental state for meeting and greeting the lwa. Just as Pavlov's dogs came to associate bells with food, you will come to associate the rattling of a maraca with magical work.

Candles

When you go to a fet, you will see many seven-day candles burning on the table. These tall candles—approximately 8 1/2 inches tall by 2 1/2 inches in diameter—are enclosed by a glass "chimney" and are designed to burn continuously for seven days. They come in a wide variety of colors and styles. You may see many red candles at a fet dedicated to Ogou, while a party for Ghede will feature many black and purple candles.

You will also see smaller Sabbath candles. Before doing any operation, a Vodouisant will typically light a Sabbath candle, to "shed God's light" on the situation. They will use this candle to light the seven-day candle or candles. When saluting the lwa, the lead houngan or mambo will be followed by a person carrying a lit candle. A candle will also be placed near the door, by the drums, and by the vévés drawn on the floor. The Petwo and Ghede lwa are not saluted with white Sabbath candles, but with *bougies,* which are pieces of rolled paper dipped in wax that resemble beeswax tapers. Yellow bougies are used for the Petwo lwa, black ones for the Ghede. If you cannot find bougies (and if you don't live in an area with a large Haitian presence you probably will not), you can use beeswax tapers in the appropriate color.

Candles have a long tradition in magic and religion. I have included a few candle magic activities in chapters 26 and 32. They are a good offering to the lwa when you want to say thank you, when you want to ask their assistance, or when you just feel the need for their presence. Lighting a candle in the lwa's color will "illuminate the way" to your place. Much as the candle flame consumes the wax and transforms it into light, so too will it transmute surrounding negativity into positive energy. (Please be sure to use caution with any open flame.)

If you're going to be doing regular work with the lwa, I strongly recommend stocking up on the appropriately colored candles. Seven-day candles with glass chimneys will be your best bet. Some will even come with decorations on their chimneys dedicating them to a particular saint or for a particular purpose. You can use these, or you can use plain, unadorned ones. Feel free to decorate the outside of your candle as you like. Glitter, decals, markers, or paint can all be used to produce a candle that isn't just an offering but a work of art. If you aren't so artistically inclined, you may be able to purchase decorated candles from botanicas or online. Sallie Ann Glassman, who has a shop at www.feyvodou.com, produces some particularly lovely candles and other Vodou-related items.

When you are done with the ceremony, you can put out the candle by snuffing it out. You can either pinch the wick with wet fingers, or, if you want to avoid blisters, you can cover the top of the candle with a cast-iron skillet or otherwise cut off the flame's oxygen. Save the candle and relight it when you want to speak to the spirit again. When you are finished with the candle, you can discard the chimney, or you can use it to create a wanga (see chapter 32). Because it carries the lwa's energy, it will be a powerful magical item.

Bottles

To call the spirits, libations are poured on the ground before the table, by the drums, and at the poteau-mitan. Each of the spirits receives specific libations: some are saluted with rum, others with sirop d'orgeat, and still others with *kleren* (an alcoholic drink made from sugarcane) or water. The proper libations are often kept in elaborately decorated bottles. Created using cast-off empties and scraps of fabric, these "Vodou bottles" are now among Haiti's most famous artwork. Bottle makers have synthesized African customs with European religious imagery and the island's limited resources to create something that is uniquely Haitian and uniquely beautiful.

Vodou bottles are created by covering empty bottles with cloth. This is then decorated with sequins or beads, because it is believed that the spirits love light and are attracted to shiny objects. Often a lithograph of the spirit is attached; at other times a vévé design is appliquéd on the bottle. Then the bottle is dedicated to the lwa. This will then be kept on the spirit's altar or with the spirit's other things. Vodouisants will take pains to ensure that these bottles always have something in them. Putting an empty libation bottle on an altar is like inviting the spirit to dinner but serving an empty plate.

A *bokor* (sorcerer) might also create a "magic bottle" as a protective amulet. These bottles are frequently covered with patchworks of red-and-black cloth—colors associated with the sorcerers of the Sanpwel and Bizango societies. These will not be decorated with shiny sequins, but they may well have small mirrors attached to deflect negative energy thrown at the owner, and scissors or other sharp objects to cut or stab an enemy. Often these bottles will contain bone fragments scraped from skulls and mixed with alcohol and herbs. The sorcerer passes the mixture through a flame while chanting or singing songs designed to "heat up" the spirit. This bottle closely resembles the *Kongo nkisi,* or spirit container. Because it is believed to contain the spirit of a dead person, many Haitians will also call this a zombie bottle.

Although you may have some difficulty finding a zombie bottle—and you probably don't need one even if you find a seller—you can definitely decorate your altar space and your home with Vodou bottles. Vodou bottles dedicated to a particular lwa can often be found on eBay, or in Haitian botanicas. If you are a crafty sort, you can create your own. Cover a bottle with cloth. (You can use sequined cloth and save yourself some sewing; many Haitians in the diaspora do this.) Affix a lithograph or image connected to the lwa to this cloth. If you are handy with a needle, you can even embroider a sparkling vévé. Once you have done this, fill your bottle with an appropriate libation: sirop d'orgeat for Damballah, rum for Ogou, rum and peppers for Ghede, rum and wormwood for Zaka. (Refer to part 3 and its chapters on the particular lwa for more ideas.)

Now present it to the spirit. When you wish to offer your lwa a drink, you can pour it from this bottle; when it is getting low, you can refill it. Be careful not to spill anything on the cloth lest you stain your bottle. I've learned this from hard experience, and now I have funnels handy. You can keep this bottle on your lwa's shrine, or, if you don't have a permanent altar, you can keep it out in the open as a decoration. They are quite beautiful and will make a nice centerpiece on a coffee table or overlooking a room.

Flags

The Fon kings of Dahomey had elaborately stitched and decorated banners. Yoruba artisans were famous for their intricate beadwork. Ghanian warriors identified their company and depicted proverbs and animals on their Fante Asafo flags. Slavery introduced these traditions to the New World, where they were combined with the Masonic aprons and liturgical vestments of Catholicism. Today we see echoes of this in the "regal flags" of Afro-Brazilian samba schools, and in the orisha flags of Grenada and Trinidad. Many art history scholars believe this synthesis reached its culmination in the *dwapo lwa,* the brightly sequined "Vodou flags" of Haiti. Today these art flags are popular with tourists and collectors, whereas *dwapo sevis* (ceremonial flags) remain important in Vodou rituals.

Dwapo sevis tend to be square, have a fringe, and feature a single lwa, who may be represented by a saint image and/or by the appropriate vévé. Ezili Freda, Ogou, and Damballah are particularly popular, as are the Ghede. Dwapo sevis are less heavily sequined than art flags; because they must be waved around, they have to be relatively light lest they fall apart from the strain. Art flags can vary widely in size, and they may feature secular imagery like angels, political figures, or even celebrities.

As a ceremony opens, two *reine dwapo* (flag queens or female flag bearers) will often enter with dwapo lwa draped over their shoulders. Between them stands the *laplas* (the peristyle guardian and master of ceremonies, often seen as second-in-command to the presiding houngan), who wields a machete. The reine dwapo and the laplas swing the flags and the sword and salute the cardinal points and the congregation. The sequins and beads sparkle in the light, capturing the attention of those present and marking the service's beginning. Some Vodouisants believe the sequins are pwens, divine sparks where the human and divine intersect. The sparkling sequins on the dwapo make it a powerful tool for calling on the lwa.

Be they art flags or ceremonial flags, they take a lot of work. Traditionally, the flags are designed by houngans or mambos, and hounsis or apprentices painstakingly stitch on the sequins. The cloth is clamped onto a wooden stretcher and each artisan works on a different area, much as American women would do at a quilting bee. Once the sequins are in place, the artist chooses a border in a complementary color. A single flag may take a month or more to complete and require more than twenty thousand sequins.

Today artisans throughout Haiti do a booming business sewing flags for tourists and collectors. They are readily available at numerous art galleries online and offline. If you want to find an appropriate centerpiece for one of your shrines, or if you just want a beautiful and reasonably priced decoration, you may want to consider purchasing one or more dwapo lwa. Although a particularly impressive flag by a "name" artist like Antoine Oleyant or Sylva Joseph can fetch twenty-five hundred dollars or more, you can get smaller flags for as little as forty dollars. They may not be ceremonial flags, but they are no less lovely for that. Your spirits will certainly appreciate a beautiful flag, and you will, too.

Scarves

Writing in 1779, Moreau de Saint-Méry described a Vodou ceremony thus:

> Each initiated puts on a pair of sandals and fastens around the body a more or less considerable number of red handkerchiefs or at least of handkerchiefs in which this colour is strongly predominant. The Voodoo King has more beautiful handkerchiefs and in greater numbers and one which is entirely red and which he binds around his brow is his crown. A girdle, usually blue, puts the finishing touch to display his striking dignity.[4]

Today, *moushwa* (head scarves, from the French "mouchoir") serve various purposes in Vodou. When preparing a table for a spirit, a moushwa may be used as a cloth. Moushwa of various appropriate colors will also be pinned to the table at a fet to represent the lwa who will be honored, and the lwa who will be attending as guests. For special occasions, a moushwa may be embroidered with the vévé of the guest of honor, or otherwise decorated appropriately. One of the mambos in our house, a talented textile artist, embroidered scarves for Danto and Freda for my wedding to these two lovely ladies. The scarves now decorate the spirits' altars along with their wedding certificates and rings.

When the lwa is saluted, an appropriately colored moushwa is draped over the shoulders of the lead houngan or mambo. Another will often be wrapped around the bottle holding the libations. The color helps to draw the lwa's attention, and it encourages the spirit to "ride" or possess the person. When a lwa arrives, its scarf will often be wrapped around the head, arm, or waist of the person who is possessed. By tying the scarf to the person's body, it is believed that the lwa will be "tied" and the possession strengthened.

In Haiti, satin moushwa made with nylon or other synthetic fabrics are most commonly used. These are relatively resistant to stains, easy to clean, and inexpensive. You should be able to find these at any store that sells head scarves or head wraps. If you want to make your own, you can certainly do so. A typical moushwa is made with about one square yard of fabric, finished all around with a simple overcast stitch to prevent fraying. Once this is done, you can embroider or otherwise decorate the scarf as you see fit. I have included the colors appropriate to each lwa, along with their vévés, in their respective chapters in part 3. Feel free to include other fitting decorations if you would like. You may also feel free to use other fabric for your lwa. A blue denim moushwa would be appropriate for Danto or Zaka, whereas Freda would certainly be pleased with a scarf made with lacy white and pink chiffon and decorated with pale pink rhinestones or other jewels.

I do not recommend that you wear moushwa while serving the spirits. I particularly do not recommend tying a scarf around your head when doing so. You do not want to encourage the lwa to possess you at this point. Possession is something that should only be done with an experienced "spotter" around—preferably a houngan or mambo, but at the very least someone with experience in African diaspora religions or trance possessions. However, you definitely can decorate your altar with moushwa and wrap them around a bottle when you are giving libations. If your space is limited and you can only put up a table for a short period, you can lay out the appropriate scarves, and then put them back in a drawer when you are done. This will allow you to serve the lwa discreetly and with minimal demands on your space.

Drums

We have long honored the divine with rhythm. Today the tradition continues. Drumming circles have become a regular part of many Pagan gatherings, as drummers celebrate the Earth and the spirits by making a joyful noise. Repetitive beats help the celebrant silence the logical conscious mind; depending on the speed and frequency, they can alter our moods and even drive us into a trance.

The drums are a major part of any Vodou ceremony. Each family and nation is honored with particular rhythms, which are played in a specific sequence. A spirit of the Rada lwa will be honored with a *yanvalou* rhythm first, and then sent away with a *zepol* beat, whereas the Ghede are honored with the racuous *banda*. Learning these complex rhythms, and the ceremonial order in which they are played, can take years. A competent *tambouye* (drummer) is assured of steady employment. In the Haitian diaspora, one must often book drum ensembles weeks or months in advance to ensure their attendance at your fet.

Vodou ceremonies dedicated to the Rada involve at least three drums with cowskin heads. The smallest, called a *boula,* is played with two straight sticks and serves as the timekeeper. The two bigger drums, the *maman* (the lead drum, played with one hand and a small wooden hammer) and the *segon* (played with one hand and a fork-shaped or a curved stick), join in. These two call and respond to each other during the ceremony, carrying on a conversation throughout the night. The drums are accompanied by the *ogan,* a flat piece of metal struck with a stick that also acts as a timekeeper.

Petwo rhythms are played on two conical single-headed drums, known as the *gwo baka* and *ti baka* (in some regions they are called the *ralé* and *manman*). These are played in call and response in some of the most intricate patterns in Vodou. At times the *kata,* a third drum smaller than the gwo baka and ti baka, is added to the ensemble to warm up the music or *chofe misik*. Many Petwo songs are also accompanied with the sound of whip cracking and police whistles. Petwo drumheads are made with goatskin, and they are played by hand only. Some of the Petwo rhythms include *petwo makaya, fran petwo, petwo doki, makandal, bumba,* and *kita.*

As is common in Vodou, the rhythms vary with geography. Some of the most popular Rada rhythms from Port-au-Prince and surrounding areas include yanvalou, *mayi,* zepol, and *dawomen,* whereas in Gonaïves, Rada rhythms take such names as *wanjale, akbadja,* and *kavalye hounto.* There are many other Vodou rhythms, including *djoumba, kongo, ibo, tchika, raboday,* banda, *nago,* and *maskawon.* In the United States, Vodou drummers will often use conga drums or other drums they have purchased instead of the traditional handmade Vodou drums. It is difficult to procure the appropriate materials to build the drums in America, and the heads will frequently crack or go out of tune in the drier American air.

After they are built, the drums are anointed with holy water and given names in a ceremony of baptism. They are then fed from time to time during special ceremonies called *kouche tambou,* putting the drums to bed, and *tambou mange,* feeding the drums. The drums are laid in the badji on a bed of banana leaves. A candle is lit on each drum, and ritual food and drink are sprinkled over them. A machete is driven into the ground before the drums and a white sheet hung over them. They are left like this for a night so their spirits may cross to the ancestral homeland and replenish their power.

Unless you are a percussion prodigy, you're not going to pick up the Vodou rhythms without serious training and study. But this doesn't mean that you can't honor the lwa with drums. Much as a parent might proudly exhibit a child's sloppy finger painting, the lwa will appreciate your effort and overlook any lapses in rhythm. If you can take classes in Haitian drumming, or any other form of African or Afro-Caribbean drumming, so much the better. This will help give you an understanding and appreciation of Haitian drumming's beauty and power, and the lwa will appreciate the efforts you make on their behalf.

If you're among the rhythmically challenged, don't fret. There are a number of excellent CDs that contain some of the rhythms and the *chante lwa,* or "songs for the spirits" used in ceremonies. (I have included some of these in Resources.) You can play these to "set the mood" when you are serving your spirits . . . or you can honor them without drums. In America, many fets are held without drums because of noise issues; the congregation simply claps and sings quietly. There are other ceremonies, like the *action de grace* (a ceremony of thanksgiving for the lwa), that require only stillness and quiet prayer. Vodou has always provided plenty of room for improvisation. You need not fear that the lwa will reject an offering presented with sincerity and good faith.

Perfume and Incense

The scent of dewy grass in springtime, the tangy odor of hot dogs and mustard at a summertime ballpark, the aroma of fresh-baked pumpkin pie in autumn, the warm fireplace smell of burning logs in wintertime—these smells, and others, add immeasurably to our experience of the world. Within days after birth, babies recognize their mother's scent; adults often find themselves transported to an earlier, long-forgotten time by a whiff of some evocative fragrance. Sight and hearing are processed by a relay center in the cerebrum before reaching the rest of the brain, but olfactory impulses have a more direct route. Whereas sight and hearing are closely connected with logic and reason, smell is associated with emotion and sexual behavior.

This ability to affect consciousness on a primal level means that scents can be powerful magical tools. By appealing to the sense of smell, we can quickly create sacred space and the sacred mind-set; we can also create other moods, if these are appropriate. (Aleister Crowley, the British poet, occultist, and alleged "Wickedest Man in the World," once noted how a high-church Anglican slips into a reverent frame of mind upon perceiving the incense wafting through the church—and how quickly he might be distracted by a patchouli-wearing woman sitting nearby.) Haitian Vodou recognizes the power of scent, and various incenses and perfumes are used for ceremonies and magical workings.

Many of the Rada lwa are saluted with Pompeii lotion, a mildly sweet, clean-smelling cologne. This is sprinkled on the floor when they come; it can also be used in baths dedicated to these spirits, or to cleanse and anoint statues or other items dedicated to them. If you can't find Pompeii lotion in your area, you can purchase it online. In a pinch, you can also use rose water. The Nago and Petwo lwa are honored with Florida water. This sharp, citrus-scented cologne is known for its purifying and cleansing effects, and it is used throughout the Caribbean. It is available at many drugstores and spiritual supply stores, or it can be ordered online. Murray and Lanman makes the most famous variety. Some female lwa like other perfumes as well. Danto is partial to Rev D'Or, a perfume produced by the makers of Pompeii lotion, whereas Freda likes just about any good perfume, the more expensive the better.

Native Americans frequently use tobacco to smudge. Like sage, the smoke from burning tobacco can purify an area and remove negative vibrations. Ogou is particularly fond of fine cigars. Lighting one for him and then blowing smoke to the four quarters is a good way to attract his attention . . . and when Papa Ogou is around, negativity runs screaming in terror. Some lwa are also fond of cigarettes. Ezili Danto smokes strong, unfiltered cigarettes like Camels, and many Ghede will bum cigarettes from the congregation upon arrival. If you don't smoke, or can't smoke indoors, you can always offer these spirits tobacco outside—or you can offer them something else entirely. (You should be careful to avoid burning tobacco around the "white lwa": Damballah, Freda, La Sirene, and Agwe. They don't like the smell.)

Vodouisants sometimes use incense for purification. Frankincense burned on charcoal will produce a high, positive vibration in the area. You can use a "church incense" blend available at many religious supply stores or Catholic bookshops, or you can just burn plain frankincense. We have also had good results with burning dragon's blood before working with the Petwo lwa. This incense is spicier and more pungent than frankincense or myrrh. I've also found you can add a tiny pinch of cayenne pepper to further heat it up. (And I do mean "tiny"—otherwise you'll find yourself fumigating the place with stuff that could be used as tear gas.)

A Mexican spirit of our acquaintance introduced us to copal, a resin that was used by the Aztecs in funeral rites and that seems to be favored by many dead spirits; we sometimes mix it with myrrh, another incense connected to death and tombs. Ylang-ylang incense and/or cologne (which is also known as kananga water) is yet another scent that strengthens the dead. In its native Indonesia, ylang-ylang flowers are scattered over a corpse to mark its departure; they are also sprinkled on the marital bed of newlywed couples. Because ylang-ylang is connected with both death and sex, it's an ideal offering for the Ghede.

Smells are a very evocative tool—and a highly personal one. If a beloved ancestor had a favorite perfume, or always smelled of a particular brand of soap, feel free to put that on your ancestral altar. If the scent of pine brings back memories of your time in boot camp, you can definitely burn some pine incense when calling on Ogou. Your spirits will let you know if they object to any scent you're using.

Statues and Images

Hellenic temples featured enormous statues of the various gods; Buddhists erected mammoth images of Siddhartha; Hinduism gave us figures ranging from tiny "pocket shrines" to huge idols. The Hebrew prophets repeatedly railed against the practice of praying to idols and honoring graven images. The fact that they devoted so much time and energy to condemning the practice gives some idea of how widespread it was throughout the region, and how many Jews found their home idols more accessible than the mighty and terrible God of the temple.

Throughout most of Christian history, the majority of Christians were illiterate. Images served as a way to teach them about biblical stories and provided them with a concrete way to grasp abstractions. Legends arose about icons that worked miracles and statues that blessed their followers. There were numerous efforts to stamp out this "idolatry." Many Protestant sects railed against Catholics and their "worship of statues." The Catholics responded by explaining that idolaters worship their images as divine, whereas Catholics believe the images are only "conduits of [God's] abounding grace. . . . The object itself is not important, but rather the fact that God is using the object to bless people!"[5] Many Vodouisants also see the images and statues as a home for the spirits. When you give your lwa a statue or a lithograph, you are providing it with a body—a means by which the spirit can interact with and work changes in the material world.

In Haiti, Vodouisants tend to use lithographs and statues of various saints and holy figures to represent the lwa. The image of the Mater Dolorosa represents Freda; the Mater Salvatoris with her scarred cheek represents Danto; St. Lazarus on his crutch represents Papa Legba, the limping old man at the crossroads. The particular saints used may vary; for example, some houses represent Danto with St. Barbara, the sword-wielding woman used for Chango in Santería, whereas others use St. Rose of Lima, a saint who bore the stigmata of Christ's coronation with thorns and who is typically shown with a bleeding wound on her forehead. I have provided the saint/lwa attributions that I received from Mambo Edeline St.-Amand and Houngan Hugue Pierre, my initiatory mother and father. In some cases I have provided alternate attributions I have seen used in other houses. This is definitely one of those cases where there is no right or wrong.

You may find that your lwa favor saint imagery. Because these representations have been used for so long, they have acquired what ceremonial magicians call an *egregore*—what Phil Hine, author of *Prime Chaos* and *The Pseudonomicon,* has defined as a "magical entity purposefully created by a group or order."[6] It may be easier for the lwa to inhabit an image to which it has grown accustomed. Just as most of us sleep more soundly in our own bedrooms than in a motel room, Papa Legba, for example, recognizes a St. Lazarus statue and feels "at home" there, so it's easy for him to take up residence. These images are relatively easy to find if you have a botanica, a Catholic bookstore, or a spiritual supply shop in your area. They can also be purchased online.

On the other hand, you may not feel comfortable with these Christian images. In that case, you certainly can substitute other imagery that resonates both with you and the lwa. In Haiti, you may find posters of Rambo decorating a shrine to Ogou, or Darth Vader figurines standing atop a table to Bawon Samedi. My Ogou resides in a statue of the Taoist war god Guan Di and has never expressed any particular interest in St. George, St. Jacques le Majeur, or any of the other saints commonly associated with Ogou. This is an interactive religion: your spirits are the final authority on what they want and what is a "proper" offering.

Not long after the September 11 tragedy, my partner and I did some work for a friend whose apartment had a clear view of Ground Zero and who had been suffering numerous signs of spiritual oppression. We decided to call on Ghede to help lead these troubled dead to their proper place, and accordingly we set up a Ghede altar in her house. Because our friend is Jewish, she didn't feel comfortable with crosses and pictures of saints in her apartment. ("My mom would have a heart attack!") We found an image that fit the purpose and was sufficiently nondenominational: Beetlejuice! Ghede apparently agreed with us: her nightmares and weight loss ceased after we placed this theatrical character in charge of cleanup duty.

6
PRACTICES: THE TECHNIQUES OF HAITIAN VODOU

Although the specifics may differ in various houses, there are some techniques that are found at almost every Vodou ceremony. Understanding these can help you to get a better feel for how the spirits are served—and can teach you some powerful ways you can honor the spirits on your own.

Song

Each lwa is typically saluted with three songs; you may hear well over a hundred chante lwa during a fet. The *houngenikon* (songleader) is most frequently an initiate who knows many songs and has a strong voice. Like the drummers, a houngenikon must know the reglamen, and the proper songs to call the spirit, greet the spirit when and if it comes, and honor the spirit as it departs. A good houngenikon may have memorized hundreds of different songs for the lwa, learned during years and decades of attending ceremonies.

These songs often appear simple; typically they are no more than four or five lines, repeated once or twice. Yet their simplicity can mask layers of irony and double meaning. In one song, the well-known diplomat

Ogou Badagris says, "I show you my teeth, I don't show you my heart." Does he "show you his teeth" like a snarling wolf, or like a grinning congressperson glad-handing supporters? Whatever the case, you can be sure that you are only seeing what he wants you to see. Another song claims that Bawon Kriminel, a spirit connected with the dead and with criminals, works "for the worms of the earth." These songs developed in a society where oppression was the rule, not the exception. Plainspoken complaints and comments could be hazardous to the speaker's health; as a result, double meanings and veiled commentary became an important part of the culture and its art.

The melodies are not complex, and these songs are easy to learn if you know Kreyol. If you don't, learning the songs will take a bit longer. There are some CDs available that will teach you some of the traditional chante lwa—but alas, they will not teach you the ceremonial order. This is one of those situations where only training with a house, and experience attending Vodou services, will teach you. However, this does not mean that you cannot incorporate songs into your service of the lwa.

There have also been efforts by some Haitian "roots" musicians to incorporate lwa songs and lwa imagery into new music. Although you might not hear these songs at a traditional fet in Port-au-Prince, there is no reason why you can't sing them for your spirits, or play these CDs in their honor. You can even incorporate other songs that fit the spirit: sea songs for Agwe and La Sirene, for example, or some lush French opera music for Ezili Freda. You may not know the exact ceremonial order, and you may get the rhythms woefully wrong, but the lwa will appreciate the sentiment.

If you have a voice that would give rutting cats pause, and if you can't think of the appropriate CD for the occasion, don't worry—you can serve the lwa without embarrassing yourself. Indeed, most Haitians who were working alone with their spirits, performing an action de grace, or standing before their table in meditation wouldn't be singing. They would open the ceremony with a prayer, and then quietly commune with their spirits or talk to them as they might talk to a beloved elder.

Dance

Many Vodouisants claim that you don't pray to the lwa, you dance for them. Maya Deren and Katherine Dunham came to Vodou not as anthropologists but as choreographers; their studies of Haitian dance paved their way to the djevo. Dancing helps Vodouisants get "caught up in the rhythm" and possessed by the spirits. There are numerous dance steps you will see at a ceremony, as well as various ceremonial movements that are used to salute the lwa. One could write a book on the various dance steps used in Haiti.*

Specific gestures and motions are used for each portion of the ceremony. When saluting the drums, the poteau-mitan, a spirit, or a senior mambo or houngan, initiates and house members will *vire* (turn three times, right left right), with hands touching in a prayer position. When Ogou is being honored, one of the initiates will carry a machete behind the houngans and mambos saluting him and strike it hard against the poteau-mitan and the floor. This clashing sound will often "call Ogou" and induce a possession. During the Petwo portion of a ceremony, a houngan or mambo will kneel before the drums or poteau-mitan and "fume" the surface by taking a small amount of rum in his or her mouth and spraying it in a fine mist.

Perhaps Vodou's most famous dance is the yanvalou. In this dance, dancers maintain a bent position, rolling and undulating their back from the base of the spine upward through the neck. (Those familiar with yoga will note that this also stimulates the kundalini.) This evokes the movements of a serpent or the waves of the sea. The yanvalou is performed during every Rada rite, and it is danced for the all Rada lwa. Other noted dances include Ogou's militant nago, and the banda, a bawdy, crotch-grinding "dirty dance" performed for and by Ghede. As members of the congregation sing the chante lwa, they will perform the appropriate dances. The drummers will supply the rhythm, occasionally

*Mambo Katherine Dunham has done just that. Her *Dances of Haiti* (Los Angeles: UCLA Center for African-American Studies, 1983) is out of print and difficult to find, but it's well worth seeking out at a university library or via interlibrary loan.

striking off the beat in a possession-inducing technique called "beating the spirits into the head."

As the dancing continues, one or more of the participants will often stumble or stagger, and the possession experience will begin. Many of the spirits have particular movements that announce their arrival. A person possessed by Damballah will slither about on the floor like a snake; Freda crosses her arms and walks delicately like a ballerina. Their gestures and bearing are unique and distinctive. You'll have no problem telling the difference between Ogou's chest-thumping combat stance and Danto's wheeling tornado spins, or between Bossou's head-butting charges and Zaka's suspicious, stoop-shouldered peering at the crowd. By watching these motions at a few different parties, you will soon be able to recognize the lwa when they come.

If you get a chance, you should definitely check out a class in Haitian dance. Even if you don't have that opportunity—or if, like me, you were born with two left feet and no sense of rhythm—you need not despair. The lwa generally appreciate your best efforts and will enjoy your "interpretive dance." By incorporating dance and movement into your service of the lwa, you will begin to "feel the spirits," not just accept them as an intellectual construct.

Possession

The Hebrews condemned any form of possession as "sorcery." Jesus spent much of his three-year career casting out demons and "unclean spirits" that had taken up habitation in innocent people. After his departure, his followers remained vigilant against demonic infestation. When a medieval Christian sneezed, those around were quick to say "bless you" so that no demon would slip in the sneezer's open mouth. Exorcists regularly plied their trade on "infested" houses and people. Devils who refused to leave were often "dispossessed" by having the "demoniac" (possessed person) burned at the stake.

With the Enlightenment and the advent of modern psychiatry, the concept of demon possession became less fashionable. Those who had once been labeled demonaics were now labeled schizophrenics. When we encountered people who screamed blasphemies or who manifested multiple personalities, we no longer murdered them as witches. Instead we locked them up in madhouses and, later, used various chemicals to lobotomize them. Intellectuals no longer believed in demons—or any other form of spirit—and now, instead of fearing spirit possession, we dismissed it as "primitive superstition" or "mental illness."

Given this, it's easy to forget that spirit possession has a long and honored history around the world. The Pythoness at Delphi would become possessed by the divine and utter prophecies that influenced Greek rulers and commoners. Hawaiian priests and priestesses were regularly possessed by their deities, and to this day the Burmese seek counsel from *nats,* ghost spirits who possess their *kadaws* (priests) at *nat pwe* ceremonies. Possession experiences are particularly common in African traditions—and possessions are one of the hallmarks of Haitian Vodou.

When you see your first Vodou possession, it's likely to scare the pants off you. As a person is "mounted" or "ridden" by the lwa, they will frequently stumble or thrash about like they have been hit with an electrical current. Often their eyes roll back in their head and their face becomes contorted. Shrieks or involuntary utterances of gibberish are not uncommon. As the possession state begins, hounsis will run over to the prospective "horse" (possessed person) and remove his or her shoes, because it is believed that contact with the earth will strengthen the possession. Depending on the spirit who is coming, the horse may be sprinkled with rum, Pompeii lotion, Florida water, or some other appropriate liquid. A houngan or mambo asogwe may begin speaking langaj in an attempt to call down the lwa and bring the possession to culmination.

Once the spirit has arrived, the horse will usually be dressed in one or more scarves of the appropriate color. It will be given its favored implements. Freda may be given soap, perfume, and cosmetics so she can prepare herself as befits a woman of substance. Ogou will be given his machete and cigar, and he may well demand a bottle of rum as well. One of the Ghede will powder his face, and then put on his sunglasses so he can stand the light aboveground. The spirit is then saluted by those present and begins making the rounds. It may make demands, propose marriage, offer blessings and advice, or chastise those who have neglected their duties to the spirit. It may kill the animal that is to be sacrificed, or consume the food and drink the congregation offers. It may also induce possession in others present.

As a sign that the possession is genuine, the spirit may perform acts that would be impossible for the horse. A horse possessed by Maman Brigitte may rub a Scotch Bonnet pepper over the genital regions; one possessed by Ogou Feray may eat a lit cigar. A horse who normally speaks only Kreyol may speak in French when ridden by Freda; a horse possessed by Zaka will reveal secrets that the mounted individual could not have known. Superhuman strength is not uncommon. I have seen a small, elderly gentleman possessed by Bossou pick up two large men and sprint around the peristyle with them on his shoulders.

Finally, the spirit will leave. Frequently the horse will collapse and need to be revived. Possessed people will typically have no memory of the events that transpired during the possession, and other than feeling dizzy and fatigued, they will show no ill effects. (I have seen people possessed by Ogou consume several bottles of rum, then awaken and walk away without any sign of drunkenness.)

Efforts by scientists and scholars to "explain" these states have not been entirely successful. Some have claimed that possession states were merely sacred dramas in which the horse took on the roles of divinities for the benefit of the community. Others have brushed this off as "mass hysteria" or claimed that the poverty in Haiti results in the peasantry being unable to obtain the nutrients (especially carbohydrates or glucose) needed for the manufacture of neurotransmitters, thereby making them prone to breakdowns in brain function, namely possession experiences.[1] None of these theories explains the amnesia that commonly occurs after a possession, nor some of the superhuman feats the possessed sometimes accomplish. Nor does it explain why possessions can happen involuntarily to spectators, not just to believers who expect and welcome possession—or why comparatively well-fed Haitians in the diaspora, not to mention American practitioners, get possessed.

The explanation Vodouisants give is more simple. In Vodou, the "individual" is actually a collective. The *gwo bon ange* and *ti bon ange* ("big good angel" and "little good angel," respectively) help to form the person's ego. The gwo bon ange is seen as the "higher self," whereas the ti bon ange may be compared to the Freudian conception of the ego. (Some practitioners reverse these ideas.) These forces, through the manipulation of *namh* ("life energy"—comparable to chi), animate the *kadav,* or body—and the body's needs, strengths, and limitations shape the selves that are joined within it. During a possession, the various selves are shuffled aside and the lwa takes over the body for a period of time. The possessed people literally are the lwa: they will be addressed by the lwa's name, not their own, and after returning to consciousness they will be told "Danto did this" or "you should have seen Ogou," not "you did this." It may not pass scientific muster, but it explains the peculiarities of the possession experience more convincingly than any of the scientific theories I've heard.

Even if you have some experience with channeling, aspecting, or "shadowing," I strongly advise against trying do-it-yourself possession experiences. Evangelical Christians may be mistaken in their belief that demonic oppression is the only form of possession . . . but that doesn't mean that demonic oppression doesn't exist. Not every spirit has your best interests at heart, and it can be far easier to invite a nasty in than to get it out. Haitian Vodouisants come from a culture where possession is not an anomalous experience; as such, they know what to expect, and where to go if things go wrong. If you're reading this book, you probably don't have that luxury.

For now, I recommend you deal with the spirits in the time-honored "talk to them, then listen for their response" style. I don't recommend trying to "aspect," "shadow," or "channel" them. You may be used to working with channeled spirits, but you're probably not ready for the sheer consciousness-rending rush of power that is a Vodou possession . . . and you may not be able to convince them to slow down and take it easy.

If you feel an unwanted possession coming on, or if you see someone who appears to be going into a possession state, you often can shock yourself or the other person out of it by pouring water on the head, or by covering the head for a second or two with a bag or cloth. (Before you do this to another person, make sure you're not actually witnessing an epileptic seizure. If the person is going into convulsions, they may need medical, not spiritual, attention.) You can also tie a knot in your hair, or wear a holy symbol of your choice. Haitians believe that these serve as a "keep out" sign to spirits, discouraging them from "mounting" or possessing you.

Sacrifice

Many from outside the Vodou community are horrified at the thought of cutting a bull's throat, or ripping a dove's head off at the culmination of a ceremony. They forget that ritual sacrifice was an integral part of most ancient pagan traditions, not to mention the Judeo-Christian traditions—and they decide that Vodouisants are sick thrill seekers who torture animals for fun, or to summon "the powers of evil." Animal sacrifice is probably one of the most misunderstood practices of Haitian Vodou—and, sadly, it has become one of the things most people think of when they hear the word *Vodou.*

Remember that most Haitians do not have the luxury of separating the death of animals from their later consumption at the dinner table. In Haiti, much of the population works at subsistence farming. When they want meat, they don't go to the supermarket. Instead, they slaughter the animal, gut it, skin or pluck it, cook it, and finally eat it. They are used to seeing pigs, goats, chickens, and bulls killed; it's a normal part of their daily life. In this environment, a Vodou sacrifice is neither gory nor unusual. In most cases, the animals killed are later cooked and fed to the congregation. Because of this, Vodou ceremonies will often attract the poorest of Haiti's poor: they come seeking not only the guidance of the lwa but also a meal.[2]

There are specific animals connected to each spirit, specific ways the animal must be prepared before the ceremony, and specific techniques for killing and later preparing the animal. I have not included these details for a reason. You can serve the lwa without killing animals. In fact, I strongly advise against do-it-yourself animal sacrifices to your lwa. Animal sacrifice is something that should only be done by trained professionals in the context of a ceremony; you cannot learn these spiritual and physical skills from reading a book (not even this one). Trying to figure this one out on your own can get you in serious spiritual and legal trouble.

Fortunately, this is not a major hurdle. You can serve the lwa without practicing animal sacrifice. Indeed, most rituals in Haitian Vodou can be and typically are performed without killing any animals. There are many offerings that are appropriate for the spirits that can be given by any servant of the lwa, initiated or not. I have included many of these offerings in the section on the various spirits; but you may find that your spirits make other, different requests. As I've said before, the spirits have the final say in these matters.

If you find that one of your spirits keeps demanding a blood sacrifice, you are within your rights to say, "I can't give you that—but if you really need this, put me in contact with someone who can do this for you, and give me the money I need to pay for this." Again, I must advise against making a blood offering without proper training and supervision, no matter what your instincts may tell you. Trust me on this one.

The idea of sacrifice shows the interdependence between the spirits and their servants. The lwa look after our needs and provide us with assistance when we need it. In return, we give them things they enjoy. We might give Ogou a new machete, or a bottle of rum, in exchange for his help in getting us a new job. Should La Sirene help us with our singing lessons, we could give her a nice mirror and comb as a token of our appreciation. By doing so, we cement our relationship with the spirit. We also give them power to help us more in the future. When Vodouisants give Ogou a machete, they believe it will help him to "cut through" obstacles that stand in our way; when we give Legba a cane, we hope it will help him travel down the road and guide us on the right path.

If you have a shrine set up for your spirits, you can place their offerings there. Otherwise, you can wrap them in an appropriately colored cloth and put them away until such time as you are calling on their assistance. Then you can set up a quick table, place their offerings there, and then put them back in their box after you are finished. Whatever you do, you should make sure that you do *not* take back anything you have given to the spirits, or use it for your own purpose. If you give Danto a knife, you don't want to "borrow" it to carve your pot roast; nor do you want to drink any of Ogou's rum. Once you have given the items to the spirit, they belong to that spirit.

In the case of food offerings, all you need to do is to present the offering to the spirit, and then dispose of it. If you can dispose of the offerings at a crossroads, in a river, or in a wooded area, that is preferable. Otherwise, place them in a bag by themselves (i.e., without any other house garbage) and dispose of them along with your trash.

Part Three

THE LWA

A comprehensive listing of all of the lwa served in Haiti could easily fill several volumes. If you included the regional and house variations in their images, offerings, and names, and all of the different oral legends that have arisen around each of the spirits, it might fill a library. Well over one hundred spirits are saluted in the priye Gineh as I learned it; and there are other houses whose priye might well honor spirits we don't know or don't serve. There are other spirits who are honored only at certain times, or who are called only for specific purposes. There are still others who receive honor only from secret societies, or from individual houses.

Fortunately, you don't have to have an encyclopedic knowledge of the lwa to serve them. Most solitary servants of the lwa will concentrate their attention on a few favored spirits—those they know well and with whom they have a personal relationship. This is the place where you should begin. Get to know a couple of the lwa—and let them get to know you. Once you are working together with your spirits, the rest will fall into place.

What I have provided here are some of the spirits with whom I am most familiar. You may be familiar with some of these names and images if you have read other works on Vodou—or even if you haven't. I have given you some idea of their likes and their dislikes, their preferred offerings and colors, and their general personality. But ultimately all of this is just a framework; it's up to you to build the sculpture. Books can tell you about the spirits, but they can't give you the kind of intimate friendship and knowledge that comes from knowing the spirit. That only comes from long acquaintance. Think of this as an etiquette book. I can tell you what to bring to a party . . . but it's up to you to attend.

I have divided the lwa into three major groups: the Rada, the Petwo, and the Ghede. These groups correspond to the rites in which each are honored. Within each group, there are numerous nachons . . . and here things can become confusing. There is a Rada nachon within the Rada group—but some of the lwa honored within the Rada rite are not members of that nachon. The Zakas are part of the Djouba nachon, whereas the Ogous are part of the Nago nachon. (And to further complicate things, there are individual Zakas and Ogous who are considered part of the Petwo group!) These nachons are largely based on the originating area of the lwa, but not exclusively. For example, most of the Rada lwa come from Dahomey, but the European saints Clare and Philomena are considered members of the Rada nachon.

If you're overwhelmed, don't be too worried. In practice, these specific divisions are only important for purposes of leading public ceremonies. You can work with each of these spirits without knowing the intricacies of how to introduce them at a fet. Indeed, you are not likely to receive that knowledge unless and until you are initiated or find a teacher.

The Rada Lwa

Most of the Fon and Ewe peoples from Africa who landed in St. Domingue were shipped out through the slave port at Arara (or Allada in some dialects), located in what is modern-day Benin. In time, the spirits they brought with them became known as the Rada lwa. These are among the most widely served spirits in Haiti. A few have become well known outside of Haiti, if not always well understood.

Many Vodouisants say that the Rada lwa work more slowly than some other spirits. They are not as quick as the fiery Petwo and are more distant than the earthy Ghede lwa. Still, their detachment has given them wisdom and an ability to see the "big picture." Their actions may take a while . . . but the results are likely to be life changing and long lasting. They are also generally easier to approach than some of the hotter spirits. (And don't be fooled: if need be, they can do things so fast they make your head spin!)

7

LEGBA

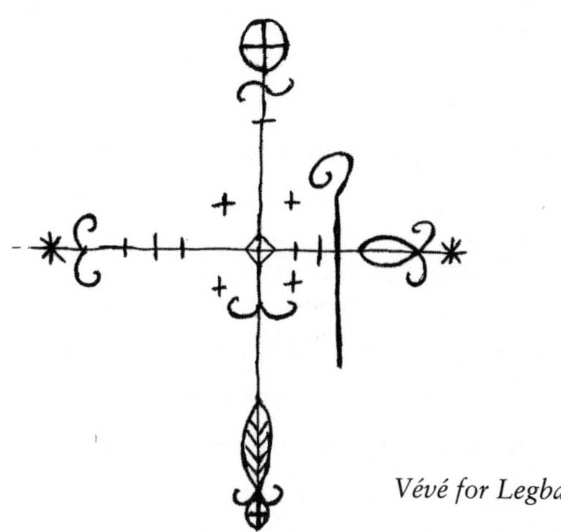

Vévé for Legba

They say if you go down to the crossroads alone, and wait for that brief moment when night turns to dawn, you might see the old man sitting there. Even if you don't see him, you might smell the faint aroma of his pipe tobacco, or see the shadow of his crutch, or hear his deep merry chuckle. Sometimes he gives you things; sometimes he takes things from you. Only one thing is certain: once you've gone to see him, you'll never be the same again.

Some say the old man is the devil himself. Others say he's an angel sent from heaven, and still others call him the lurker at the threshold. If you ask him about this, he'll tell you "yes." And then he'll chuckle to himself, his eyes brighter than the waning stars as he puffs on his pipe and dawn becomes daybreak.

The crossroads is the point where possibilities intersect, the point where we must make a choice. If we choose to travel down one path, we have also chosen not to travel on the other; traveling toward destination A takes us away from destination B. It is the place where travelers separate—and the place where they are introduced.

The cosmology of various African tribes has always placed great importance on the crossroads, and on the meeting points of heaven and Earth. For tribal Africans, the cross did not represent the crucifixion, but the creation of the universe. When the Godhead created the world, she moved to the four corners of the universe, thereby creating a cross.[1] The cross still symbolizes the creation and the communication between the two worlds, that of the spirits and the humans, in many western African religions still practiced today. This emphasis survived the Middle Passage, and today in Haiti we go to the crossroads to meet Legba, the guardian of the gate.

At first glance, Legba looks like an unassuming old man. Accompanied only by his faithful dogs, he leans against his cane for support as he limps down the road. With nothing to his name but shabby clothes, a corncob pipe, and a straw bag, you might mistake him for a beggar. But when you are dealing with Legba, you must remember that appearances can be deceiving. The cane he leans against is actually the poteau-mitan, the gateway between heaven and Earth by which the lwa enter ceremonies. He limps not because he is crippled but because his feet are in different worlds—the material kingdom and the land of spirit. He may seem frail, but he can bring the best-laid plans of kings and generals to nothing . . . or raise the poor and the humble to heights they never thought possible.

Legba is the first one saluted at any Vodou ceremony. Because he is the keeper of the gateway, no spirit can enter the peristyle without his permission. He is the one who facilitates communication with the spirit world. Houngans and mambos say that Legba knows all the languages of people and gods. He is the one who brings our messages to God and to the other lwa—and the one who brings their responses to us. In this he resembles the Greek Hermes, and, like that Greek god, he can be a trickster. We must remember that Legba is the great communicator, but also the great miscommunicator. He is fond of riddles, paradox, and ambiguity. He allows us to speak with the gods, but he often plays tricks with their messages. He gives diviners a glimpse into the future—knowing full well they will misinterpret his statements. In yet another of the paradoxes so beloved by Legba, he governs both destiny and uncertainty.

Legba's home is itself a crossroads, where various cultures and traditions have mingled for centuries. Long before the Yoruba and Fon peoples were brought together in chains to St. Domingue, they were trading, making war, and exchanging ideas, religious and otherwise. The crossroads guardian whom the Yoruba honored as Exu or Alegbara became Legba in Benin. Today, he remains one of the most revered spirits in Benin. In downtown Cotonou, a gas station has gone up beside a famous shrine to Legba. At Station Legba, as the sign says, you can fuel up and leave a priest instructions to pray for you. (I have no doubt that Legba finds this endlessly entertaining.)

In Haiti, images of St. Lazarus, the lame beggar who walks with a crutch, are frequently used to symbolize Legba. Other houses will use lithographs of St. Peter, because Peter is seen as the guardian of the gates of heaven and is often pictured standing before a doorway and holding keys. Still other houses use St. Anthony of Padua (the patron saint of lost items), whereas in other houses you may see Legba represented by St. Jude, St. Christopher, St. Roch, or other saints who are pictured leaning against a staff. One can hardly be surprised that Legba would choose to wear multiple masks before his followers; it's only par for the course. Nor should we be surprised to find that some congregations honor him with yellow scarves, whereas others salute him with red and white and still others with red and black. Some swear that he is served on Wednesday, whereas others pay him homage on Tuesday and still others say Monday is his day. (You could ask him yourself—but don't be surprised if he insists that you serve him on Thursday.)

Honoring Legba

Legba does not demand a lot from those who serve him. An occasional cup of black coffee, some grilled corn or peanuts, and a little tobacco for his corncob pipe will make him happy. Other offerings he may like include cane syrup, palm oil, plantains, salt cod, yams, gin, rum, and cassava bread. To warm his old bones, you may want to add a liberal sprinkling of cayenne to his food. This can be given to him on whatever day you prefer, along with whatever else he may request. His needs are typically modest, if sometimes bizarre. Our Legba has asked us to serve his beans with a chopstick. Not two chopsticks; just one.

You can use an image of St. Lazarus to represent Legba; these are readily available in most Haitian and Cuban botanicas. (In Cuba and Cuban-derived traditions, St. Lazarus represents Babalu Aye, a powerful spirit of healing and disease who is not served in Haiti but who is wildly popular in Cuba.) You may also use one of the other images referenced above, or some other figure that calls to mind the crossroads. You can also represent him with a scarf of the appropriate color, or with his vévé.

Before you honor any other lwa, you must honor Legba. This doesn't have to be fancy, elaborate, or drawn-out. All you need do is sprinkle a few drops of cane syrup or some other drink of his choice on the ground, give him a cup of coffee or some roasted corn, or even say "Legba, please open the door for me. You remember me: I gave you [offering] on [whatever day you fed Legba]." When you do this, you ensure that he will open the door and let the other spirits through. If you forget to do this, he will not bring your offerings to the other lwa until you've provided him with appropriate payment and respect.

Working with Legba

Legba is not difficult to please. If you give him some spare change, some peanuts or candy, a bag in which he can keep his belongings, or a crutch to help him along his way, he will generally be satisfied. Of course, if he really does something special for you, you can reciprocate in kind: give him a nice statue, or have a houngan or mambo prepare him a makoute Legba—a special bag that contains his things and that has been activated by ceremonial means. We keep his things by the door—his St. Lazarus statue, his makout Legba, his straw hat, and some toys and other things he has collected along the way. If you can, you may want to keep a shrine to Legba by your door. He will guard the gate and bring you good fortune, while sending bad things elsewhere.

Before you ask Legba for any favors, remember that he has a keen sense of humor and loves taking you by surprise. When he comes through for you, it's likely to be in a totally unexpected and surprising way. He may even make you feel like a fool on occasion. If this happens, the best thing to do is laugh with him and learn from the experience. Everyone's ego can use a little deflating from time to time, and Legba's jokes are generally pointed in that direction. He's often fond of concealing great wisdom in puns and verbal games—so you may want to contemplate his jokes and see what you can learn from them.

Another thing to keep in mind: Sometimes Legba may leave you asking, "What have I done to deserve this?" I can speak from personal experience here. In April of 1999, after an absence of some years, Legba reappeared in my dreams. He told me it was time I started studying Vodou seriously, and that I needed to travel to Haiti. I paid him little mind. I had a job and a steady relationship. Although neither was particularly satisfying, I wasn't about to throw my career and my partner to the winds so that I could travel to some far-off land, all because of a couple dreams.

On May 8, my partner informed me that she had fallen in love with one of her coworkers and was moving in with him. On May 10, I came into work to find the office closed.

Needless to say, I was none too thrilled by these developments. Yet, as time went on, it became abundantly clear that I had been stagnating. My partner and I had been drifting apart for over a year. There had been problems at work for at least that long. I had talked about finding a more fulfilling job at a more stable firm, but I had never turned that discontentment into action. I bitched about my problems, but I wouldn't take the initiative and actually do something about them. Legba had opened the door for me; then, when I hesitated, he pushed me through. Today I am a houngan *sipwen* (the rank below asogwe). I also have a solid job at a much better company, and a more satisfying and emotionally fulfilling relationship. I have regained everything I lost, and more. At times it was a rough trip, but I'm quite satisfied with the final destination, and I recognize that I would not have arrived here had Legba not given me a swift kick.

If you feel like you're spinning your wheels and unable to get where you really want to be, Legba can help you out of your rut. Light a candle for him; give him some rum and some peanuts and roasted corn, sprinkled liberally with red pepper. Explain your problem to him, and ask him to remove the obstacles that are keeping you from your goals. Ask him for his help, and promise him that you'll do something nice for him in return if he helps you out. Then get ready for some changes. (Needless to say, you shouldn't go to Legba unless you really want those changes.)

If you have a hobby or a job that requires a great deal of manual dexterity, you can ask Legba to give you limber fingers. An old Fon legend describes how Mawu-Lisa (the highest god) told the other spirits that whoever could come before her and simultaneously play a gong, a bell, a drum, and a flute while dancing to their music would be chief of the gods. All the other gods attempted this and failed; only Legba succeeded. Throughout the American South, dice players and guitarists alike have "gone to the crossroads" to gain the skills that allow them to triumph at their trade.*

In Africa, Legba is a solar god; accordingly, you should go to the crossroads before sunrise. Bring along any items required for your skill, if possible. (If you're a pianist, you may have to content yourself with carrying a portable keyboard or some sheet music. If you play the guitar, you can carry your instrument on your back.) Don't forget a small bottle of cane syrup, a corncob pipe full of tobacco, and some pocket change. You can bring along other offerings if you'd like.

Sit down beside the crossroads. Don't sit too close to the shoulder of the road lest you get struck by an errant car. If possible, you should be hidden from view entirely. Now take the cane syrup and pour it out on the ground. Say, "Legba, I come to the crossroads so that you can teach me to . . . ," and then explain the skill you want to learn. Place

---

*This is the source of the legend about bluesman Robert Johnson "selling his soul at the crossroads." For more information on this ritual in African American hoodoo, see Catherine Yronwode's "The Crossroads in Hoodoo Magic and the Ritual of Selling Yourself to the Devil" at www.luckymojo.com/crossroads.html.

the corncob pipe full of tobacco and pocket change on the ground. Say, "Legba, so you will teach me to [insert skill], I've brought you a pipe and some money." Now, as you wait for the sun to rise, sit there and practice your craft. Keep doing so until the sun rises. Take careful note of anyone you see passing on the road. One of them might be Legba, come to teach you . . . or just to bless you by his passing. After the sun has fully risen, you can go home. Leave the offerings there.

8
THE MARASSA

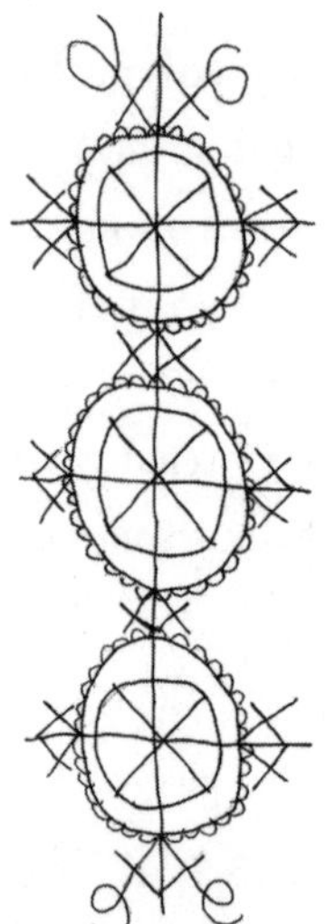

Vévé for the Marassa

Before they became husband and wife, Isis and Osiris were twin children of Nut and Geb; later they became parents to the twins Bastet and Horus the Avenger. The Mayas tell of how the twin brothers Xbalanque and Hunahpu defeated the lords of death before ascending to the sky to become the sun and the moon. The Romans sang of their city's founding fathers, Romulus and Remus. Mythmakers around the world have respected the power of twins. Sometimes their birth was an omen of blessing, sometimes a harbinger of doom, but it was always important.

The Marassa know they're something special. You can see it in their innocent yet impish identical smiles. They are always together; many say they are one soul born in two separate bodies. The people smile with them and rejoice in their laughter. Even their occasional misbehavior is indulgently tolerated. They are bringers of fertility and good fortune . . . and besides, everyone knows that children will be children.

Twins in Africa

Once the Yoruba people considered twin births a bad omen; twin babies were often taken to the wilderness and left to die so they would not bring ill luck to the village. This proved unsuccessful, and the already high rate of infant mortality among single and multiple births skyrocketed. Desperate for a solution, the chiefs consulted a diviner, who informed them that twins were a blessing, not a curse, and that from this point forward they should be honored. The chiefs followed the diviner's advice, and to this day the Yoruba consider *ibeji* (twins) a sign of great good fortune. Throughout western and central Africa, twins are still seen as powerful and magical.

Many African tribes believe that twins are two people who share one soul. If a twin dies, it is believed that it will become lonely in the underworld for the other half of its soul and will try to kill its twin so that it will have company. A Yoruba family that loses a twin will buy a memorial figure. The soul of the deceased twin is transferred to this statue, which is placed on an altar in the family home. The mother then cares for this ibeji figurine as she cared for the twin in life, giving it food and clothing. In return the ibeji—and the figurines of other twins in the family lineage—protect their home and ensure the family's continuing success and prosperity.

For obvious reasons, twins are seen as emblematic of fertility in all its variations. They are often called upon by farmers to bless crops, and by merchants to bless the marketplace. Yet even African cultures see them as a double-edged sword. Because they are so powerful, they can cause harm to those who displease them. An angry twin can bring illness, misfortune, or even death to those who cross them. The Bali of Cameroon place two bells in a room where twins sleep. These must be quietly rung before a person enters, lest the twins be startled and cause unintentional harm or sickness to the person. Since the twins' power can also attract the attention of negative spirits, a fence is traditionally built around their house to keep out evil.[1]

The Marassa: The Twins in Haiti

In Haiti, the twins are honored as the Marassa. They are seen as identical twin children, and they are represented by images of the twin saints Cosmas and Damien. Some houses serve the Marassa with white scarves; others serve them with pale blue and pink. Like most children, the Marassa are known to be temperamental and will sometimes throw tantrums if they are ignored or neglected. To keep them pacified, a large wicker plate filled with popcorn, cookies, and candy is brought out near the beginning of every ceremony. Handfuls of this are thrown to the four corners of the peristyle to "feed" the Marassa; afterward, the plate is passed around to the congregation, who will eat a small bit of this to "gain the luck" of the Marassa.

When a fet is held in honor of the Marassa, a *plat Marassa* will be prepared for them. These dishes consist of two identical sections, in which will be placed candy, cookies, sweet porridge, and rice pudding. Bottles of Kola La Caye (a sweet fruit cola drink popular in Haiti) will also be left for the children, as will two cups of coffee, one with sugar and one without. When the Marassa arrive in possession, they arrive hungry. Sitting down at their plate, they will eat and drink until they are satisfied before doing anything for the congregation. They are often petitioned for aid with luck and fertility. Childless women seeking to conceive may ask the Marassa for assistance, as will those faced with a difficult pregnancy. As in Africa, Haitian farmers and small businessmen will call on the twins for help. Although they are capricious, they are also known to be powerful.

One popular ceremony for the Marassa is the *mange Marassa*. A party is held for the Marassa; cakes and other goodies are prepared. Neighborhood children are invited to partake of the fun and food. They are told to eat with their hands, and after they are finished, they are encouraged to wipe their hands on the heads of adult participants. It is thought that the Marassa will be amused by this party and by the antics of their playmates and will bless the adults and children who indulged them. A mange Marassa may be held by a family that has just given birth to twins, or as a reward to the Marassa for their assistance in other matters.

Because twins are so important throughout Africa, the Marassa are honored in other rites as well. The Petwo twins are honored as *Marassa trois* (Marassa three); they are represented by the image of the "three virtues" (faith, hope, and charity). Some Vodouisants will also refer to these spirits as the three queens of Egypt. They are generally honored at a distance, because they are seen as even more capricious and prone to anger than *Marassa dossu-dosa* (the twins served in the Rada rite). I would advise strongly against using the "three virtues" image in place of the pictures of Cosmas and Damien (or any other twin image that strikes you as appropriate). The twins can be a handful. There's no reason to further complicate your life by calling on the triplets!

Working with the Marassa

If you are a twin, or if you have twins in your family, you probably should pay homage to the Marassa. Set up a small table for them with white cloth (or with pink and light blue cloth). On that you can place some small children's toys, a "twin" image, and some sweet things—candy, cookies, rice pudding, ice cream, and the like. When you have set up the table, state that you are doing this to honor the Marassa and ask them to protect you, your home, and your family. Do this for them once a year, on or around your birthday. This will keep them happy and will ensure their continuing support in all of your endeavors.

Many African traditions hold that twins live "between two worlds"—the physical and the spiritual world. Because of this, they are believed to have the gift of clairvoyance and what Celtic practitioners know as "second sight." If you do a lot of work with divination, you may want to give an occasional gift to the Marassa and ask them to help you with your readings and your intuition. You may notice a definite improvement in your readings. Be careful, though. Like children, the Marassa may blurt out the truth even when it's embarrassing or inconvenient. In the long run, this will prove helpful; more often than not, they're saying something your client needs to hear. But in the short term, it may lead to bruised egos and hard feelings. (If you've been doing readings for a while, you have probably found that many clients don't want to hear the truth, but want to hear instead that they are doing the Right Thing. The Marassa aren't good at that sort of dissimulation, and they may wind up telling your clients more than they care to know about themselves and their situation.)

The Marassa are frequently called upon by those who want to be parents. If you want to have a child, you can ask them for their assistance. If you promise them something, though, be sure that you follow through on that promise. Vodouisants take care not to make the Marassa angry. Like children, their anger knows no bounds when provoked—and if you don't give them what you promised, the ensuing temper tantrum may turn your life upside down. If you are a parent, you can ask the Marassa to look after your child. They love children, and they will happily take care of their new playmate. Don't be surprised if your child starts talking about his "imaginary twin playmates." Children are very sensitive to the spirit world, and they may see things that jaded adults miss. Encourage your child to treat the new friends with respect, just as if they were human friends. Before long, you may well find your child is teaching *you* about the Marassa.

You may also find that other people will see the Marassa around your house. One member of our société is particularly close to the Marassa. She was awakened one night by her guest screaming. When she ran to her room, the guest blurted out, "Your house is haunted! I woke up and there were two children standing on my bed giggling . . . and I know you don't have any children!" Despite our sister's best efforts, her guest insisted on staying in a hotel for the rest of her visit.

If you are looking for help with your business, or with your creative projects, you can work with the Marassa. They can be especially helpful if your business deals with children or with things that appeal to children. With their blessing and support, your toy store, ice cream parlor, or career as a children's author is sure to flourish. Set up a small shrine to them in an appropriate place—your office, for example—and talk to them regularly. Like any children, the Marassa love attention. Don't be afraid to tell them stories, play children's games with them, or otherwise treat them like you would treat any youthful guest in your home. Give them regular offerings of small toys, children's literature, and similar items. One small warning: Do *not* give them any kind of leafy greens. Like many children, the Marassa don't like vegetables. Although you wouldn't want to give your own children sugary soft drinks, candy, or other overly sweet treats, you can and should give them to the Marassa in lieu of healthier snacks.

9

LOKO AND AYIZAN

Vévé for Lok

Vévé for Ayizan

Before there were temples, there were priests and priestesses. There has always been a class of people consecrated to the divine. Sometimes they held high rank within their society; sometimes they were outcasts consulted only when absolutely necessary. Loved or hated, they were always respected by the people who came to them for counsel and knowledge.

In Africa, priests and priestesses were entrusted with preserving the knowledge of the ancestors and spirits who watched over the tribe. Alas, in the New World, the slave owners were not respectful of their status. Holy men and women walked in chains alongside farmers, warriors, and criminals; many priests and priestesses ended their lives working on St. Domingue's plantations. Some fell into despair, convinced the divine had abandoned them. Others continued to serve their spirits, and they passed that service down to their spiritual and biological ancestors. Many of the materials that were common in Africa were no longer available. As a further hardship, under the watchful eye of overseers, and later the police, many customs could no longer be practiced. The images, the songs, the language—all changed with time. But Loko and Ayizan, the first houngan and the primeval mambo, made sure the important wisdom was preserved.

Papa Loko

In Dahomey, Loko was one of the royal ancestors, a spirit served only by the priest-kings who ruled the people. In Haiti, he has become the patron of houngans and mambos. He is the guardian of the peristyle, and he is considered the first priest of Vodou. He was taught the secrets of herbs and healing by the trees and leaves themselves, and as such he is a master healer. It is he who grants the grade of asogwe. Houngans and mambos who aspire to that grade must go to the demambwe, the sacred ground, where they are given the asson by Loko himself.

Loko is diligent in his efforts to preserve the ancestral traditions, and he is known to become violent if those traditions are disrespected. An experimental filmmaker named Stan Brakhage got a firsthand look at Loko's anger during a wedding over which author Maya Deren was presiding. Some people present at the ceremony made disparaging comments about the ritual objects that Deren had chosen for the ceremony. Papa Loko arrived to set them straight. Brakhage watched in horror as Deren, possessed by Papa Loko, hurled a refrigerator across the kitchen while screaming out a blood-chilling chant.[1]

Because he is seen as the father of all houngans, he is most often syncretized with St. Joseph, the father of Jesus. His feast day is celebrated on March 19, the Feast of St. Joseph; most Haitian houses in the diaspora will hold a combined party for Papa Loko and Damballah, whose feast day is March 17. His colors are white and harvest gold; he is given white rum and a white rooster or rice. The Fon believe that if their king is seen eating, his soul may escape through his mouth and an evil spirit take its place. Because of his royal status, Loko will not eat while he is being watched; instead, he takes his food away, or it is left for him in a ceiba tree.

Working with Loko

Loko is connected with the mysteries of the djevo, and with the initiation of priests and priestesses of Haitian Vodou. As a solitary practitioner, there is probably no reason for you to work with Loko or to call on him. Although Loko is a great teacher, he confines his teachings to initiates who have been introduced to him by people who have already met him. Because you have not been introduced to Loko, he is generally not concerned with you. Asking him to do things on your behalf will be futile at best; at worst, he might see your requests as presumptuous and arrogant.

The only exception might be if you are looking to become associated with a société, or if you are seeking to learn from a houngan or mambo. Light a gold or white candle to Papa Loko. (If you'd like, you can decorate the glass chimney with his vévé, or with a picture of St. Joseph.) Ask him to help you find a teacher who can introduce you to the spirits and who has the proper respect for the tradition. Papa Loko is known for his sense of justice; he will help steer you away from liars, cheats, and con artists, and he will lead you toward people who will provide you with the initiation you need. As with other lwa, you should expect Loko to work with you, not for you. A little healthy skepticism and caution on your part will also be in order.

Mambo Ayizan

According to Houngan Max Beauvoir, a Haitian Vodouisant and chemist who was one of Wade Davis's major sources for the book *Serpent and the Rainbow,* Ayizan's name comes from the Fon people of Benin for whom *ayi* means "the earth" or "the land" and *zan* means "sacred." Accordingly, the name Ayizan means "sacred earth" or "sacred land."[2] Author Alfred Métraux claimed that Aizan was the name given to the eldest ancestors, those spirits older than the mythical founders of the tribes. These ancients watch over the founders and also guard the houses and markets. Their symbol is a mound of earth that's sprinkled with palm oil and surrounded with fringes of palm leaves.[3]

In Haiti, Ayizan is seen as the first mambo. Some say she is the wife of Papa Legba; others say she is married to Papa Loko. She is seen as an old woman with deep pockets. She is known to exorcise evil and protect her devotees from malevolent magic. Her sacred tree is the palm, as in Africa; she gives her name to the *chiré Ayizan,* or palm branch on which the leaves have been split, so that the branch becomes a huge plume. Ayizan is also considered the ruler of the fringed palm frond that covers the faces of new initiates as they come out of the djevo. Along with Loko, Mambo Ayizan leads the *kouche*—the kanzo, or initiation, ceremony—and ensures that the ancestral knowledge is transmitted from generation to generation. Her role in the initiation ceremony is so important that some Vodouisants refer to the djevo as the womb of Ayizan.

Practitioners sometimes represent Ayizan with images of St. Anne. In my house, no saint image is used to represent Ayizan. Instead, she is represented by her vévé and by her palm branch, the chiré Ayizan. Her color is white (although some say white and silver, and still others say white and canary yellow or white and gold). Her sacred tree is the palm and she is served with bananas, palm hearts, and boiled white yams.

Serving Ayizan

Like Papa Loko, Mambo Ayizan is primarily concerned with the initiation ceremony and with the transmission of knowledge. However, she also has other spheres of influence and may be approached by noninitiates seeking assistance in those areas. As in Africa, Mambo Ayizan is seen as patroness of the marketplace. Women who own small businesses may seek her protection. Burn a white candle and ask for her assistance; you can also offer her palm hearts or dates. Because Ayizan is an elderly woman and considered one of the oldest lwa, she is not fast acting—but she is very maternal and protective. Her blessing will be subtle but powerful.

You can also call on Mambo Ayizan to purify your home and cleanse you from negativity. Get some blessed palms from a church (most likely this will entail attending a Mass on Palm Sunday). Use them to form the shape of a cross, and then place that cross over your door. As you do so, ask Ayizan to bless and protect your home. Ayizan is known to drive away evil by her very presence, and she is a strong protector of homes.

As with Loko, you can ask for Ayizan's assistance if you are looking for a teacher. She will help steer you toward the place where you need to be, and she will keep you away from people who would harm you or take advantage of you. You can burn a yellow candle for Loko and a white candle for Ayizan and ask both of them to look after you. Because they are an old married couple, they will be glad to work together to see that you get the spiritual education you deserve.

10 DAMBALLAH

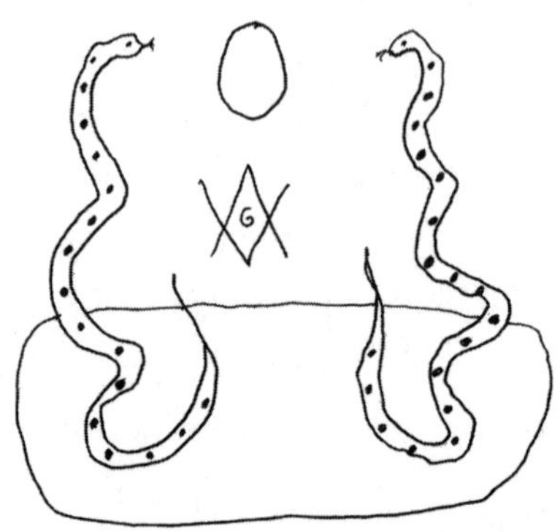

Vévé for Damballah

Most of the dragons died with the first snow. Deep beneath the ocean, Serpent barely noticed the cold. The years became centuries and the centuries became millennia. Occasionally, Serpent ventured aboveground to amuse himself with the antics of the small, furry animals who chattered amidst the dragon bones. Mostly he slept, dreaming of jungles and oceans and of the time before the great fire fell from the sky and the clouds blocked the sun.

Bones became fossils and millennia became eons. The furry animals learned to stand upright; their yips and growls blossomed into speech. Serpent became fascinated with these strange, unpredictable creatures. They wallowed in mud and filth, yet climbed the mountains where even the dragons had not traveled; they were capable of great cruelty and great kindness, sometimes at the same time. Serpent began to attend their dances, warming himself over the fire they had stolen from heaven. Teaching them was a slow process, but Serpent did not mind. He had all the time in the world.

Because the snake periodically sheds its old skin to reveal a new one, our ancestors connected it with rebirth, immortality, and healing. Snakes were associated with the underworld because they were often seen crawling from holes in the ground; they were associated with the heavens because they were just as frequently seen climbing trees. Their undulating motion as they slithered reminded our ancestors of waves and water; their forked tongues and venom evoked lightning and fire.

The Norse had Jörmungandr, the snake whose coils embraced the world. The ancient Persians had Azhi Dahaka, serpent creator of all the planets in the sky. The Gnostics had the Ouroboros devouring his own tail. Religions throughout the world have honored serpents, and Haitian Vodou is no different. One of the most revered and powerful of the lwa is Damballah Wedo, the great white python. "Wherever Damballah goes he leaves tracks," one song says . . . and today Damballah's tracks can be found around the world.

The Beginnings: Africa

Some Fon and Ewe tribesmen spoke of an androgynous serpent named Da who encircles the entire world. Above the Earth, the serpent has thirty-five hundred coils that support the sky; below, it has thirty-five hundred coils that bear the weight of Earth. They claim that the serpent existed before the world was created, and that the mountains were formed from its dung. Because this serpent cannot stand heat, the oceans were created—and it has remained at the bottom since the beginning of time. There it remains, fed iron bars by red undersea monkeys. One day, the storytellers say, the monkeys will run out of iron . . . and the snake will then arise, writhing until the whole world falls into the sea and all creation comes to an end.

Others say that the serpent lives not beneath the ocean but in the sky. The faint cloudy light we call the Milky Way is starlight reflected off its scales. It regularly comes down to visit after the rains in the form of a rainbow shimmering above the fertile plains.

But whether they place the snake above the ground or under the ground, all in Dahomey agree on the snake's importance; indeed, the region's name means "belly of Da." The architecture of Benin displayed serpent images prominently, and serpent motifs are found on the earliest artifacts found in the area.

Skeptics may scoff at claims that snake worship helps keep the fields fertile, but they can't deny that it helps Dahomey farmers. For centuries, villagers throughout the region have stored grain in granaries raised on stilts—and for at least that long, pythons have been venerated. Priests encourage villagers to bring pythons into the villages, and no religious villager would think of harming a ball python. These pythons are kept near the granaries, where they and their offspring help to keep the rodent population down, thereby saving much of the grain for the hungry populace.

Serpents are still venerated today throughout Africa. The Temple of Serpents remains one of the most important buildings in Ouidah, Benin. Many happy, well-fed pythons are kept there for good luck; it draws more tourists than the Portuguese cathedral that still stands across the street. In the Kongo and Zambia, people sometimes leave beer and pearls at basins and ponds that are known to harbor particularly large and ancient pythons, and pictures of Mami Wata (Mother Water) holding a snake can be found throughout central and southern Africa.

Damballah Comes to Haiti

The colonists considered all African religious practices "heathenism" and "witchcraft," but they were particularly horrified by snake veneration. In Catholicism, the snake was not the bringer of wisdom but the tempter, the one who had tricked Adam and Eve in the Garden of Eden. When the colonists saw evidence of serpent worship among the slaves, it could only mean that they were calling on demonic forces to overthrow their God-fearing masters. They whispered of "blood-soaked orgies" where women held enormous snakes in their arms as they danced, and where the blacks groveled before the enormous serpents they worshipped. These images had little to do with anything but their overheated fantasies—but they persisted even after the revolution and became staples of pulp fiction.

Although "snake worship" was ruthlessly suppressed, the colonists encouraged their slaves to honor the saints. Catholicism was seen as a "civilizing" influence on the "savages"; the colonists could assuage any nagging guilt they felt about their brutality by saying they had "saved the souls" of their slaves. St. Patrick's image frequently featured snakes (because Patrick had allegedly driven the snakes out of Ireland), and so St. Patrick became a "mask" for Damballah. March 17, St. Patrick's Day, became the day on which Damballah was honored, and today images of Ireland's patron can be found in peristyles throughout Haiti and the diaspora.

Damballah is known for his love of purity and cleanliness. He dislikes the smells of alcohol and burning tobacco; when he is being saluted, everyone present must close any open containers and put out their cigarettes. He is served with a mound of white flour that's placed on a white saucer; atop this rests a white egg that's been rubbed with Pompeii lotion (if available) or rose water (if not). Pompeii lotion is also sprinkled through the peristyle as Damballah arrives, to make the room smell nice for him. His drink is orgeat syrup, a sweet almond-and-sugar concoction, and his color is pure, snowy white. Because Damballah was originally connected with the ocean, and because large snakes tend to favor wet areas, many peristyles will keep a large shallow basin of water for Damballah. Damballah also does not like the smell or sight of blood; an animal that's given to Damballah will be shown to him, and then taken away and killed.

When Damballah comes in possession, the participant will fall to the floor and writhe like a snake. Most houses will keep white sheets handy when Damballah is being saluted. At the first sign of an oncoming possession, they will throw these sheets on the floor so that Damballah does not have to crawl in the dirt. Another white sheet will be thrown over the possessed horse. This gives Papa Damballah some privacy and surrounds him with his favorite color. The possessed person will be presented with Damballah's offering; the egg is cracked and Damballah licks some of the raw egg and eats some of the flour. Damballah's horse will sometimes slither around the poteau-mitan or into the basin. At other times, he will climb a nearby tree without using hands or feet. When this happens, the presiding houngan or mambo will try desperately to coax Damballah down, so that the horse does not awaken in the high branches and fall to the ground.

In Africa, Da and Aida were two names for the same entity as served by different tribes. In Haiti, Da and Aida became two spirits who were served together. Damballah Wedo was the serpent of Earth, and Ayida Wedo became his primary wife, the rainbow serpent. Both took their surname from Ouidah, the center of python worship in Benin. Ayida Wedo and Damballah Wedo are coiled together, like the DNA double helix. Although Ayida Wedo is seen as a spirit in her own right (and is frequently represented by images of the Immaculate Conception), she is only served alongside her husband.

Damballah is also married to Ezili Freda, the lwa of love and luxury . . . and to many Haitian women who seek his benevolent protection. Generally Vodouisants who marry Ogou will also marry Damballah and Zaka. Some say that marrying Ogou alone will make your head too "hot" and that you need to be grounded by Zaka and cooled by Damballah. Others have a more simple explanation: they say that if you only marry one, Zaka will spread gossip between the two and make both jealous. In some houses, men will marry Damballah; this is uncommon, but, given Damballah's androgynous nature, it makes sense.

Working with Damballah

Damballah is a very clean lwa. If you're going to set up a permanent table to honor him, you should make sure the surrounding space is immaculately scrubbed, dusted, and polished—and that it stays that way. You should never smoke tobacco near Damballah's table, nor should you use alcohol (or any other kind of intoxicating substance) in his presence. You should refrain from using profanity when you are near his table; you should also avoid arguments, idle chatter, and other "hot-tempered" speech. You also should never make any offerings to him unless you have first bathed and changed into clean clothing—and you should make sure never to touch his things if you are menstruating or if you have an open wound.

Needless to say, many people can't meet these rigorous demands. Some of us live in small spaces; and some of us aren't confident that our housekeeping will measure up to Papa Damballah's rigorous standards. If you don't feel like keeping a permanent Damballah shrine in your residence, you can create a temporary table for him in his honor. You can do this on St. Patrick's Day or on any occasion when you need Damballah's counsel or when you wish to thank him for his blessings.

You can start a Damballah shrine by cleaning and dusting the table thoroughly, then wiping the surface down with Pompeii lotion or rose water. When it is completely clean, you can cover it with a clean white cloth. Atop the cloth, place a clean white saucer, with a mound of flour and a white egg that has been cleaned with Pompeii lotion or rose water. Place some orgeat syrup (available in many gourmet-food stores or coffee shops; look for Torani Orgeat Syrup or similar brands) in a small shallow bowl for him, and place a white basin filled with cool water beneath the table. You can use an image of St. Patrick, or if you can find a nice image or representation of a white snake, that will work as well. (The Damballah altar in our home has a small white jade dragon that we purchased in Chinatown.)

Sprinkle a little Pompeii lotion or rose water on the floor, and then light a white seven-day candle and thank Damballah for everything he has done for you. Tell him about your worries, and ask for his wisdom and assistance. Instead of asking Damballah for specific things, you can ask him to give you guidance and to cool your troubled mind. Sit before his altar and empty your mind, then relax and wait for his guidance. Generally Damballah doesn't speak (although there are some Vodouisants who have the gift of understanding what he says when he hisses), so you may not get words, or even images. What you will get is a feeling of serenity and peace. You may also discover that problems that appeared insurmountable really aren't all that bad . . . and that the solution was right in front of you all along, and you were too flustered to see it.

Damballah is one of the richest of the lwa, and he can also help you with money worries. If you come to Damballah to help you get some shiny trinket or something you don't really need, he's not likely to respond. If, on the other hand, you come to him because you are at the edge of bankruptcy and you can't sleep at night, he may very well take pity on you and ease your burdens. Damballah isn't a lwa you approach with trivial problems—but he is a powerful and compassionate elder who will not let his children suffer. When you receive his assistance, be sure to thank him and treat him with the respect and reverence he deserves. A nice crystal egg, a clean white cloth, or a bowl of orgeat syrup left beneath a tree, along with a heartfelt, "Thank you, Papa Damballah," will be greatly appreciated and will help to ensure that he keeps his eye on you in the future.

You can ask for Damballah's assistance in keeping your living quarters or your workplace free of negativity and "bad energy." Sprinkle a tiny bit of Pompeii lotion or rose water on the floor—a very little will do—and ask Damballah to watch over this place and keep all harmful influences away. Do this and you'll find you have less arguments and strife. The area will feel less oppressive or stifling and more open and peaceful. Your work will improve, your relations with those around you will become smoother and more harmonious, and you'll find that many of your problems slowly but surely disappear.

11
AGWE AND LA SIRENE

Vévé for both Agwe and La Sirene. Some practitioners will draw a mermaid near the boat when specifically calling on La Sirene.

In Haiti, the ocean is never far away. The waters off the Haitian coast are among the deepest in the region: within a mile from Cap Haitien, the sea is over three thousand feet deep. Well-developed coral reefs fringe long stretches of coastline, along with highly productive and spectacular barrier and atoll reefs, and walls of coral, along the shelf edge. Thousands of seamen work the waters immediately surrounding Haiti, harvesting conch, crab, scampi, and shrimp.

During the colonial era, the Middle Passage brought millions of Africans to the New World. Many must have looked longingly at the oceans that separated them from their homeland. In time, Guinea became Gineh, a land that lay not across the sea but beneath the ocean like the Celtic Land Under Wave. And presiding over this underwater paradise was Met Agwe, king of the ocean, and his wife La Sirene, queen of the mermaids.

Met Agwe

Met Agwe—often referred to simply as Agwe—is one of the "root lwa," one whose origins are easily traced back to Africa. His Ewe name is Agoueh (pronounced og-HU-way) and his Fon name is Hu. Like other Rada lwa, Agwe is considered a "cool" and merciful spirit. Despite this, his wrath can be terrifying: when he is angry, he is as terrible as a hurricane at sea or a towering tsunami.

Agwe is traditionally seen as an admiral, and he is most often pictured in a naval officer's uniform. His color can vary; he can appear as a white man, a black man, or a mulatto. Often he is pictured with green eyes, but they can be another color as well. Some stories describe Agwe as female. Despite this, he is not androgynous; rather he can be either very masculine or very feminine. He can also appear as any kind of sea creature. The image of St. Ulrique, a bearded bishop holding a fish, is also frequently used for Met Agwe.

A person possessed by Agwe will sit on a small, low chair as if sitting in a boat. The hounsis present will give him an "oar" (often a stick or a cane), and he will then "paddle" around the peristyle. Often he will pour water over himself; as a sea spirit, he likes to stay wet. If the service is taking place in a boat or on the beach, the possessed person may try to swim away—or will dive and then surface holding a fish. Agwe does not speak, but there are certain Vodouisants who can "hear" him when he comes in possession and who can make his wishes known to the congregation.

In Haiti, Agwe's offerings—white rice; cake with blue, green, white, and/or silver icing; champagne and liqueurs; white candles; and a white sheep whose fleece has been dyed blue—are put onto a wooden raft or bark and then taken out to sea and thrown overboard. Maya Deren describes an Agwe service in her book *Divine Horsemen*. She portrays Agwe as a "gracious host" and shows him crying when he sees the feast his worshippers have prepared for him.[1] This is a very lengthy and expensive ceremony, which is why it doesn't take place that often. Some American Vodouisants take Agwe's offerings to the beach and either throw them into the ocean or leave them near the edge of the water and let the incoming tide take them.

Serving Agwe

You can place model boats or images of boats atop Agwe's table. If possible, decorate them with the word *Imamou*. Imamou is one of the langaj used to serve various lwa. Some scholars believe this comes from the Arabic *Imam,* the prayer leader of a mosque; others dispute this. Whatever the original meaning, *Imamou* now appears in many of the chante that honor Agwe. An oar or paddle can be placed on Agwe's altar, along with driftwood, netting, and other naval artifacts. You can also give him seashells, especially conch shells. In Haiti, a *lambi* or conch shell is blown like a horn during songs for Agwe.

You can use a St. Ulrique lithograph to represent Agwe, or some other image of a naval officer. I've seen images of Poseidon used on Agwe shrines, and I've also seen statues of St. Raphael (the archangel connected with water) used in place of St. Ulrique. In Tarot terms, Agwe can be represented by the King of Cups—particularly because this card represents the lord of water and "great emotion held in dignified reserve."

Agwe likes things done properly. He would rather have one elaborate service a year than dozens of smaller ones done carelessly, or with a cheap substitute for one of the offerings. He'd rather have a split of real French champagne, for example, than a magnum of Cold Duck or sparkling wine. He also likes cleanliness almost as much as Damballah does, although he doesn't have Damballah's taboo against alcohol. Because he is a "white" lwa like Freda and Damballah, you should avoid smoking around him. Remember that Agwe is an emperor, the ruler of the ocean and all its riches. Talk to him as you would talk to any other friendly but high-ranking official—not with fear, but with the proper respect.

If you are going to be making a voyage by sea (a cruise, perhaps) or flying over an ocean, you can ask Met Agwe to bless your trip. Burn a candle for him before you go, and promise that you will burn another after you return. You can also do this on behalf of friends or relatives who are crossing the ocean. Vodouisants believe Agwe looked after the slaves and ensured their survival through the Middle Passage. Today, many Haitians are forced to emigrate to the United States or to other Caribbean islands in search of jobs, educational opportunities, and a better life. Some depart as *virewon* (stowed away aboard a cargo ship) or via *kannot* or *batimann* (small boats). Before leaving, many will petition Met Agwe for his protection. They believe that Agwe will look after them during their dangerous journey, and that he'll help them avoid the patrol boats that seek to return them to Haiti.

As king of the ocean, Agwe is considered one of the wealthiest of the lwa. He is also known for his generosity, and he may be able to help you in times of financial need. You should treat him with respect—and give him your best—and in return you will find that he looks after you. If you are having money difficulties—and most of us have these to some extent—you can light a white, green, or light blue candle for Met Agwe. Pour him a glass of champagne or a nice liqueur, particularly a cordial imported from overseas. (My partner's Agwe enjoys an occasional drink of sake.) Tell him that you're having money problems and ask him to assist you. Offer to buy him some flowers, a nice statue, a conch horn, or some other appropriate gift if he assists you. Although he doesn't need gifts, he will appreciate your gratitude and your good manners.

If you have access to the ocean, you can bring Agwe's offerings to the beach and leave them there, letting the tide take them away. You may also want to go to the beach when you are troubled or when you wish to speak with Agwe. It will be helpful; but if you're landlocked, you can make do with an appropriate shrine, or a candle burned in his honor. If you have the resources, you might even want to set up a saltwater tank as a shrine to Agwe. It will provide him with a little taste of the ocean, and it will also make a lovely decoration for your altar room.

Agwe's bounty has always provided a humble living for Haitians . . . and it may, in the future, provide them with real wealth. A lack of modern equipment hinders Haiti's fishermen; the catches of reef fish and crustaceans are only sufficient to supply local markets. At present, fishing, like farming, is largely a subsistence industry. With proper care and investment, the fishing industry could become one of the major engines propelling Haiti's economic recovery. Yet even that might pale next to the windfall Haiti might receive as OTEC technology develops.

OTEC, or ocean thermal energy conversion, converts solar radiation to electric power. The ocean's layers of water have different temperatures; as long as the temperature between the warm surface water and the cold deep water differs by about thirty-six degrees, an OTEC system can produce a significant amount of power. The cold, deep seawater used in the OTEC process is also rich in nutrients, and it can be used to culture both marine organisms and plant life near the shore or on land. Conditions off the Haitian coast are particularly well suited for this technology. OTEC plants could provide Haitians with much-needed power, as well as desalinated water and sea products. In the near future, Haiti may find itself sitting atop a Saudi Arabia–sized gold mine.

La Sirene

On January 4, 1493, Columbus and his crew witnessed mermaids breaking high from the sea off the coast of Haiti. Some skeptics claim they couldn't tell the difference between a fair maiden and a sea cow or a porpoise. Those who know better pay tribute to the woman Haitians revere as La Sirene, Met Agwe's mermaid queen.

For as long as there have been sailors, there have been tales of mermaids. The ancient Syrians worshipped a fish-tailed moon goddess called Atargatis; the Philistines knew her as Derceto. In Cornwall, England, grandfathers still tell tales of merrymaids who live beneath the ocean; Irish poets wrote of *muirruhgach;* and Japanese sailors spoke of the *ningyo,* a fish with the head of a beautiful woman.

For much of their history, sea maidens have also been connected with music. Hindu mythology honors *apsaras,* flute-playing water nymphs; the Greek poet Homer spoke of the singing sirens. In *A Midsummer Night's Dream,* the faerie-king Oberon pays tribute to a mermaid who sang:

> *. . . such dulcet and harmonious breath*
> *That the rude sea grew civil at her song*
> *And certain stars shot madly from their spheres,*
> *To hear the sea-maid's music.*[2]

But despite their beauty and their beautiful voices, mermaids were often more feared than loved. Odysseus could only enjoy the Sirens' music by having his crew tie him to the mast, so that he wouldn't jump into the water and drown himself. Russians feared the Rusalkas, singing water spirits who murdered sailors and unwary passersby. The haunting, lilting voice of the mermaid was said to forecast stormy weather. And it was believed that injuring a mermaid could bring misfortune upon an entire crew—or an entire coastline. Still, there were tales of mermaids helping sailors who had fallen overboard, and rumors of men who had married these strange, lovely creatures.

La Sirene (literally "the Siren" or "the mermaid") is as ambivalent as any other mermaid. She is as changeable as the sea, capable of great love and great cruelty. She is known for her long beautiful hair, for her great wealth, and for the haunting beauty of her voice. In one hand, she carries a mirror; in the other, she carries a comb. Some say that La Sirene "walks on both roads." In her Rada aspect, she can bring luck and good fortune, whereas the Petwo La Sirene lures people to a watery death. Some images of La Sirene will show her with two sides, one white and one black.

In Haiti, many Vodouisants will avoid putting their heads beneath water while swimming in the ocean. They believe that if they do they may be captured by La Sirene, who will take them to Gineh. There they will stay for years, if they come back at all. When they return they will be powerful magicians. La Sirene's comb, mirror, and fish tail come from European stories of mermaids—but stories of female teacher-spirits who take people under the water can be traced back to southern Africa.

John Takawira, a sculptor living in Harare, Zimbabwe, describes the spirit the Shona call the *njuzu* or *nzuzu*. According to Takawira, the njuzu come as a very beautiful woman. Those she favors are enticed to the bottom of her pool. There they are treated harshly for a time. If they obey her orders, she will become kind and offer delicacies, as well as a basket with *mushonga* (magic medicines). Then she will let them leave the pool, but thanks to her gifts they will become rich and famous.[3]

Interestingly, La Sirene is sometimes saluted with Kongo rhythms—rhythms from the south of Africa—rather than the Rada rhythms that originated in central and northwestern Africa and that are used to honor Agwe and other Rada lwa. This also suggests that her African origin may lie further south, among the Kongo tribes that gave us Mami Wata and other seductive and powerful water spirits.

People possessed by La Sirene will sometimes fall to the ground and begin swimming. Often they will make motions as if blowing a horn. (Flags to La Sirene often show her with a horn in her hand.) At other times, La Sirene will sit down and begin combing her hair, or she'll whirl about on her tiptoes like a ballerina. La Sirene does not speak when she comes, although occasionally she will sing in a high-pitched voice. When she arrives, hounsis will throw a sheet on the floor so that she doesn't have to "swim" in the dirt; they will also sprinkle Pompeii lotion or some other sweet perfume around to make the place presentable for a queen.

Many people have tried to equate La Sirene with Yemanja, the Yoruba sea mother honored in Ifá, Cuban Ocha, and Brazilian Candomblé. It is easy to confuse the two: both are intimately connected with the ocean, and both are often represented using the *stella maris* (star of the sea) icon, an image of a beautiful white-robed lady with a star crown rising from the ocean waves. However, there are important differences between the two spirits. Yemanja is a maternal spirit, connected with fertility and children. Although some legends talk of La Sirene's lost child Ursule, she is not particularly known for her motherly tenderness or for inspiring fertility. Rather, this role is associated with Ezili Danto (see chapter 17). La Sirene is literally a Siren—a spirit who charms with her beauty and her voice, a seductress who can grant you favors but who should be approached with care. She and Yemanja may be cousins, or even sisters, but they are not the same spirit. Treating them that way is likely to offend both.

Working with La Sirene

Not surprisingly, La Sirene loves images of beautiful mermaids. If you want to create a shrine to La Sirene, be sure to include some mermaid imagery. Like Agwe, La Sirene also enjoys nautical materials and items. Seashells, driftwood, sea glass (particularly light blue, clear, and green sea glass), sea floaters, and other things that have been taken from the sea or that are connected with marine or ocean imagery will be appropriate for her altar. You should also give her a comb and a mirror—the finest you can afford. As Agwe's wife, La Sirene is a wealthy lady . . . and she expects gifts befitting a woman of her station. Gold and pearl jewelry will also be appreciated; if you can't afford that, she will accept anything aquamarine. Like any noble lady, La Sirene is gracious to those beneath her status, and she will appreciate their honest efforts to please her with the best they can give.

Some occultists connect La Sirene with the Tarot trump The Moon, a card that represents the subconscious and hidden. Others use the Queen of Cups (queen of water) or Seven of Cups (illusion and daydreams). You can use these in place of, or along with, images of stella maris, mermaid pictures and statues, or anything else that resonates with you. Because she is connected with water and the ocean, you should put a nice crystal bowl on the shrine; in this you can place water along with some sea salt.

La Sirene likes sweet things, particularly cakes with white and light blue-green icing. She doesn't eat these cakes, but she enjoys looking at them. She also likes parties and celebrations—particularly when they're held in her honor. You can also give her champagne, orgeat syrup, or other liqueurs. She will take most libations that are given to Agwe, although she tends to favor sweeter drinks. You can leave her offerings at the beach, or you can place them on her shrine for a day. Be sure to take them off her shrine before they start to spoil, and then put them in a clean bag and throw them out immediately.

If you want to be a musician, you couldn't have a better teacher than La Sirene. She is famous for her singing, and she can help you to become a much better vocalist. In fact, she can help you with any instrument or in any type of musical endeavor. La Sirene can also make you a more magnetic and charismatic actor or performer. Writers, painters, and other artists can ask La Sirene to make them more creative and imaginative. Place a white, light blue, or light green seven-day candle in La Sirene's crystal bowl; when you light it, ask her for her assistance. (You should place a saucer between the bowl and the candle, because candle chimneys can get hot enough to crack crystal!)

You may want to take a La Sirene bath to improve your magnetism and charm. Combine some sea salt, condensed milk, sugar, and light blue flowers in a white basin, and then offer it to La Sirene and ask her to bless it. (You may also want to put it in the refrigerator to cool it a bit, because La Sirene is a "cool" spirit.) Pour it over yourself—but *do not* pour it over your head. Getting it on your head may allow La Sirene to "take you away" and can result in a prolonged period of, at best, dreaminess or spaciness, and at worst, mental imbalance. La Sirene can make you beautiful and rich, but she can also make you insane. In working with La Sirene, you will do best to treat her like the powerful, capricious queen she is. Give her due respect, and keep her happy, and she will reward you as a loyal companion and subject.

12

EZILI FREDA

Vévé for Ezili Freda

When she comes into the room, you can't take your eyes off her. She's everything you ever wanted, everything you will never have. She doesn't walk so much as dance, floating gracefully above the ground as if she is too beautiful for the earth. Maybe she is. Nobody could ever love her the way she deserves to be loved . . . and she has long since realized that no one ever will. Even the prettiest half-caste girls learn early that dreams don't always come true. The rich old men can't take their eyes off her either. When you look at the lust in their eyes, you know what they're dreaming. Of course, they wouldn't take her home. That would be . . . unacceptable. But there's no harm in showering her with presents, in exchange for a sweet sad smile or a kiss or maybe a night or a weekend. If you look closely, you can see how her immaculate makeup hides the trails of her tears.

Ezili Freda has become nearly as popular among Pagans as she is with Haitians. Many witches have installed her picture beside their Hathor statue, or placed her dwapo above their Aphrodite altars. Although Freda is no doubt flattered by all this attention, a bit of caution may be in order. As Haitians say, Freda is no small lwa. She can grant favors to those she loves, but she is also quick to anger when she feels neglected, spurned, or offended.

Who Is Freda?

In Benin, Ezili is seen as a river divinity and is one of the most well known of the "Mommy water" spirits found throughout the western coast of Africa. She is both beloved for her beauty and feared for her jeweled dagger. When they arrived in what was then St. Domingue, the slaves saw images of the Virgin Mary wearing rings, necklaces, and a shining crown, her heart pierced by a knife to symbolize her suffering at the foot of the cross. They came to identify this beautiful, pale woman with the spirit they had known in Africa, and to this day the Mater Dolorosa (suffering mother) is identified with Ezili Freda.[1]

On St. Domingue, in addition to white plantation owners and businessmen and black slaves, there was also a sizable population of affranchis. They were allowed to own land and property, but they were subject to numerous restrictions and humiliations. St. Domingue's laws kept them from, among other things, marrying whites, participating in colonial government, wearing European clothing, carrying swords or firearms, or attending social functions with whites. In 1790, Vincent Oge, the Paris-educated son of a mulatto woman, tried to organize the affranchis and demanded they be given the rights recently afforded to them by the French National Assembly. The colonial government responded by crushing his elbows and knees with hammers, and then tying him faceup to a wheel and leaving him in the sun to die. Afterward, they cut his body into pieces, and then sent one of his limbs to each of the four provinces of St. Domingue as a warning to those free persons of color who might wish to rise above their station.

Despite their low status, the affranchis had little sympathy for the black slaves. Some of these affranchis were slave owners themselves, and most feared and loathed the Africans as much as they hated the *grand blancs* (white plantation owners). They wanted freedom from the French—but they wanted a freedom in which they took the place of the whites as lords and masters. Most sought to distance themselves from their black ancestry, and they were said to be "more French than the French."

These cultural scars and chasms are reflected in Vodou's service to Ezili Freda. Freda is a beautiful mulatto woman, with pale skin and long straight hair. People possessed by Freda will often powder their face, apply makeup, and don an outfit that is in the peristyle especially for Freda's appearances. When possessed by Freda, people will often begin speaking French, even if they normally speak only Kreyol. All these things still represent status and wealth in Haiti, where French-speaking mulattoes long controlled most of the resources while poor Kreyol-speaking blacks labored for them. Freda represents a romantic ideal that's beyond the reach of most Haitians. As Mama Lola says poignantly, "Poor people don't got no true love. They just have affiliation."[2]

Freda is married to three lwa: Met Agwe, lord of the ocean; Ogou Ferraille, the bold warrior; and Damballah, the wise white serpent. Yet for each she is more mistress than wife. Agwe's primary partner is the mermaid La Sirene, Damballah favors the rainbow goddess Ayida Wedo, and Ogou is partial to Freda's sister, the hard-working country woman Ezili Danto. Freda constantly seeks an unattainable love, and she is continually disappointed. More often than not, Freda possessions end with her breaking down in tears, sobbing uncontrollably as her dreams are crushed by hard reality.

Freda loves men. When she arrives she will flirt with the men, kissing and caressing them and basking in their attention. She is not so affectionate with other females; at best, she will respond to them with a nod and a wave of her hand. Women who wish to work with Freda must treat her like a maid treats a beloved mistress. She will generally respond to devotion like any well-bred woman will respond to a caring servant: with gratitude and gifts.

Freda's favorite colors are white and baby pink. She likes flowers, particularly pink roses; candy and sweet things; cosmetics, fine clothing, and jewelry. When she comes, Haitians throw perfume about the room because she loves the smell; they also will wet the dirt floors with water so that she does not get dust in her throat. The lady of luxury, she is as generous as she is demanding. She particularly rewards those who are handsome, or who dance well, or whose personality pleases her.

Serving Freda

Those who serve Freda well will be richly rewarded; those who treat her casually or disrespectfully will soon encounter her wrath. Still, those problems can be avoided easily enough by following a few simple rules.

Freda is particularly noted for her jealousy; she doesn't like sharing the spotlight with anybody. If you want to serve Freda, you should give her individual attention, rather than just including her name in a list of "love goddesses." Don't treat her like an "archetype"; treat her like a person you admire for her grace, charm, and beauty. The lwa are not abstractions or unapproachable deities. In Haiti, they regularly come down and talk with their servants, giving them aid and assistance. You wouldn't treat a stylish, classy lady as some generic pretty woman or consider her interchangeable with any other pretty woman—and you shouldn't do that with Freda! If you're going to serve Freda, spend a few minutes every day meditating beside her shrine. Talk with her—and be sure to tell her how beautiful she is and how much you love her. When working with Freda, flattery will get you everywhere.

While you're talking with her, you can also say things like, "I'm having a problem with X. What do you think I should do, Freda?" or, "I wish I had more money; then I could buy you a nice crystal champagne goblet." Don't try to order Freda to do things; instead, trust in her generosity and her kindness to her devotees. Freda will often send good luck your way casually, the same way a wealthy heiress might give a devoted servant an enormous tip. Those who are beloved of Freda are frequently blessed with uncanny luck. They're the sort of people who move to a new city and a few days later find a perfect apartment in the best neighborhood for far less than the going rate. They meet some casual stranger in a nightclub, only to receive a lucrative job offer from him. If Freda decides she likes you, she can give you that kind of good fortune.

In Haiti, poor Vodouisants will scrape pennies together for weeks to buy Freda a bottle of perfume or a pretty dress. When she receives the finest you can give, Freda gives the finest in return. As the lwa of luxury and riches, she is not going to be satisfied by second best. You will do better giving her a small bottle of fine perfume than a bunch of cheap cosmetics; a few Godiva chocolates will make her much happier than a big bag of stale candy.

You must be careful, though. If you try to meet all of Freda's demands, you will find yourself in the poorhouse. By her very nature, Freda cannot be satisfied. Don't let yourself be talked into spending more than you can afford. If Freda seems particularly insistent about something, tell her, "If you give me the money for this, I will do it for you." It's okay to bargain with the lwa; it's also okay to set up conditions for your gifts, such as, "If you help me get that raise at work, I will buy you a bottle of perfume." If you do this, though, be sure that you keep your promises. You may forget that you told Freda you'd buy her something—but Freda won't forget, and there are few things more frightening than a woman scorned.

When working with Freda, there are a few taboos. You should never give her anything black. You should never have sex in front of her shrine; do not put it in front of your bedroom if you can avoid it. (In Haiti, where space is frequently at a premium, Vodouisants will put up a screen between their bed and their altar, so that she doesn't have to watch them having sex.) Freda is a jealous lwa, and if her shrine is placed in your bedroom, she is likely to wreck any relationship you have. Never keep Freda beside a shrine to your ancestors or the gods of the dead. Freda dislikes the Ghede, the foul-mouthed spirits of death and the graveyard. You also should never smoke cigarettes or marijuana around Freda's shrine. When she arrives at a sevis, all the smokers immediately put out their cigarettes, because Freda doesn't like the smell of burning things.

Freda is a demanding lwa, and many Vodouisants will not "put her up" in their house. They may offer her service, but they do not give her a shrine. If you cannot meet her demands (if, for example, you are a smoker who lives in a studio), you may want to consider making occasional offerings to her without creating an altar in her honor.

Working with Freda

Do you want to be more attractive? Get Freda's assistance as a beauty consultant! Buy her a nice bottle of perfume, and place it on her shrine. (If you don't have a shrine for her, wrap the bottle in a pink silk cloth, and then put it in your closet or drawer.) When you want to look your best, ask Freda if you can borrow a drop of her perfume, even if you don't normally wear scents. Don't use a lot of it; you don't even need to be able to smell it. Place this tiny drop over your heart. When you do this, some of Freda's charm and beauty will rub off on you. If you're sensitive to perfumes, you can give Freda a glass of sugar water, and then ask her if she will bless it for you. Sprinkle on a little bit of this when you need to look your best. (Men can use a tiny bit of her perfume, or they can ask her to recommend a nice cologne.)

Freda is also frequently consulted in matters of love, and many "love wangas" are made with her assistance. This may offend some of the readers of this book who have learned that it's wrong to "control the will of another" by casting a love spell. Most Vodouisants would scoff at this. To them, love spells are no more coercive than wearing a sharp suit or a revealing dress to catch your prospective partner's eye. Mambos and houngans do a brisk business in love charms; at ceremonies the lwa are frequently asked to intervene on behalf of love-struck or heartbroken devotees. In this they are following an ancient tradition. Some of the earliest magical amulets were made to bring back straying lovers or win the affections of a target. The idea that "no witch would ever cast a love spell" would be greeted with amusement by most historical witches and folk magicians in any tradition.

I generally do not recommend casting love spells against a specific target for practical reasons. I've found that love spells are 100 percent effective—on the person casting them. If you think you were hung up on your target before you started casting, just wait until you burn a few candles or petition the lwa. I have also found that love spells are only good at getting you the person you desire as she or he is—not the person you might imagine. An unfaithful partner will remain unfaithful even if a love spell works; an abusive partner will remain abusive. It's rather like discussing the ethics of cutting high-tension wires to steal the copper. A simple "that's a good way to get yourself seriously hurt or killed" should be sufficient for most people, without arguing about property rights.

If you wish to ask Freda for her assistance in love, you're better off asking her, "Help me find a partner" instead of asking, "Make X fall madly in love with me." You should also be aware that Freda is a hopeless romantic. She will often bring you a lover who is beautiful and charming but who is not very good at practical affairs. Brilliant but impoverished poets, lovely but free-spending models . . . those are some of the results you can expect from love spells done with Freda's help. If you are looking for a more stable, practical partner, you may want to ask another spirit for help.

13

FILOMEZ AND KLEMEZIN

Vévé for Filomez

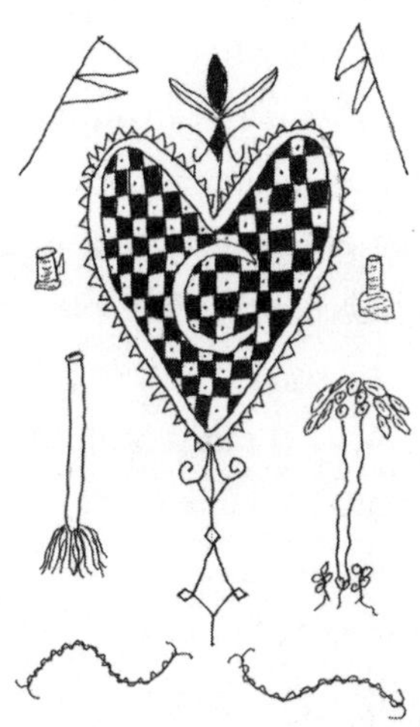

Vévé for Klemezin

"To practice Vodou, you must be Catholic," said a Haitian peasant to ethnographer Alfred Métraux.[1] The influence of Roman Catholicism in Vodou extends far beyond mere usage of imagery. The priye Gineh combines supplications to God, Jesus, the Virgin, and various saints with hymns in praise of the lwa. New statues of the lwa are "baptized" with holy water; the maryaj lwa (marriage to the spirits) features a *prêt savann* (bush priest) who recites the wedding litany and accepts the vows. Vodou's African and Native American roots have received a great deal of scholarly attention, but the influence of Roman Catholicism has often been downplayed.

Some writers seek to dismiss all Catholic elements as "masks" or "blinds" used by the slaves to avoid unwanted attention from overseers.

There is some merit to this, but Catholicism has remained in Vodou long after the overseers have gone and the persecutions have ceased. Vodouisants no longer need to "hide" Ezili Freda behind the Mater Dolorosa; nor do they have to pay homage to the Immaculate Conception or take their children to a priest for baptism. And yet images of the Mater Dolorosa are still found in peristyles and shrines throughout Haiti and the diaspora, and many of the same Haitians who attend fets on Saturday night can be seen at Mass on Sunday morning.

Others wish to "purify" the African traditions from "corruption" by "white," European influences. Their anger is understandable, but their quest is doomed from the beginning. If you strip away the Catholicism from Haitian Vodou, what remains is not Haitian Vodou at all: it is a reconstruction that uses some elements of Haitian Vodou. This is not necessarily a bad thing; Wicca is both a reconstructed religion and a valid spiritual path. Still, those who try to pass their new creation off as "authentic" while scorning the original as "corrupted" are guilty of bad history at best and cultural imperialism at worst. And, ultimately, the very idea of "pure African practices" is based on a myth. By the time the slavers came, the religions practiced in Dahomey and Yorubaland had been exposed to the "religions of the Book" for centuries. Christian missionaries, Islamic conquerors, and Jewish merchants all passed through sub-Saharan Africa and left their mark on African culture centuries before the "triangular trade" began.

Catholicism speaks of "intercessors." Although anyone can and should worship God and his son Jesus, Catholics believe that some holy people and angels are particularly close to him. They might ask the Virgin Mary to intercede on their behalf, thinking Christ will not refuse a request from his mother. Certain saints were even given to specialized miracles. St. Peregrine, a devout man miraculously cured of cancer, has become the patron saint of cancer patients, and St. Lucy, who lost her eyes during the Roman persecutions, is patron of the blind and those afflicted with eye diseases. A peasant who would shudder before the King of Kings might feel more comfortable talking to a humble tailor like St. Gerard Majella or a pious farmer like St. Isadore. Protestants might call this veneration of holy men and their images and relics "idolatry"; but to the Catholic Church, the saints provided models for a holy life and guides who would help lead their devotees to the light.

This worldview is similar to that found in many traditional African religions. They held that after creating the world, God withdrew and left everyday affairs to a whole host of spiritual beings. Some of them were celestial beings from the beginning; others were heroic men and women who became honored ancestors and later guardians for their families, clans, villages, or tribes. A person raised in these African faiths would have little trouble believing in celestial choirs of angels, or of holy men transformed into powerful spirits after their deaths. In the best Catholic tradition, they were guided to the faith by the example of those who had gone before them . . . even if their interpretations and practices weren't always quite so orthodox as their local clergy might have hoped.

In Haiti, some of the saints do double duty as both saint and lwa. Ogou San Jak is seen as Ogou in his manifestation as St. Jacques, the heroic crusader. Haitians call him "St. Jacques Majeur (St. James the Greater)" but the image used is St. Jacques de Campostelle, the crusader (and Moor slayer). The painting of the Black Madonna of Czestochowa, with her dark skin, piercing gaze, and small child, is honored as the Virgin and used as a representation of Ezili Danto. And still other spirits have no African or Indian parallel, but rather come straight from Catholicism. In homes throughout the Haitian diaspora, you will find crosses, statues of the Virgin and the Holy Family, and other Catholic images. These are not all "masks" or "images" for the lwa. Many of these saints and holy figures are seen as powerful spirits and benevolent protectors in their own right.

Christianity and Paganism

Wiccans and Neopagans often have ill feelings toward Christianity and active hostility toward its symbols. Many will state that "all religions are valid" . . . and then enter into long tirades about all the sins and failings of Christianity. Equating evil with "the other" is often far more comfortable than dealing with moral complexity—or with our own shortcomings. For some Pagans, Christianity is a convenient bogeyman. They can rail about the evil Christians while feeling self-righteous about their own "enlightened" rejection of all things Christian.

There is no question that horrible excesses have been committed in the name of Christ and his various churches. But Christianity is not alone in this. In India, Hindu rioters have murdered innocent Muslims and perpetrated centuries of oppression against the Dalits (the untouchables). Africans who practiced their traditional faiths happily sold conquered tribes to slavers, and the long and bloody tradition of human sacrifice by indigenous Central Americans is well documented. People have killed and have been killed in the name of Marxism, democracy, liberty, monarchy, and any number of principles. Human stupidity and human evil are not confined to any particular creed; nor are Christians alone in suppressing indigenous religions. The Roman soldiers who persecuted the druids were not Christians or even monotheists.

Although we should not sugarcoat Christian atrocities, neither should we overlook the good things that have been done by Christians. Christian charities have fed many who would otherwise have gone hungry and provided medicine and treatment for many who were ill and indigent. Christianity has also provided a spiritual framework for billions throughout history. It has helped them to endure adversity and given their lives meaning. Dismissing all of these people as "ignorant" or "benighted" is, in the end, no less condescending than referring to "poor unenlightened heathens" and downplaying the positive contributions of their cultures.

Many—perhaps most of us—come from homes that were at least nominally Christian. We may express our spirituality through Wicca or Buddhism; but most of our ancestors honored the Divine via Christian rituals. We may find that they request Christian symbols—crosses, rosaries, holy cards, and the like—on their altars. (See chapter 25 for instructions on honoring your ancestors.) Studying the faith of your parents (and grandparents) can help you to understand the forces that shaped them, and, by extension, shaped you. A simple-minded rejection is of no more use, in this quest, than unthinking acceptance. Ultimately you will do best to accept both the strengths and the weaknesses of their creed. (You may also be surprised to find how many of those "Christian" preconceptions you still retain. I've met many former fundamentalists who are now Wiccans and who merely switched sides, with evil Christians in the role once played by "the devil and his minions.")

Vodouisants will happily recite psalms or petition saints if they think that will help them achieve their goals. Like most folk-magic traditions, Vodou is geared toward results. Vodouisants work with the saints because they have found that the saints will work with them. Given that veneration of saints has been part of magical and religious practice for thousands of years, in any number of traditions, they may well be on to something.

You do not have to be Catholic to honor the saints. In Trinidad and Tobago, the Spiritual Baptists pay tribute to Philomena as an aspect of Oshun, lwa of love and beauty. In this section, I have left the Christian imagery intact. If you wish to alter these because you feel uncomfortable with honoring Christ or Jehovah, you are of course free to do so. (I know one Jewish houngan who remains silent during those sections of the priye Gineh that honor Christ, the Virgin, and the Catholic saints.) You may find you get the best results by using the words that have been used for centuries—or you may use your own words. In any event, you'll find the saints are less concerned with religious orthodoxy than many of their leaders: they'll happily intercede on behalf of the deserving, whatever their religious orientation.

Filomez (St. Philomena)

On May 25, 1802, excavators in Rome's catacomb of St. Priscilla discovered a hitherto unknown tomb, which was sealed with terra-cotta slabs in the manner usually reserved for nobility or for great martyrs. Upon those slabs were three tiles, inscribed with the words LUMENA/PAXTE/CUMFI, and with the symbols of a lily, arrows, a scourge, an anchor, and a lance. When the excavators opened the coffin, they discovered the remains of a girl of about twelve or thirteen years, along with a vial of her dried blood. When the tiles were rearranged, the inscription "Pax Tecum Filumena" (peace be with you, Philomena) was revealed.

The relics of this new martyr might have remained in obscurity had it not been for a priest named Francis de Lucia. Father de Lucia wanted the relic of a martyred saint for his chapel in Mugnano, a small Italian town. On pausing before Philomena's remains, he was suddenly filled with an unaccountable spiritual joy and begged for those relics. After some difficulties—and many prayers asking Philomena to intercede for him—he was given what he requested. The relics were encased in a special statue and brought to Mugnano.

The day the statue arrived in its new home, a long drought was broken by a much needed rainfall. And that was just the first of many miracles attributed to her. Visitors to her shrine reported cures of cancer, healing of wounds, and the Miracle of Mugnano, in which Pauline Jaricot was cured of a severe heart ailment overnight. Pilgrims from throughout Europe came to know Philomena as a wonder worker and as powerful with God. By 1837, just thirty-five years after her exhumation, Pope Gregory XVI officially recognized her as St. Philomena and declared her Patroness of the Living Rosary. This made her the only person recognized by the Church as a saint solely on the basis of her intercession; nothing historical was known of her except her name and the evidence of her martyrdom.

Decades later, Mother Mary Louisa of Jesus, a nun known for her devotion to St. Philomena, claimed that she had received a revelation from the virgin martyr. According to Mother Mary Louisa, Philomena was the daughter of a prince who governed a small state in Greece. Raised as a Christian from birth, Philomena had betrothed herself to Christ at the age of eleven. Unfortunately, two years later the Roman emperor Diocletian asked for the young maiden's hand in marriage—and, being an emperor, he was sorely offended by her refusal. Philomena was sent to a dungeon and chained hand and foot. Despite the pleading of her parents, and the emperor's threats, she refused to accept Diocletian's proposal of marriage.

Whipped, at the emperor's order, until her body "resembled one open wound," she remained obstinate. Finally, Diocletian ordered her cast into the Tiber River with an anchor around her neck, only to be foiled when two angels cut the rope and carried her back to shore before a multitude, "many of whom were converted to the faith."[2] Now infuriated, Diocletian commanded that Philomena be dragged through the streets of Rome and shot with arrows, and then returned to her dungeon to die. His fury became blind rage when he awoke to discover that during the night, Philomena's wounds had been healed. When one of his magicians suggested that fire would be effective against her sorcery, he commanded that she once more be dragged through the streets and wounded, this time with flaming arrows. Alas, his magician was proven wrong: when the flaming arrows were fired at Philomena, they reversed course and killed six of the archers instead, causing still more of the crowd to renounce paganism. By this time, Diocletian's anger was tempered by fear. In place of a messy (and potentially embarrassing) public execution, he instead ordered a simple beheading. This was accomplished without a hitch, and Philomena attained the crown of virginity and the palm of martyrdom.

You may think this all sounds a bit far-fetched—and many Catholic leaders would agree with you, albeit privately. During and after the Vatican II era, as the Church sought to modernize itself, many saints were dropped from the liturgical calendar, among them St. Philomena. Although Catholics were still free to honor Philomena on August 11, it was no longer officially recognized as her feast day. This was greeted with outrage among traditionalist Catholics—but it made little difference to many of St. Philomena's most devoted followers. High-ranking Catholic clergy may feel that Philomena no longer deserves a place in the liturgical calendar, but she still has a place in the hearts of millions of devotees. Many of the faithful still bring their petitions to her shrine in Italy, and she remains a well-loved saint throughout the Caribbean. In Haiti and the Haitian diaspora, St. Philomena is regularly asked for aid and makes frequent appearances at Vodou fets.

Working with Filomez

Vodouisants serve Filomez (the Kreyol form of "Philomena") with pastel-colored scarves, typically light blue, light pink, light yellow, and pale green. When she arrives she dances around the room, and she is often given a bouquet of flowers, which she scatters about the floor. Some say she is a cheerful merchant girl who brings prosperity. Others petition her in matters of love and claim she is a sister to Ezili Freda. All agree that she is a powerful intercessor with a long history of granting miraculous favors to those who honor her.

If you want to petition Philomena, you should have little problem finding an image of her online or at a local Catholic supply store. Provide her with fresh flowers (preferably in pastel shades—pink roses, light yellow carnations, etc.) and ask her to help you. I have included a popular Catholic prayer to St. Philomena. You may use this or you may petition her using a prayer or speech of your own.

Prayer to St. Philomena

O faithful virgin and glorious martyr, St. Philomena, who works so many miracles on behalf of the poor and sorrowing, have pity on me. You know the multitude and diversity of my needs. Behold me at thy feet, full of misery, but full of hope. I entreat thy charity, O great saint! Graciously hear me and obtain from God a favorable answer to the request, which I now humbly lay before thee. [Specify your petition here.] I am firmly convinced that through my merits, through the scorn, the sufferings, the death thou didst endure, united to the merits of the Passion and Death of Jesus, thy Spouse, I shall obtain what I ask of thee, and in the joy of my heart I will bless God, who is admirable in His saints. Amen.

Klemezin (St. Clare of Assisi)

Although she would become renowned as founder of the Poor Clares, Clare Offreducció had an early life that was anything but poor. The daughter of a wealthy count and countess in Assisi, Italy, she spent her youth in a palace. Even as a child surrounded by all the trappings of luxury, she was known for her piety, and for her disdain of worldly things. This disdain was inflamed when she was eighteen and heard a friar named Francis preaching in the streets. Like her, Francis had also been born into wealth and privilege, and yet he had forsaken everything for the sake of God. His example spoke to Clare, and she resolved to follow in his footsteps. On March 20, 1212, young Clare ran away from her parents' house, and with the aid of the friar who would later become St. Francis of Assisi, she entered religious life.

Her father had hoped to marry the young countess off to a worthy nobleman, and he was infuriated with her decision to join a convent. He tried to persuade her to return, and he even tried to drag her off by force; but young Clare was steadfast in her decision. Ultimately, she and a few other women who had turned their backs on the world followed St. Francis to a rough dwelling on the outskirts of town. There these "poor ladies" spent their days in prayer and mortifications. They owned nothing, not even property in common, and they relied on begging for their daily bread. They wore no shoes, ate no meat, and kept silent most of the time. Some people thought they were too severe in their poverty and their mortifications, but Clare responded, "They say that we are too poor, but can a heart which possesses the infinite God be truly called poor?"[3] By 1215, Clare had been declared abbess of this new convent, despite her wishes to be nothing but a humble member. Her position did not stop her from working alongside her fellow nuns, nor did a delicate constitution that left her battling with frequent and severe illnesses. She arose early in the morning for prayers; she would get up late at night to tuck in her sisters who had kicked off their covers.

In 1234, the army of Frederick II prepared to attack Clare's convent. Rising from her sickbed, Clare took a monstrance (a container for the Eucharist) from the chapel that adjoined her cell, and then faced the invaders at an open window against which they had placed a ladder. As she raised the Blessed Sacrament on high, the soldiers on the ladder fell backward as if dazzled by a bright light. Blinded, they ran away in terror. Later, when a larger force arrived to attack Assisi, Clare gathered the other women of the convent and led them in an earnest prayer that they and the townspeople might be spared. As if in response to their prayers, a furious storm arose, blowing away the soldiers' tents and causing them to once again retreat in panic. Henceforth no one troubled the convent, and Clare was able to continue her rulership until her death in 1253. Near the end, she was forced to spend much time on her sickbed, but even this was not enough to keep her away from Mass. Even as she lay ill, an image of the service would display on the wall of her cell. By that time, orders of Poor Clares could be found throughout Europe, as women sought to follow her as she had followed Francis. Her legacy continues. Today there are over twenty thousand Poor Clares, living in seventy-six countries around the world.

St. Clare is most commonly pictured holding a monstrance, in honor of her triumph over invaders. Because of her ability to see the Mass without being present, she has also become the patron saint of clairaudience and television. In Haiti, she is beloved as Klemezin Klemay, and her image is seen on peristyles throughout the country.

Working with Klemezin

Although St. Clare died of natural causes at the age of sixty after years of illness, Vodouisants envision Klemezin as a young, healthy, and beautiful woman. When she arrives, she bounces up and down on her toes and will spring around the peristyle. Sometimes she scatters flower petals about; at other times she takes a broom and "sweeps away" negativity and bad luck from the area and from participants. She is served with light blue and white scarves; when she is saluted, flower petals and perfume are sprinkled on the floor, as befits a noblewoman. (St. Clare would likely be horrified at this indulgence and request that the perfume and flowers be sold and the money donated to the poor; but as many others before and after her have found, you can't always control your admirers.)

Vodouisants petition Klemezin for clarity of vision and clear dreams. They will sometimes make an offering to her that consists of a bowl of spring water in which they have placed some coconut water, some shredded coconut, and some white flower petals. They will place this under their bed; they believe that by doing so Klemezin will grant them clarity of vision and insight into ways they can solve their problems. If you want to do this, you can certainly do so. Clean your space beforehand and place clean sheets on the bed, and then put the bowl under your bed. In the morning when you awaken, sprinkle the water about the room; you can also rub a drop or two on your eyes. This will help you to achieve clarity.

You can offer Klemezin sweet white or light blue cakes, white or light blue flowers, and perfume. You can also make offerings in thanksgiving to charity; the Poor Clares will appreciate your contribution, as will any charity dealing with children or with the poor. If you work regularly with St. Clare, you will find that you are more able to "see a solution" to tangled problems; you will also discover that your instinct and intuition becomes more clear.

Sample Prayer to St. Clare of Assisi

Blessed St. Clare, illuminate the darkness of our hearts and our minds, that we may see what we need to do, and perform our duty with a willing and joyous heart. Have pity on our struggles and comfort us in our mourning. Obtain from God for us the grace we ask, and help us to submit to the divine will. Let the divine light pierce through the darkness of evil and corruption. Be a light to us in our sorrows and anxieties, and lead us into the eternal light of heaven. Amen.

14
ZAKA

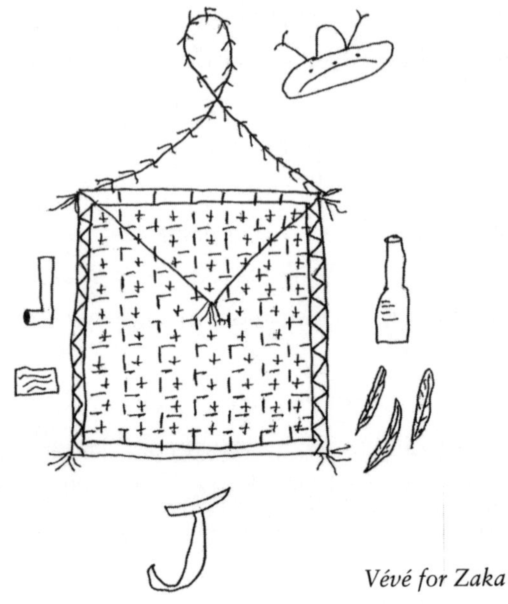

Vévé for Zaka

The tools have not changed that much—the hoe, the shovel, the bag full of seeds. Nor have the long days of backbreaking labor under a pitiless sun. For thousands of years, we have scratched the dirt and survived off what crops we could raise. Many in Haiti still scratch at what is left of St. Domingue's fertile soil, planting the food they will later eat, barring flood or drought or any of the other disasters waiting to happen.

If you go far enough into the countryside, you'll still find him there. It might take a while before he warms up to you—but once you gain his trust he'll be happy to teach you what he knows. For the right price, of course. A working man knows the value of money, and he knows that all you damn fool rich people have plenty to spare.

Among Pagans who are interested in Vodou, Zaka is generally little known and infrequently served. The lwa of agriculture and farming isn't as pretty as Ezili Freda or as boisterous and fun loving as the Ghede. Still, he deserves more attention than he receives. In Haiti, Cousin Zaka, as he is sometimes called, is a major lwa and a beloved friend to the poor, with a reputation as a hard worker. Understanding this powerful spirit can help you understand the forces that have shaped Haitian culture and Haitian history. If you treat Zaka with the respect he deserves, and honor your commitments to him, you'll find that he's a faithful helper and a tireless assistant.

The Origins of Zaka

Vodou is an oral tradition, and one that received little attention from scholars until the twentieth century. As a result, it can be difficult to determine exactly where many of the lwa originated, and when they were first served in Vodou. Zaka's roots are particularly obscure. Finding his history requires a lot of digging, a fair bit of speculating, and more than a few educated guesses. It is easy to see how Da, the Great White Serpent of the Fon people of Ewe, became Damballah, and how Elegbara became Legba; but it is more difficult to find an African equivalent for Cousin Zaka.

Maya Deren, author of *Divine Horsemen,* thought Zaka was originally a spirit from the Arawak and Taino peoples, inherited from the Indians by the escaped African slaves who hid in the rugged Haitian mountains.[1] Zaka is said to be the first lwa who spoke with the Indians, who introduced him to New World crops like corn. Some scholars believe the Ghede also has Taino roots, and many Vodouisants say the Ghede are Zaka's brothers. Houngan Aboudja believes that some of the spirits who are named Zaka do have an Indian origin. However, he traces the "root" Zaka, or first Zaka, to western Africa, where even today a spirit named Zaka is honored in Savalou, an area in Benin.[2]

If Zaka's origins are unclear, his connection to Haiti and Haitian culture is undeniable. During the slavery era, St. Domingue was largely composed of massive plantations, which produced sugarcane, indigo plants, and other crops for export. After the Haitian Revolution of 1804, the plantation owners were gone, but vast tracts of fertile land remained. Haiti's first leaders, Jean-Jacques Dessalines and Henri Christophe, attempted to enforce *fermage,* a serflike system, onto the people. Most of the newly freed slaves, unsurprisingly, wanted nothing to do with this. They took their leave of the new plantation lords and retreated into the

Haitian interior. There they set up small farms, growing the food they needed to support themselves and their families. Later, Alexandre Pétion tried to appease the black majority by distributing small parcels of land to soldiers and later to other beneficiaries. This helped Pétion stay in power, but it proved disastrous to the Haitian economy. These small family plots were more suited to subsistence farming than to the export crops grown on the large plantations. The sugarcane industry that had made St. Domingue France's wealthiest colony diminished until, by 1822, sugar exports ceased altogether.

These subsistence farmers, and their children and grandchildren who followed in their footsteps, were well acquainted with hard work and poverty. Within twenty years after the Haitian Revolution, Haiti had become divided into a rural black majority and an urban minority of mullatoes and *gens de coleur* (free persons of color). The rural blacks mistrusted their urban "leaders"—and with good reason, given Haiti's long history of misrule and bloodshed. For the most part, they preferred to be left alone. They had little in the way of health care, education, or clean water—but they were also largely free of tyranny. Although their lives were not luxurious, they were better than the horrors of the plantations—or the press gangs and forced military conscription that awaited many of them in the cities. They became especially close to Zaka, who also farmed for his supper. Today, Zaka is one of Haiti's most popular and revered lwa. His image is still found throughout the Haitian countryside. It is also found in peristyles in many major cities in Haiti and the Haitian diaspora. Erosion and deforestation have washed away much of the once-fertile Haitian soil, and many rural peasants have been forced off their land. They may no longer be farming, but they have not forgotten their roots, or Cousin Zaka.

Zaka Today

There are several different spirits who answer to the name Zaka. Zaka Krebs is one of the Zakas who may have Taino origins. When he arrives, he is celebrated with an "Indian war whoop" and given a burning stick so that he can burn the sores on his bare feet. (Zaka Krebs suffers from yaws, a tropical disease that was eradicated from Haiti decades ago.) Zaka Mini (Minister Zaka) is a "minister of agriculture," known for his almost comical sense of self-importance. Zaka Mede is an old Zaka who sits on the ground when he arrives.

Zaka's wife, Kouzenne, will also arrive at a fet on occasion. She is a practical country woman who handles Zaka's money for him; she also looks after small merchants, particularly women. In Haiti, women have traditionally handled market duties. Because any able-bodied man who went into town risked conscription into the military or into civil service "work gangs," it was safer to send your wife or your daughters to the marketplace to buy and sell items. (This is not to say that Zaka doesn't know how to count. I have found that Zaka is well aware of exactly how much you owe him, and when you promised to pay him. . . .)

All Zakas dress in the sturdy blue denim of a peasant and wear a peasant's straw hat to protect their head from the driving Haitian sun. Over their shoulder they carry a makoute (sack) in which they keep their few earthly possessions: a pipe and tobacco, a coconut and brown sugar, and what little money they have been able to save from their toil. Zaka's vévé shows that makout along with two of a farmer's implements, the scythe and the rake. Drummers call Zaka with Djouba rhythms, and, like the Petwo lwa, he is saluted with a cha-cha instead of the asson. However, he is honored during the Rada portion of the ceremony, along with the cooler and more benevolent Dahomey spirits like Damballah and Ezili Freda.

Like many rural people, Zaka is suspicious of "city folks." He believes that they are out to take advantage of him, because they consider him unsophisticated. Zaka cannot read or write, and he leaves money matters to Kouzenne. That doesn't mean that he's stupid—and those who take him for a simple-minded rube will find this out the hard way! In small rural communities, gossip is often a favored pastime—and Zaka is a notorious gossip. He has a keen eye for detail, and he will share your business with the crowd if you offend him, all the while feigning innocence. ("I'm sorry . . . I wouldn't have said nothing about your girlfriend if I knew your wife was here. I don't know nothing about those city manners, I'm just a poor man.")

Because Zaka must work so hard for everything he has, he is very protective of his possessions. His makout is kept hanging in the peristyle; no one disturbs it, for fear Cousin Zaka will take a fearsome revenge on the thief. In Haiti, Vodouisants will ask Zaka to look after things for them. They will place money they have put aside for some purpose in his bag, giving him a small percentage in exchange for his protection. They feel that even the most foolhardy and desperate thief will think twice before rifling through Zaka's things. Vodouisants will sometimes borrow money from Zaka. They believe that Zaka's money will bring good luck, and they are willing to pay the exorbitant interest he charges; often he will demand ten dollars for every dollar he lends, to be repaid at the next party when he arrives.

Zaka is also known to be a flirt. When he arrives, he will often propose marriage to one or more women at the party. Most women who are going to marry a lwa will marry Zaka along with Ogou and Damballah. (It is believed that Ogou's heat must be tempered by Zaka's earthiness and Damballah's cool, airy nature. Others say that if Zaka doesn't receive a wedding ring he will spread gossip about your other husbands and cause you trouble.) Although Zaka loves women, he sometimes feels insecure around them, because he is poor and black. A woman who shows him respect and returns his affection will find Zaka to be a faithful provider and loyal protector, despite his wandering eye.

Working with Zaka

Many Pagans who work with Zaka mistake him for a fertility spirit, one connected with growing things and wildlife. Zaka is actually an agriculture spirit. Instead of the untamed woods and verdant fields, Zaka is connected with working the land and using it to meet your needs. This is a subtle distinction, but an important one. Fertility spirits are generally benevolent and generous, giving from their abundance. Agriculture spirits, on the other hand, tend to be associated with hard work. Preparing a plot, tilling the land, harvesting crops—all require backbreaking labor. Zaka will help you, but he expects to be paid for his efforts.

Zaka's colors are dark blue and dark green; you can burn seven-day candles in those colors, or provide him with the appropriate bandanas or scarves. Zaka is syncretized with St. Isadore, a poor farmer who also wears ragged blue denim and who is usually pictured kneeling at prayer in his field. You can place a lithograph of St. Isadore or a St. Isadore statue on Zaka's altar and use that as his image. You may also want to give him a walking stick (useful when walking through the fields) and some old farm tools, like a scythe or a hoe.

If you are going to create a shrine for Zaka, be sure to include a straw hat and a bag. If you can get an actual straw makout, that will be ideal, but in a pinch a canvas shoulder bag will do. In that bag, you should place a coconut, a block of brown sugar (if you live near a bodega or store that sells Spanish groceries, look for a panela or piloncillo), a clay pipe and some tobacco, and some money (at least ten dollars). Once you have filled this bag, tie it shut, using a bandana. After you have done this, *do not open it again* unless you are putting something else inside. This is very important: you do not want Zaka to think you are stealing from him.

Zaka enjoys chaka, a dish made with red beans, tripe, corn, chayote, and coconut. He will also take red beans and rice, cassava, or just about anything you prepare for him. (He may grouse about the food, but he's not a picky eater. Those who are raised in poverty rarely are.) When preparing chaka, or anything else you will give Zaka, you must not taste the food before it is served. If you take so much as a spoonful from the pot before Zaka has eaten, he will accuse you of "stealing" his food. At best, he will refuse to eat it; at worst, he will cause the person who "stole" it to become deathly ill. You should prepare Zaka's food with a wooden spoon and serve it to him without silverware. Zaka does not know how to use a spoon or fork and eats with his hands; if you provide him with table implements, he may become self-conscious about his humble upbringing. You can also provide him with a bottle of his favorite drink, *absente* (absinthe). This is kleren (you can use overproof rum or other high-octane alcohol) in which wormwood has been steeped. If you can place this in a Vodou bottle that's dedicated to Zaka, so much the better.

When you ask Zaka for a favor, be sure to set a price with him. ("Zaka, if you help me, I will give you a plate of chaka and put twenty dollars in your bag.") You may discover that he wants to negotiate with you. ("How about something to wash down that chaka?") Be generous, but be firm. Zaka is a shrewd bargainer, and he will overcharge you if you let him. After he does his work for you, be sure that you fulfill your end of the bargain. If you do not have a shrine for Zaka at home, you may leave his gifts at a farm, or, if you live in an urban area, a flea market. Once you establish a history with Zaka and gain his trust, you'll find that he is one of your most hardworking and reliable spirits.

As deforestation and erosion gradually destroy Haiti's farmland, the population is becoming increasingly urban. Former farmers find themselves forced into Port-au-Prince and other cities in the diaspora. As the culture has changed, Zaka has also become patron of day laborers, factory workers, and others who earn their daily bread by the sweat of their brow. Those who wish to go into business for themselves will often petition Zaka for assistance. They believe that he will help them earn a living from their shop as he earns a living from his land, and as his wife earns a living from her small market stand. If you need help at your job, or if you want to join the ranks of the self-employed, you may want to ask for his assistance.

To get Zaka's help at work, purchase a small St. Isadore figurine or holy card. If you don't feel particularly drawn to saint imagery, you can use a small Zaka vévé. (For best results, you should draw this yourself.) Keep this at your workplace; it does not have to be in plain view and can be placed in a drawer or even carried in your wallet or purse. Ask Zaka for his assistance whenever you feel overwhelmed, when it's time for a performance review, or when you could use a little bit of help. If you have your own business, you can even put your Zaka shrine there instead of at your home. At the very least, you may want to keep a Zaka image or candle displayed at all times. With Zaka on the case, you will soon see beneficial results. Zaka may not help you "get rich quick"—but he will provide opportunities to make your hard work pay off, and give you the strength to endure difficulties and triumph over adversity.

In the remote mountains of rural Haiti, there is little in the way of organized medical care. Those who are injured or ill are forced to rely on leaf doctors who know the medicinal properties of the various herbs that grow in Haiti and who combine herbalism with prayer and petitions to the spirits. Zaka is well known for his expertise in herbs, and he is often asked for assistance in healing magic. If you are an herbalist or want to learn more about herbs, you should offer Zaka a candle and ask for his guidance. Once you do that, you'll find yourself grasping the nuances of herbalism and herb magic more quickly than you would have thought possible. (If you are fortunate, you may even get instructions from Zaka in a dream visit.)

Zaka is well known for his powers of observation and his blunt honesty. Vodouisants frequently seek his counsel. You may want to bring your questions to Zaka. Either set up an illumination (see chapter 26) or just mediate in front of his image or shrine. Zaka's advice is not sugarcoated; if you're behaving stupidly, he won't hesitate to tell you just that. He won't flatter you, but neither will he lie to you. You may not like what he says—but you'll do well to listen. Zaka may not be eloquent, but his plain-spoken wisdom will prove invaluable if you take it to heart and act upon it. When Zaka offers his assistance, he will expect you to do your part. He has little patience for laziness and will be quick to call you a "damn fool" if you don't heed his warnings and follow his advice. (Especially when you come back asking him to help you get out of the mess that will inevitably follow.)

If you're going to serve the lwa, make sure you give Cousin Zaka due respect. Getting to know Zaka will help you to understand Vodou, and the Haitian culture from whence it came. He may be gruff, and a bit lacking in social graces, but he is a reliable friend and a tireless worker. Cousin Zaka drives a hard bargain, but he makes good on his promises, and he will reward those who serve him faithfully.

15
OGOU

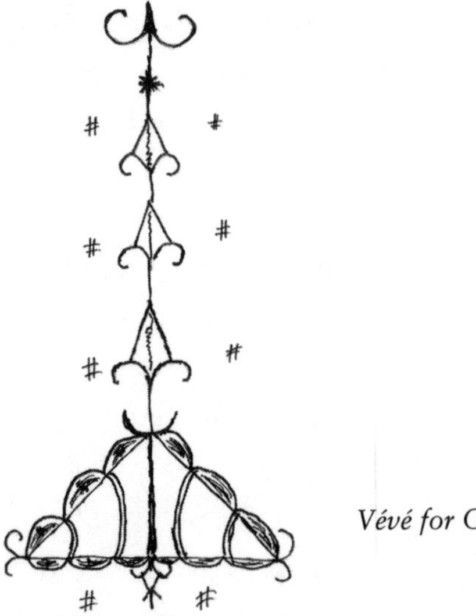
Vévé for Ogou

Faced with heavy losses both from guerrilla warfare and yellow fever, the French colonists began a campaign of genocide against any blacks they could find. By some estimates, as many as 60 percent of the blacks of St. Domingue were killed between 1791 and 1803. Possessed by Ogou Feraille, Jean-Jacques Dessalines took a French tricolor and "ripped the white out," giving his troops the red and blue banner that would become the Haitian flag . . . and a mandate to slaughter every white person they could lay hands on. By 1804, when Dessalines declared himself emperor, there were no whites remaining in the Free Black Republic of Haiti.

Today Ogou, the hot-tempered, rum-swilling lwa of iron and warfare, remains one of the most popular spirits in Haitian Vodou, and with good reason. He's rough, loud, and macho, but he's also a staunch friend and a faithful protector. Ogou can be intimidating—but when the chips are down, you can count on him.

Ogou in Africa

West Africans knew iron as both giver and destroyer of life. With iron machetes, they cleared underbrush and prepared the land for farming.

With iron hoes, they tilled the soil before planting; then they used the same hoe to weed and chop the growing crops and to aid in the harvest. Yet iron was also used to make spears, and later guns. The knife that cut the umbilical cord and the spade that dug the grave were both made of iron. Life and death, protection and destruction, building and destroying—all these things required iron.

Ironworking was a religious ritual. Master smelters led invocations, dances, songs, praises, and other esoteric activities to ensure ore's transformation into iron. Blacksmiths, and the iron objects they produced, were believed to have mystical powers. They created items that were both beautiful and functional: elaborately decorated and razor-sharp hunting knives, blades for scarification and body modification rituals, iron staffs that showed the wielder's authority while providing a history of the tribe for those who could read the engravings.[1]

Iron was fundamental to the rise of several African kingdoms—Dahomey, Benin, and the Yoruba kingdoms like Ife and Oyo. All of them shared similar spiritual beliefs concerning iron and ironworking methods.[2] Ogou was recognized by all of them. He was the first blacksmith, the first hunter and warrior, the clearer of fields and the founder of dynasties. Ogou, who's also known as Ogun, protected those who could not defend themselves—or, when he fell into a blind rage, he slaughtered them. He was both the oppressor and the freedom fighter struggling against oppression; the skilled craftsman and the bloodthirsty berserker, the protector and the predator. The red of dried blood, hot iron, and rust was his color. The hook with which the smelter stirred hot ore, the warrior's blade, and the blacksmith's anvil were his symbols.

As with other African spirits, the worship of Ogou, and the stories told about him, varied from region to region. In all areas, he was known for his strength, his skill, and his hot temper. He was also known for his honesty and his hatred of liars; to this day Nigerians who practice their traditional religions swear oaths not on Bibles but on pieces of iron. They believe that if they lie before Ogun he will punish them with death or grievous injury.

Ogou Comes to the Americas

In the New World, Ogou retained his ambivalent nature. He ruled over the iron chains that bound the slaves, and the machetes with which they hacked their way to freedom. In Cuba, those who practiced La Regla de Ocha ("The Way of Ocha," also known as Lucumí) gave him rulership over trains and automobiles, and over accidents involving machinery. He was also the orisha in charge of prisons: he could unlock prison doors if he saw fit, or, if he was angry, he could put you behind iron bars. Slaves from different areas brought with them different and sometimes conflicting stories about their spirits. In La Regla de Ocha, they accounted for these by attributing different *caminos* (roads) to each of the orishas, including Ogou. While each camino was identified with Ogou, each was also connected with particular items or activities that caused the different caminos to behave in very different ways when they came in possession.

Ogou was honored throughout the African diaspora, but he was particularly important in Haiti. There, Ogou is a family name attributed to the Nago nachon. The Ogous are seen as relatives, separate spirits who are all part of an extended family. Each Ogou carries a machete and favors red, but each works in his own sphere. Ogou Balindjo walks with Met Agwe, lord of the seas, whereas the fierce Ogou Ge Wouj (Ogou Red-Eyes) walks with the fiery Petwo spirits. Ogou San Jak is a crusading soldier; Ogou Badagris a wily general and politician. The spirits of heroic soldiers are numbered among the Ogous. Dessalines, hero of the Haitian Revolution, is honored as Ogou Dessalines. Several Cuban orishas are also included in the Nago nation. Obatala Ajaguna, one of Obatala's warrior roads, was honored as Ogou Batala, and Ogou's rival Chango became Ogou Shango among Vodouisants.

Remember that this energy manifests in different forms. Your Ogou may not be my Ogou, and those differences do not mean that either of us are wrong or misguided. Above all else, Vodou is a practical faith. If your Ogou prefers gin, or a pipe, or Coca-Cola, then you should be concerned first and foremost with keeping your Ogou happy, not with slavishly adhering to a set of instructions.

Ogou for Pacifists?

In modern times, war has become less popular than it once was. Romantic stories of heroism and valor have been replaced by graphic images of carnage, bloodshed, and senseless violence. For the most part, this is a good thing. In an age of nuclear weapons, poison gas, and cluster bombs, peaceful coexistence is preferable to wanton slaughter. Nor should war be romanticized or idealized. Rather, it should be shown in all its ugliness, so that we think long and hard before sending people to kill and be killed.

Still, this raises the question: Why honor a spirit of war in an age striving desperately for peace? This is especially true in Neopaganism, a tradition in which "an it harm none" has replaced "an eye for an eye," and the avenging god is downplayed in favor of the Mother Goddess. A machete-swinging spirit like Ogou may seem anachronistic. Is there a place for this energy among people who prefer consensus and cooperation to conflict? Should we be honoring this mind-set . . . or should we be trying to move beyond it?

One answer to this question lies in the Kabbalistic Tree of Life, a diagram that organizes the mystical and mundane world into ten *sephiroth* connected by twenty-two paths. Many of the items associated with Ogou—iron, blades, the color red, warfare—are attributed to the fifth sephirah, Geburah, and to the planet Mars. This sephirah sits opposite Chesed, the sphere of the merciful father. The two counterbalance each other. When Geburah is too prominent, it manifests as uncontrolled aggression, violence for the sake of violence, and all the things we associate with modern warfare. However, when Geburah is lacking, and Chesed becomes too prominent, we get an unbalanced mercy—a mercy that tolerates evil and allows injustice.[3] There are times when one must say, "This is wrong, and I won't stand for it." And this is where Ogou can give us the strength to fight for justice.

Suppose you have decided that our government's latest war is unjust and you should do something about it. Are you going to sit around the coffeehouse with friends who share your view and talk about how awful this war is? That may leave you feeling warm and fuzzy and self-righteous—but it's not likely to change the world, or slow down the war machine. Are you willing to stand up for your beliefs if it means getting arrested, or losing your job? Would you be willing to sabotage trains that haul war supplies? Ogou asks, "What will you sacrifice for what is right?" Sometimes pacifism requires greater courage than warmongering . . . and Ogou is far more impressed by courage than bluster.

Ogou is immense energy—but he is controlled energy. He is fire contained in a blast furnace; he is the soldier whose skills are harnessed in the service of his commanders. He teaches important lessons about discipline. The drill sergeant doesn't take "I can't" for an answer but forces cadets to overcome their weakness and become "all that they can be." Ogou does the same for us: he goads us to triumph over our fears. He despises lies—and that includes the lies we tell ourselves. His guidance is loving but stern. He demands our best, and he will not be satisfied with anything less. Much as he turns raw ore into fine steel, he shapes his servants into stronger, better people. This process of transformation will be challenging, and frequently painful, but it is a necessary part of our spiritual and personal development.

Working with Ogou

As I said, Ogou is served in Haiti with red scarves. Some Ogous will use other colors in addition to these. If you have a strong feeling that your Ogou also wants a white scarf or a blue scarf, feel free to give him this as well. You can also provide him with a machete, and with an appropriate image. If you don't feel any particular connection to the saints, you can instead use a symbol that has more meaning to you. (On my Ogou altar, I have a red statue of the Chinese war god Guan Di.) Ogou also likes rum and fine cigars. You can place these on his table, preferably on a red plate or on a piece of iron.

In Haiti, Wednesday is Ogou's day. Many Vodouisants will start their Wednesday morning by banging his machete on a hard surface to get his attention, and then pouring a little bit of rum into a plate or an iron cauldron that's been given to him. They next ignite this rum, and then they quickly run their hands through the flame and slap their arms with this fire. While doing this, they ask Ogou to provide them with strength and courage. Ogou will also look after you if you do this—although caution is advised. Ogou doesn't want you getting second-degree burns, or setting your living quarters on fire!

Ogou looks after those who serve him. If you are feeling threatened by a person or a situation, you can ask for Ogou's assistance. There is no concept of "an it harm none" in Vodou. Typical Vodouisants would have no qualms about making wanga to gain the affections of a person they desired. Neither would they see anything amiss with asking the lwa to help them get revenge against those who have done them wrong. Indeed, many would say that a preemptive "first strike" is acceptable. Although this may seem harsh, we should consider the environment in which these norms of behavior have developed. In Haiti, 80 percent of the population lives below the poverty line, and social amenities like a welfare system and police force are utterly absent in much of the country. Those who have been injured may well have no avenger but the lwa. I don't recommend using Ogou as an attack dog—although you *can* use the lwa to do malevolent work against people, it usually comes back to haunt you—but there is nothing wrong with asking Ogou to look after you and protect you from evildoers. Those who regularly face physical danger, as do police officers, soldiers, and people in other hazardous occupations, are particularly advised to honor Ogou.

Africans swear oaths on Ogou's sacred iron; you can do the same thing. If you have a habit you truly want to break, or something you really want to do, you can make an oath to Ogou that you will break that habit, start that exercise regimen, and so on. Think long and hard before doing this, and, after you make this oath, be sure that you follow through. Ogou doesn't take oaths lightly, nor does he suffer oath breakers gladly. If you break a promise to him, you will regret it. However, he will provide you with the strength and the discipline to follow through on that promise if you ask him for it.

You can talk with Ogou at his altar, or, if you don't have room for an

Ogou altar in your house, you can talk with him elsewhere. The Africans who were brought to the New World in chains couldn't set up elaborate shrines to their spirits; they had to serve them in secret, and take pains to ensure the slave owners didn't catch them in the act. If you live near railroad tracks or an industrial area, you can go to these places to honor Ogou. Pour a little rum on the ground, and leave him some change and a cigar.

"People sleep peaceably in their beds at night only because rough men stand ready to do violence on their behalf," wrote British writer George Orwell. He could have been speaking of Ogou. Ogou is not cuddly and benevolent—but he is loyal, protective, and, in his own way, nurturing. He can help you make positive changes in your life, and he can teach valuable lessons about honor, courage, and standing up for what you believe. Ogou can be a harsh spirit, but sometimes the world can be a harsh place. When times are tough, you need a strong and reliable friend . . . and they don't come any stronger or more reliable than Ogou.

The Petwo Lwa

Because the Petwo lwa can be fierce, they should be approached with caution. Some mistakenly refer to the Rada lwa as "good" and the Petwo as "evil." This is misleading. The Rada lwa can be used to make malevolent magic, and the Petwo can heal and do beneficial workings. However, they are more forceful than the more easygoing Rada lwa. Vodouisants say the Rada are cooler and the Petwo are more hot. They can be great allies, but they can also burn you if you are not careful.

I have included only a sampling of Petwo lwa in this book. Many of these spirits are patrons of the secret societies like the Sanpwel and the Zobop. They are seen as powerful but demanding—and quick to take offense if they are not greeted in the appropriate manner or if they are called by one who presumes to approach them without the proper ceremonies. If you choose to become initiated, you may receive the introductions and passwords you need to greet them and work with them. The Petwo spirits I have listed here are hot and strong, but they are a bit more forgiving of error than some of the other Petwo, and they can be approached by a curious and respectful newcomer.

16
KALFOU

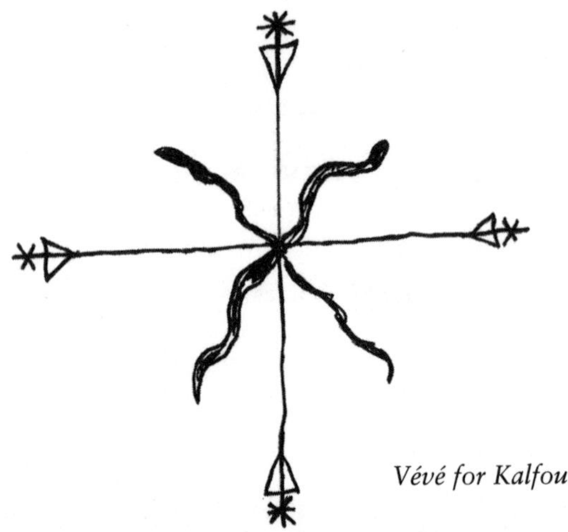

Vévé for Kalfou

We can choose between destinations when we reach the crossroads . . . but what happens if we choose to leave the road altogether and go wandering outside? There are corners, and then there are the spaces between the corners. There are roads, and then there are the pathless wastes beyond the road. Pathless, maybe—but not barren. If you go walking there, you won't be walking alone.

There are stories of people who left the road in the dead of night. Some came back insane. Some didn't come back at all. Those who came back were . . . different. The way they carried themselves, the way they spoke, the look in their eyes. You could tell they had seen things people weren't meant to see.

If you want to learn the difference between Legba and Met Kalfou, all you need do is look at their vévés. Legba's vévé is symmetrical, with emphasis placed on the four distinct cardinal points. It represents the cosmic order. Legba may be a complicated and sometimes unpredictable spirit, but there's always a method to his madness. The cross on Kalfou's vévé has snakes wrapped around it, slithering through the empty spaces between the cross. Kalfou rules the chaos that dances at the edge of order. Like H. P. Lovecraft's Lurker at the Threshold, he is the lord over forbidden and unknown realms. Legba opens the door so that the spirits can visit humanity. Kalfou opens the door so humanity can enter the realm of spirits.

Legba is associated with healing, benevolent magic, and preservation; Kalfou is connected with death, the cemetery, and destructive magic. When you want to do magic for destruction, or when you want to work outside the rules, go to Kalfou for assistance. When Legba comes, he arrives as a little old man limping down the path. Kalfou arrives like a mighty warrior. A person possessed by Kalfou will sometimes eat fire or handle red-hot metal. This shows Kalfou's strength and gives us evidence of his "hot" nature. He is a strong and aggressive spirit, quick to work but equally quick to punish. Those who approach him casually or carelessly, or who do not pay him proper respect, will learn how terrifying his wrath can be.

Legba was honored in Benin. In Yorubaland and the Kongo, there was another crossroads spirit: Exu. Exu was not so benevolent as Legba. Rather than calling on him, people often bribed him to stay away. Wherever Exu went, discord and strife followed; he was fond of starting wars and stirring up trouble. Exu's emphasis on trickery and vengeance made him an ideal orisha for slaves, who imagined him as the saint of revenge against the whites. In Brazilian Umbanda, Exu became syncretized with the devil; his altars frequently featured pitchforks, buckets of blood, and burning sulfur. In Cuba, Exu became Ellegua—more a childlike prankster than a bloodthirsty killer, but still not a spirit to be trifled with. Those Cuban slaves who preserved La Regla de Congo—the traditions we now call Palo—knew Exu as Lucero Mundo. Like Met Kalfou, Lucero's colors were red and black, and many of his *firmas* (sigils, or signs) featured crosses with lines intersecting the cardinal points.

Kalfou in Haiti

Much Christian theology is Manichean: it postulates an absolute good against an absolute evil. African and African diaspora religions tend to concentrate more on the balance of forces. In Vodou, there's more than a little suggestion that this Higher Power may not be all-good and all-loving. Although one Haitian proverb says, "God is good," another says, "When a man strikes a man, God laughs." The spirits of Vodou are the spirits of Haitian life—the good parts and the bad parts. Masters talk about mercy from the comfort of their privileged position. Slaves are far more likely to cry out to heaven for justice and vengeance. It is easy to talk about forgiving your enemies after they no longer pose a threat to you. It's easy to "turn the other cheek" when you don't have to worry about getting slapped. Those who face poverty and oppression on a daily basis know that the universe is not always a kind and benevolent place and that not all of the spirits that populate the universe are kind and benevolent.

Kalfou is intimately connected with the feared secret societies of Haiti. He is also served by houngans and mambos asogwe. They have the training and knowledge required to approach the powerful master of the crossroads. They can petition him to work magic for good or for ill: they know how to enter the realms of shadow and return unscathed. Bokors and *sorciers* (sorcerers), independent practitioners who serve the lwa, will sometimes go to Kalfou for "work with their left hand"—in other words, a sinister wanga. Most, however, prefer to leave Met Kalfou alone.

Working with Kalfou

Generally, Kalfou is one of those spirits who should not be approached without a proper introduction. If you don't know what you're doing, or if you approach him carelessly or casually, you may well find yourself in over your head, and quickly. Calling Kalfou "evil" may not be particularly useful; but calling him quick tempered and aggressive is definitely appropriate. Instead of asking him to come to you, you may be best off asking him to stay away.

If you're having a lot of serious problems, particularly serious interpersonal problems, you may go to the crossroads and give Kalfou an offering so that he will leave you alone. Kalfou gives sorcerers and evildoers their power, and so he can take that power away. By giving him an offering, you can petition him to "close the gates of hell."

Many people believe they have been "hexed" or "psychically

attacked." Psychic attacks are actually quite rare. Most of the people who want to be "powerful black magicians" lack the discipline and determination required to cast an effective curse, or to command a negative spirit. Many cases of "haunting" or "spirit infestation" can be chalked up to overactive imaginations; many "ghostly chills" are caused by bad insulation or drafty windows. That being said, there are some nasty things and nasty people out there. If a basic cleansing doesn't work, you may want to ask Kalfou to take your problem with him.

Get a small red flannel bag, and place three dollar coins inside. Get a little dirt from a hospital, a jail, or a courtroom. Place this in the bag along with the coins. Add a pinch of red cayenne pepper as well. Now, wait until nightfall, and then go out to a crossroads. (Midnight will be the best time for this.) Make sure you are wearing some kind of holy symbol: a crucifix, a pentagram, a star of David, whatever you'd like, but make sure you have something to protect yourself.

When you are at the crossroads, say, "Kalfou, I want you to take your spirits away from me. I want you to close your doors so that no one can send your spirits against me. Here is a gift so you will leave me alone." Now, turn around. Throw the bag over your shoulder, off the road. Walk away . . . and *do not look back*. When you threw that bag away, you threw your problems with you. Go home by a different path than the one you took to get there. When you get home, take a cleansing bath and cleanse and purify your living quarters.

This is a serious curse-breaking wanga. You should only do this one if other things have failed, and don't do it too often. You don't want to bring out your suitcase nuke when a flyswatter will do the trick, and you don't want to trouble Kalfou if you can avoid it.

17

EZILI DANTO

Vévé for Ezili Danto

She made her first appearance in 1791, at the Bwa Cayman ceremony. She fed her children a black pig's blood, and then made them swear they would drive out the French slave masters or die trying. A week later, one thousand settlers were dead, the rich plantations of Cape François were in smoldering ruins, and the Haitian Revolution had begun.

Some say slavers cut out her tongue as punishment for participating in the revolution. Others say Danto was made mute by the black guerrillas so that she could not betray them under torture if captured. All agree that thirteen years after she made her first appearance, the last French soldiers were gone, and the Free Black Republic of Haiti was born.

Although she remains one of the most popular and frequently propitiated lwa, Ezili Danto—often known simply as Danto—has a mixed reputation. Many Neopagans (and even some Vodouisants) see only her tooth-grinding rage, deeply scarred face, and razor-sharp dagger, and they label her an "evil spirit." I speak from experience here: for a long time I feared Danto and avoided working with her. As I became more deeply involved in Vodou (and was married to Danto and Freda in January 2004), I discovered that Danto is above all else a loving mother who gives her children the strength to face any obstacles. She may be a fearsome warrior, but she is also a faithful protector who works hard and quickly for her devotees. Now that I have been fortunate enough to meet Danto face-to-face at several ceremonies, and now that I can call her my wife, my fear has been replaced by love and a deep respect for this powerful spirit.

The image of the Mater Salvatoris (the Madonna) is common, and the aspect of the Mater Salvatoris associated with Danto is based on the Black Madonna of Czestochowa. St. Luke supposedly painted this icon atop a table made by Jesus when Jesus was still an apprentice carpenter. Later, the icon was brought to Constantinople by St. Helena, then to Eastern Europe, and finally to Poland, where it was venerated and richly decorated with jewels and gold. In 1430, foreign marauders roughly removed many of the gems with swords, leaving two deep cuts in the Madonna's face. The vandal who slashed the picture allegedly fell screaming in agony and was still screaming hours later when he died. To this day, pilgrims flock to Czestochowa and attribute miraculous power to the battle-scarred icon. In Haiti, the scratches on Danto's face are attributed to her battles with Freda. Some scholars believe that these wounds point to Danto's roots in the Kongo, where decorative facial scarring is common; others compare them to the war paint worn by the Carib and Taino Indians and place her origin among the indigenous people of Hispaniola (i.e., Haiti).

Red and blue (a few houses say red and green) are Danto's colors, and altars to Danto are usually covered in red cloth. Whereas Our Lady of Czestochowa's clothing is decorated with lilies, the image of the Mater Salvatoris, commonly used in Haitian Vodou for Danto, wears a plain red-and-blue cloak with a simple green dress. Danto is frequently envisioned wearing the simple blue denim dress of a Haitian peasant woman, and sometimes those possessed by her are also garbed in blue denim.

Danto is considered the mother of the Petwo nation and is one of the most important Petwo lwa. Whereas her sister Freda is known for her softness and gentleness, Danto is known for her strength. When faced with harsh reality, Freda breaks down in tears; Danto's response is an inarticulate shuddering tantrum. Grinding her teeth and clenching her fists, she stutters over and over, *"Ke! Ke! Ke! Ke!"* as the veins pop out on her neck and her forehead. Once seen, Danto's rage is not soon forgotten.

Danto's vévé features a heart pierced with a dagger; Danto is well known for her love of knives. Those possessed by her are typically given knives to hold. One well-known song to Danto says, *"Prete'm kouto, prete'm pwenyad"* ("Lend me a knife, lend me a dagger"). An altar for Danto will always feature a sharp blade, prominently displayed. Danto is familiar with both sides of the knife. Sometimes a person possessed by Danto will vomit blood. This is seen not as proof of Danto's weakness but of her power; even though she has been stabbed and injured, still she keeps on going. In Haiti, a land where injustice and grinding poverty are all too frequently the norm, even the lwa are not above injury. Their strength lies not in their invulnerability but in their ability to survive. In this, Danto shows her kinship to those who serve her. What she gives them is not the ability to conquer so much as the ability to endure.

In addition to the knife and red head scarf, one often finds a black doll on Danto's altar. Typically the doll is dressed in denim or in blue-and-red calico and holds a smaller doll in her arms; frequently scratches will be drawn on her cheek to represent the scars on Danto's face. Other altars will feature a plaster statue of the black Madonna and child, or a figurine of La Madama (a heavyset black woman wearing a red kerchief and carrying a broom). A Mater Salvatoris lithograph usually hangs on the wall above her, and there will often also be a Vodou bottle decorated with her image.

Danto's sacrificial animal is a black pig and her favorite meal is *griot,* a spicy Haitian dish made with marinated and fried pork cubes. Most often today's sacrifice to Danto will become tonight's griot, but vegetarians need not despair. Sallie Ann Glassman, a mambo and vegan who is the author of *Vodou Visions,* recommends coarse brown bread as well as pepper jelly and honey with cinnamon and pepper. Others have found that Danto likes pan-fried corn with peppers, black beans, fried bananas, and *riz djon-djon* or "black rice," a dish made with rice and mushrooms. Some people give Danto rum, whereas others say she prefers a dark red wine. Many Vodou peristyles in New York serve Danto Manischewitz Passover wine. I have even seen one house that serves her with 40s of malt liquor!

Cigarettes are kept on her altar as well. In Haiti, she smokes Comme il Fauts, but in America, any strong, unfiltered cigarette will do. (Those who don't like the smell of tobacco can take Danto's statue outside and light her cigarette for her, and then bring her back in when the cigarette burns out.) Danto also likes Florida water. In Vodou, as in many other Afro-Caribbean traditions, it is believed that the smell of Florida water purifies the air and drives away negativity. Sometimes, a person wavering on the edge of trance will be splashed liberally with Florida water in an attempt to bring on full-scale possession.

Like Our Lady of Czestochowa, the Mater Salvatoris holds the Christ Child in her arms. Vodouisants say this child's real name is Anais, and they identify her as female. Danto has other children as well. Ti-Jan Danto, her son by the lwa Jan Petwo, is a popular and well-liked lwa, especially in northern Haiti. (Many say that Jan Danto is not just her son, but also one of her lovers.) Some say that Ezili Danto and Jan Petwo are mother and father to the entire Petwo nation; others say that Danto has seven children, and they place seven dolls on her altar to represent them.

In Haiti, the marriage ceremony is largely reserved for the wealthy. Cohabitation is far more common. As a reflection of this, although Danto is romantically linked with several lwa (Jan Petwo; the herbal magician Simbi Makaya; the warrior Ogou Badagris; and Bawon Samedi, lord of the cemetery and the dead), she is also seen as a single mother. Jobs are scarce in Haiti. Men must frequently travel to the United States, Cuba, or the Dominican Republic to find work, leaving their partners behind to survive as best they can. Although these men may share Danto's bed, she does not rely on them but rather supports herself and her children through hard work. Danto is seen as a special patron of single mothers and has been known to wreak a terrible vengeance on men who abuse women.

Although Danto has children and male lovers, there are many who claim she is actually a lesbian. (Still others believe she is a hermaphrodite, with both male and female sexual organs.) In Haitian culture, exclusively homosexual behavior is rare. It is more common for a gay man to live with a lesbian woman and father her children while both pursue romantic same-sex affairs. Vodouisants will often claim that lesbian or "butch" women have Danto as their met tet (ruling lwa), much as they claim that effeminate or gay men are particularly loved by her sister Freda.

Mama Lola speaks about a ritual in which a doll representing Ezili Danto is sent after an enemy. She cautions that the forces released by this ritual will cause Danto to begin behaving toward you like a *baka* (evil spirit) until she ultimately kills you as she kills your enemy.[1] Although there is no "threefold law" per se in Vodou, Vodouisants recognize the importance of balance. Most Vodouisants would see aggressive magic as an option of last resort, after all other means of addressing the situation have failed; they would also want to make sure that they were in the right. Otherwise, their call for justice might result in them getting what they deserved—but not in the way they had hoped. You would be well advised to follow their example. Instead of dealing with a boss from hell by calling on the lwa, try calling some numbers listed in your local paper's Help Wanted section. If you are dealing with an abusive spouse or stalker, call on the lwa for protection, but be sure to contact your local authorities about a restraining order as well. There's nothing wrong with asking Danto to guard you and protect you from trouble; she'll be happy to do so. But if you buy into the "evil red-eyed she-devil" myths and decide you're going to send her after your enemies, you're likely to find yourself in a whole heap of trouble.

Working with Ezili Danto

If treated with kindness and respect, Danto will protect you from danger and help you to triumph over obstacles. If you have children or work with children, she will also look after them, helping to keep them safe and ensuring that you have the resources to care for them properly.

Danto is not the sort of spirit who will give you "easy money" or help you get rich without effort. What Danto gives you instead is opportunities. Danto can help you get more overtime at work or help you to find a job if you are unemployed. She can also give you the strength to overcome adversity and the confidence to stand up for yourself.

When working with Danto, you must remember to keep her and Freda separated. In Haiti, peristyles keep two rooms, one for the Rada lwa and another for the Petwo. You also should never ask both of them for the same thing. If you do, they will fight between themselves and never get around to giving you what you want. Either or both may also be offended by your presumption and take their anger out on you. You must also make sure that you keep your promises to Danto. She may not be the evil spirit that some make her out to be, but she is not a woman to be trifled with. Those who anger Danto are sometimes plagued with stabbing pains. If she is especially angry, they may even begin vomiting blood.

Danto can be intimidating, but she also can be appeased by sincere repentance. She is a stern mother, but she is also loving and quick to forgive her children once they have learned their lesson. The product of a harsh land where resources are limited, Danto is willing to accept most gifts if they are given to her with a sincere heart. She is less fussy in that regard than many other lwa. If you treat her with devotion, you will find her to be a caring and powerful protector.

18
BOSSOU

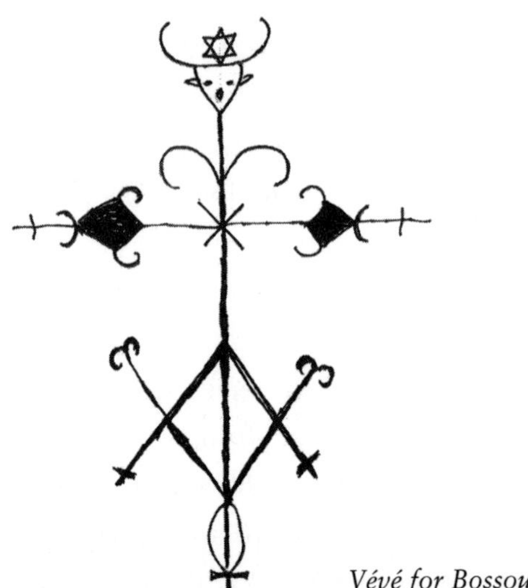

Vévé for Bossou

The Egyptians honored the Apis bull. The gods slew Enkidu after he assisted Gilgamesh in slaying the Bull of Heaven. The Canaanites represented their god El as a bull and his son Baal as a calf. Since before history began, we have honored the bull as a symbol of courage, strength, virility, and fighting spirit.

Like most bulls, Bossou is generally easygoing. He's in no hurry to get anywhere. He knows that nothing is going to stop him once he decides to move.

Throughout much of world history, children born with mental or physical deficiencies were looked upon as cursed. When they weren't killed at birth, they were often segregated from "normal" people. By contrast, the people of Dahomey saw deformed children as *tohossous*, "powerful guardian spirits." Families with a deformed child would create a small sanctuary to the tohossous in their home. Instead of an omen of doom or disaster, their birth was seen as a blessing that would bring benediction and prosperity to the lucky family.

Even royal families would sometimes have tohossous. Dossou Agadja, king of Dahomey from 1708 to 1732, was the father of a child who was born with hornlike protrusions on his head. That child was honored for bringing prosperity to the kingdom: under Agadja's watch, they were able to conquer the cities of Allada and Ouidah and gain access to the lucrative slave trade with the Europeans. Today, many of the descendants of people sent across the ocean as a result of that trade still honor Agadja's totem spirit as Bossou, the bull lwa.

Bossou in Haiti

As a general rule, the Rada spirits have their roots in Dahomey, and vice versa. The situation with Bossou is a bit more complex. Although his origins are clearly Dahomean, he is served in both the Petwo and Rada rites, and some Vodouisants classify him as a strictly Petwo spirit. There are several Bossous. Kadja Bossou is one of the older "root" Bossous. Bossou Twa Kon (three-horned) has three hornlike protrusions on his head. Bossou Towo is Bossou the Bull, and Djobolo Bossou is Bossou the Devil. (The reason for this name is unclear, given that Djobolo Bossou is not one of the more fierce or "evil" Bossous. Perhaps his horns reminded some houngans and mambos of the classical depiction of a horned Satan.) In our house, Djobolo Bossou and Kadja Bossou are saluted during the Rada portion of the ceremony, and Towo and Bossou Twa Kon are saluted during the Petwo portion of the rite.

Those who classify Bossou as Petwo may do so because of the violence of his possessions. Those who are ridden by Bossou will frequently be tossed about like they are getting gored by a mad ox. Others will ram their heads into the poteau-mitan or any other hard object, like a bull butting a red flag. Sometimes Bossou will dance through fire or through rum that's been poured on the floor and lit; at other times he will take burning brands from a bonfire and eat the glowing embers. I have seen a small, slender, elderly gentleman possessed by Bossou Twa Kon run about the peristyle with two grown men over his head, snorting like a bull as he wheeled about. (I was one of the people he was holding over his head, so I had a particularly impressive view of the proceedings.)

Bossou's bottle is red and has two large cloth horns sewn onto the fabric. His image is also found on many dwapo lwa. He is served with kleren or rum, which is poured on the ground and is frequently ignited to call him. He can be saluted either with an asson or a cha-cha, depending on the rite in which he is being honored. In Haiti, his fet is celebrated with the sacrifice of a red bull, which is later cooked and fed to the congregation. Because this is a considerable expense, festivals for Bossou are uncommon.

A number of different saints are used to represent Bossou. In our house, Bossou is generally represented by the image of St. Charles Borromeo. Other houses use St. Vincent de Paul, and still others use El Cristo Rey (Christ the King), an image of Christ with three beams of light shining from his head. Some Haitians in Miami represent Bossou with Buddha, since both Bossou and Buddha are seen as large, bald, and jolly men.

Bossou is not considered one of the faster lwa; he is generally slow-moving and deliberate in his actions. However, once he gets going, few things can stop him. He is often called on by people who have major problems. Although he may take a while to get moving, if there's a real problem, he's going to charge straight ahead and destroy any obstacle standing in his path, or yours.

Working with Bossou

If you have a big problem—a lingering health issue, persistent unemployment, or some other long-standing difficulty—you may call on Bossou for assistance. Light a red candle for him, and give him a glass of rum (some Bossous like whiskey or vodka). Explain your difficulty to Bossou, and ask him to knock away the obstacles that stand in your path. You don't have to promise him a bull, but it would be nice to offer him a roast beef dinner, or some barbecued chicken.

After you're done asking Bossou for his assistance, wait for the bull to charge. It may not happen overnight, but you can rest assured that you'll see results. Of course, you should also take any other reasonable and necessary steps to solve your problem: consult a physician, apply for work, create and follow a budget, and so on. You'll have much more success in asking the lwa to work with you than in expecting them to work for you.

Bossou is also a great protector of those who honor him. If you live in a troubled neighborhood, or if you have reason to fear for your physical, emotional, or spiritual safety, you may want to ask Bossou to keep an eye on you and yours. You can set up a small table for him. Use any of the saint images listed above, or a Buddha, or a bull or minotaur picture or figurine. Place a red scarf on the table; burn a red candle when you wish to speak with Bossou. (In Haiti, he is typically honored on Tuesday.) You can occasionally feed him beef or chicken; Bossou likes his food spicy, with a red sauce. In exchange for your dedication, you can count on Bossou's vigilance—and those who wish to harm you will learn the meaning of "mess with the bull, get the horn."

In many cultures, bulls are seen as emblems of fertility and sexuality, and you can ask for Bossou's assistance in those spheres as well. In Haiti, mambos and houngans frequently consult with clients who have "lost their nature"—in other words, they will call on Bossou to restore their client's virility. If you're having problems with sexual dysfunction, you should consult a professional to rule out any physiological or psychological difficulties. But in conjunction with their help, you can petition Bossou for his assistance. Burn a red candle; you may even want to burn a "red penis candle" (available in many hoodoo botanicas and online) and ask Bossou to transfer some of his bullish nature to your loins.

19
SIMBI

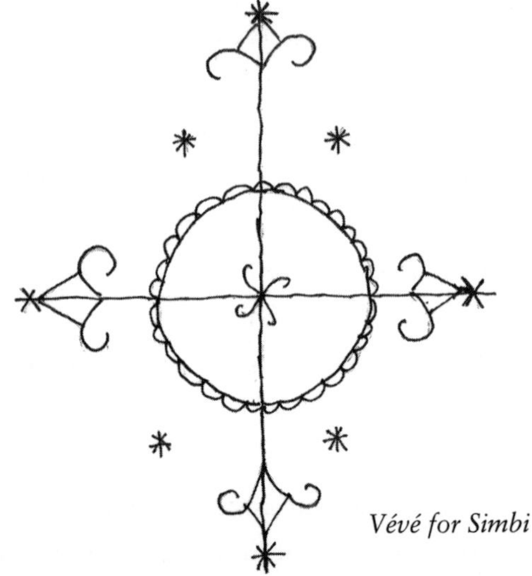
Vévé for Simbi

There is magic in the places where salt water joins with fresh, magic in the places where farmland meets forest, magic in the places where springs bubbles up from the earth. You may hear the water whispering when you least expect it. You may see something out of the corner of your eye. But when you turn to look, when you listen intently, there is only water and shadow. Magic rarely makes itself obvious.

Simbi hides in all these places. You can find him in the streams, in the trees, in the places between places. It may take you a while to find him. But once you've made his acquaintance, he'll be a great friend and a powerful ally.

There are several theories as to where the Simbis originated. Some trace their roots to the Zemi spirits, local deities or ancestral cult figures worshipped by the Taino and Arawak Indians who lived in Hispaniola, or Haiti. Two of their major spirits were Yucahu, lord of the sea, and Atabey, the goddess of fresh water and human fertility. Perhaps this explains why Simbi is known to live in two waters, salt and fresh. Maboya, on the other hand, was a feared nocturnal spirit who destroyed the crops. Elaborate sacrifices were offered to placate him. He may have become Simbi Makaya, the sorcerer propitiated by secret societies like the Sanpwel and Bizango.

Others claim that the Simbis come from Africa. In what was formerly known as the French Congo, they honored the spirit who ruled the rains, sent the lightning, and gave them rainbows by the name Nzambi Mpungu. His wife, also named Nzambi, was a mighty princess and judge. Yet another theory suggests that Simbi stems from the Kongo *basimbi,* spirits who occupy a position between the deities and the human dead and who can be either helpful or harmful, depending on their mood. Other scholars point to Kongo-influenced African American folktales about the *cymbees,* magical but mischievous child-spirits who are sometimes seen in streams, swamps, and ponds.

We do not know for certain who is correct. It could be that all of these traditions came together to give us the Simbi served today. Simbi is no more forthcoming with anthropologists than he is with the Vodouisants who serve him. Even those who know Simbi best, those who honor him in Vodou rituals, find him mysterious. Although he is classified as a Petwo spirit, many houses serve him in both the Petwo and Rada rites. In this, too, Simbi resides "between two waters," bitter and sweet, resisting all efforts to classify or define him.

Simbi in Haiti

Freda is associated with rivers and La Sirene and Agwe are rulers over the ocean. As Simbi Andezo ("in two waters"), Simbi rules over the brackish water of salt swamps. Whereas Damballah is a huge python, the Simbis are envisioned as small, slender, fast-moving water snakes—and like water snakes, they are timid. Most of the Petwo spirits have a reputation for being fierce and aggressive, but the Simbi spirits are generally shy and retiring. Often they will stay in the shadows at the edge of a ceremony, frightened by the commotion. Houngans and mambos must coax them into the peristyle.

But, once he arrives, Simbi is a more forceful character. Like many other Petwo spirits, Simbi's possessions can be violent. I have seen a woman possessed by Simbi Makaya go into convulsions so intense that four men could not hold her down. When Simbi arrives, a whip is wrapped around the horse's chest and upper body. This may be because the whip is long and slender like a water snake; it may also be reflective of the way Kongo power objects are tied with string or rope to bind the spirit into the material.

As with other lwa, Simbi is a family name. There are a number of spirits within the Simbi family. A few have been mentioned above: Simbi Andezo is connected with brackish water, and Simbi Makaya is a sorcerer and magician. Simbi Gangan is a fierce warrior and protector. He may be the Haitian version of Samba Gana, a folk hero and dragon slayer honored by the Soninke of western Africa, or he may take his name from the Bantu word for "chieftan," *gangan.* Other popular Simbis include Simbi Dlo (connected with springs and rainwater) and Simbi Anpaka (a skilled herbalist and leaf magician).

Different houses will use different colors to honor the Simbis. Some houses serve Simbi Makaya with red and green, whereas others serve him with red and black. Simbi Dlo is served with red and turquoise by some; others serve him with green and blue. Simbi Gangan is generally served with red or red and blue, whereas Simbi Andezo is most frequently honored with red and white and Simbi Anpaka with white and green. Some Vodouisants use a lithograph of St. Andrew to represent Simbi, whereas others use an image of the Three Kings and still others use St. Charles Borromeo.

When Simbi arrives at a fet, he is typically asked to do magical work. The Simbi spirits are often called upon for protection against negativity. Much as Danto will give a *gad migan* (stomach *garde* or guard—a ceremony that protects against spiritual or physical poisoning) using the blood of a black pig, Simbi will sacrifice a turtle and use its blood to make a mixture that will protect against poisons and baneful magic ingested through food or drink. At other times, he will wave a live chicken over the congregation, and then break its neck after it has absorbed bad energy from the bystanders. (Those who were raised in the Jewish faith may see some parallels between this and the *kapporos* chicken sacrifice performed by some orthodox sects before Yom Kippur.)

Simbi is a powerful healer in the physical realm as well. Those who are ill will ask for his herbal advice. He can prescribe medicinal leaves and gather roots and flowers that he uses to make healing teas and tinctures. He is also a lwa connected with communication: people waiting for messages from relatives abroad may petition Simbi so that he will bring word of their success. As befits his nature, it is difficult to define him conclusively.

Working with Simbi

All of the Simbis are known for being shy. They are also known for ignoring those they do not fancy. Even if you have Simbi, it may take you a while to coax him into working with you; if you do not have him, you may call on him for years but all your efforts will be in vain.

Being so advised, you may want to start out your work with Simbi by leaving small offerings in his favorite places. You can put some lemon drops on a small white china plate and leave them by a stream or well. You can leave a small bottle of rum in a salt swamp; you can leave a cup of black coffee under a tree. When you do this, say something like, "This is for you, Simbi. You can come for it when you're ready."

After you've done that, keep notes in your dream diary. (See chapter 26 for details.) If you begin dreaming of water snakes, or if you meet any figures who introduce themselves as Simbi, you know that you've made his acquaintance. These dreams may be brief and Simbi may not have much to say at first, but note them anyway. Keep leaving him offerings, and keep talking to him. Don't ask him for anything at first. This is a time for getting to know each other. Once you have gained Simbi's trust, you will find that he is a powerful ally—but if you don't gain that trust, he will never do any work on your behalf.

Once Simbi has revealed himself to you, you will find he is an undemanding spirit. He will be satisfied with small offerings, and he will happily offer his protection and services in exchange for your occasional attention. A candle lit on his day (November 30), along with a glass of white rum or other small offerings, will generally be enough to keep him happy. You can offer him other gifts as the mood strikes you. If he arrives in a dream and requests something, or you get a strong feeling that Simbi would like you to do something on his behalf, feel free to follow his instructions.

Many houngans and mambos connect Simbi with computers, telephones, and other electronic and high-speed communications devices. If you're having computer troubles, you may find that having Simbi around helps ease the crashes. Get a saint lithograph, a copy of Simbi's vévé, some picture that reminds you of Simbi, or an object in the colors you use to work with Simbi. Sprinkle it with spring water, or with a mixture of spring water and salt water, and say, "I offer this to Simbi, so it can remind me of Simbi and so Simbi will look after me and protect me." As you do this, imagine a small, appropriately colored water snake curling around the item, and then nesting inside it. Place this near your computer or workstation. When you're having problems with your machine, turn to the charged object and ask Simbi for his assistance. With Simbi's help, you may find your computing time more productively spent. You may also find your programming or network administration skills improve after you start giving props to Simbi. Like a snake navigating in tangled underbrush, he can provide you with sudden flashes of insight that will help you get through the most difficult computer problems.

Simbi can act as a catalyst for other Petwo lwa. He may stand back unobtrusively, but his quiet presence can encourage other spirits to work faster and harder than they would otherwise. Much as you honor Legba before beginning a ceremony, you may find it worthwhile to give Simbi a little rum, a cup of strong black coffee, or some other small gift before you do any kind of Petwo work. He can also be called upon to assist in any kind of magical ceremony or spell work. If you do ceremonial magic, Simbi can help you to make powerful contacts with other realms.

Simbi can also help you in situations where you want to remain unseen. Carry a talisman dedicated to Simbi—a vévé, an image of the Three Kings or some other saint, a piece of shed skin from a water snake, or something else you associate with Simbi. When you need to be unnoticed—when your professor is asking hard questions, let's say—you can whisper under your breath, "Hide me, Simbi." He understands that sometimes you want to avoid attention, and he can help you be overlooked.

20

GRAN BWA

Vévé for Gran Bwa

When Columbus first set foot on the island, it was a verdant, thickly forested paradise. Today, there is almost nothing left but bare rock and trucks kicking up dust as they haul away the last scraps of wood. Every year, Haiti loses more than 30 million trees. Some say that within a few years, there will be nothing left of the Haitian forests.

Once his kingdom stretched as far as his eye could see. Now, like everyone else in Haiti, Gran Bwa is struggling for survival. If you peer through the dusty haze and the faint bluish tinge of charcoal smoke, you can almost see him tied to a stump and pierced with arrows.

Reverence for forests and trees is found throughout Africa. Particularly old or large trees are seen as home to spirits; offerings are often left in their branches. Much as the Hebrew prophets went out into the desert to commune with their deity, African priests went out into the bush to seek visions. This reverence for trees and the wild survived the Middle Passage. Houngans and mambos who are taking their asson must visit the demambwe, the uncultivated ancestral land that's the domain of Loko's close friend Gran Bwa, ruler of the forest and all its plants and animals.

Trees are also are important sources of folk medicine in Haiti. There is little in the way of organized medicine in Haiti. At present, there is one hospital bed for every fourteen hundred Haitians, and one doctor for every ten thousand Haitians. What little medical care is available is often prohibitively expensive for those who are ill. Lacking access to clinics and hospitals, Haitians often rely on the services of a Doktè-Fèy (leaf doctor), Fanm-Chaj (midwife), or Ganga (healer). They will also call on Gran Bwa. As ruler of the forest, he is considered one of the great masters of herbal healing and a maker of powerful medicine.

The forest is a place of power and mystery, a place where one can find both sustenance and danger. Like the other Petwo lwa, Gran Bwa can both help and harm. Many sorcerers who work "with the left hand"—that is, make magic for ill—will seek him out. Much as Gran Bwa knows how to cure with leaves, he also knows how to kill. His skill with medicine is matched by his skill in making poisons. Decades before the 1791 revolution, Makandal used Gran Bwa's herbs and roots to kill hundreds of white plantation owners. Today, many of Haiti's secret societies pay homage to Gran Bwa and leave sacrifices in his domain. Some say the Bizango and Sanpwel come to him for plants like Kokomb Zombi (a relative of America's Jimsonweed) to transform their victims into soulless, shuffling zombis.

Gran Bwa has long been one of the most important lwa, and he is venerated throughout Haiti. And yet his domain is in danger of disappearing altogether.

The Disappearance of Haiti's Forests

Those who visited the Haiti pavilion at the 1904 St. Louis World's Fair were informed that, "Forestry is in an undeveloped stage; trees which appear like forbidding shrubbery proving to be very large and such as might be useful in commerce. Some of these bear delicious fruits and some are laden with flowers of enchanting odors which can often be distinctly perceived for miles at sea." Potential exports were listed: "logwood, mahogany, guaiac, (lignum vitae), boisjaune, and bayarondes."[1]

Today, only 1 percent of Haiti remains forested. Desperate to survive, Haitians are slowly cutting away the last of the forest, turning trees into lumber, firewood, and charcoal, and burning the grounds to plant vegetable patches. Haiti's once abundant mahogany forests have been almost completely cut down, leaving the mountainsides eroded and infertile. For the most part, the government's actions have been too little and too late. The few national parks that have been set aside as ecological preserves are thinly guarded by poorly paid security; loggers and charcoal makers travel through them with impunity, cutting the few trees that remain. Four Haitian ministries—agriculture, tourism, environment, and planning—argue over how they should be run; they squabble, and the deforestation continues.

This deforestation has wreaked havoc on Haiti's once-fertile farmland. Without tree roots to hold it, the topsoil is entirely at the mercy of the elements. Much has been eroded and even entirely swept away in some cases. Over 6 percent of Haitian land is completely stripped of arable soil and will never be able to support crops. Another 33 percent is seriously eroded and facing imminent conversion into desert. Deforestation and erosion in the mountains have blocked up irrigation systems on the plains, leaving land that once produced half the world's sugar unable to produce enough food for its own people. It has also left many who live in the valleys and on the slopes vulnerable to mud slides and flash floods, like the May 2004 flooding, which killed over two thousand Haitians and wiped out entire towns.

Faced with an imminent ecological collapse, organizations like USAID have been financing reforestation projects. But, although peasants can earn a few dollars planting seedlings, there is still more money to be made in charcoal. Few of the seedlings survive; certainly not enough to replace the trees that are still being destroyed. Other, small-scale reforestation efforts by local groups around the country have been more effective. Unfortunately, these efforts are usually starved for resources and receive little if any funding from Haitian or international sources. We can only hope that Gran Bwa's forests will be restored while there is still soil left for planting trees.

Working with Gran Bwa

In Haiti, Gran Bwa is considered one of the more affable Petwo lwa. His possessions are sometimes violent; he is known for making a great deal of noise when he comes and for throwing his horse about rather forcefully during the early stages of the possession. Still, he's generally in a jovial mood once he arrives, and quick to offer his wisdom and protection to the société. If you approach him with respect and reverence, you're sure to find him a good friend as well.

Gran Bwa's colors are red and green; if you wish to create a shrine to him, you can use red and green scarves. In Haiti, Gran Bwa is represented by the image of St. Sebastian, an early Christian martyr who is typically shown tied to a tree and pierced with arrows. This lithograph is relatively easy to find in botanicas or Catholic supply stores. (I've heard of people using images of Treebeard from *The Lord of the Rings* to represent Gran Bwa. This wouldn't be standard Haitian practice—but it would definitely be appropriate.)

Gran Bwa lives in the forest, where he has easy access to food. Generally when he comes he isn't hungry—but the Vodouisants still provide him with food to be polite. You can give him rice and beans or cornmeal prepared with honey; place these on his shrine or leave them in the woods if you have easy access to a forest. If you can find banana leaves, serve the food on these; otherwise a plate will do. Haitian Vodouisants will fill a straw makout, like the ones carried by Legba or Zaka, with food, and then hang it high in a *mapou* or cypress tree as an offering to Gran Bwa. If you live near a high tree, you can place a bag full of his food in its branches. He drinks white rum, whiskey, or coffee. You can give him these in a mug, or you can pour them out at the base of a large tree. (A little bit will do: poisoning a plant is not a good way to honor the lwa of the forests.) You can even make a donation in Gran Bwa's honor to a charity that seeks to preserve the forests or clean up ecological catastrophes. He'll definitely appreciate the gesture—and your money will help to fix some of the mess we've made in our wild lands.

If you're working with herbs, or if you are a gardener, you can surely benefit from Gran Bwa's assistance. He can help you get that green thumb you always wanted; he can also help you in mastering herbcraft. Light a red or green candle for him before you start studying your texts on herbology, or before you go out in the field to gather herbs. When you pick herbs, leave him a little bit of rum or some change as a thank you. He will help you find the best herbs, even if you're not in Haiti. Although Gran Bwa's home is in Hispaniola, he is the master of all forests and plants.

If you can, try camping in a wooded area. Go out into the forest by yourself. Stick to a path, and carry adequate illumination if you're going to be walking at night. Spend some time listening to the woods and its various sounds. Learn the way the forest smells; feel the moss on the grounds and trees. Explore the woods with all your senses. Bring along a present for Gran Bwa; introduce yourself, tell him why you've come, and ask him to look after you. When you awaken in the morning, be sure to record all your dreams. You may well find that Gran Bwa has paid you a nocturnal visit and provided you with some important insights.

21

IBO

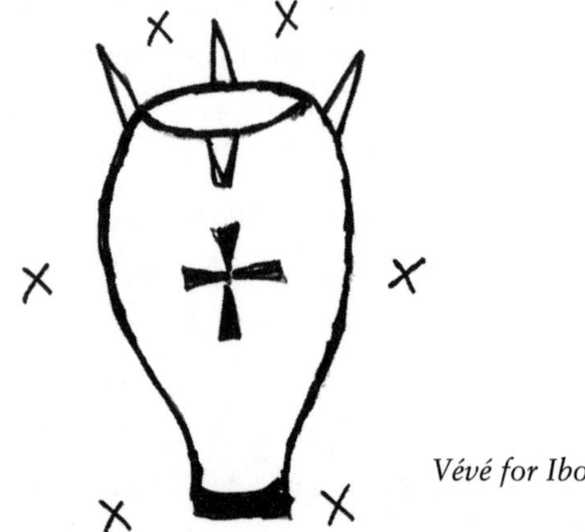

Vévé for Ibo

There are all kinds of bravery—but few are more moving than the bravery of the utterly defeated. The conquering hero may gloat and rejoice, but what can he do when the conquered refuse to grovel? Is there any greater dignity than dignity without hope? Is there any greater strength than weakness without submission? The Ibo know this well. As often as they have been beaten, they have never been vanquished.

While the kings of Yorubaland and Dahomey were building walled cities and empires, the Igbo were living in small villages, ruled by councils of elders. Decisions that affected the whole village, such as the declaration of war, would generally be put to all the free adult males of the town. A man who had proven his skills at war in the past might be selected to lead the people through a battle, but he would be expected to relinquish this leadership once the time of crisis was past. This society was not entirely egalitarian. The *osu* or hereditary slaves formed a despised and disempowered class of untouchables, and barren women and childless men were subject to scorn and marginalized in their community. Still, the typical Igbo had far more say in village affairs than a Yoruba or Dahomey subject. Alas, this more open and peaceful society came at a terrible price, as the Igbo were regularly subjected to raids from African and European slavers.

This persecution has continued to the present day: when the Igbo tried to secede from Nigeria and form their own country, Biafra, in 1966, they were attacked by the Yoruba- and Hausa-controlled Nigerian army. A later blockade resulted in widespread famine and the deaths of over 3 million Igbos before the Nigerian government regained control of Igboland in 1970. In May 2004, rioting broke out between the Muslim Hausa and Christian Igbos in Nigeria's Plateau State; thousands were killed on both sides and untold thousands more forced from their homes.

The Igbo in Haiti

Many plantation owners in St. Domingue preferred Igbo slaves because they were strongly attached to one another. Newly arrived Igbo (also known as Ibo) slaves could find help and care from those Igbo who had arrived before them. Others were reluctant to purchase Igbo because they were known for a propensity to suicide and were reportedly prone to "melancholy." Finally, some overseers began beheading and mutilating the corpses of Igbo who committed suicide. Because the Igbo saw death as a "return to Africa," they believed that a mutilated corpse would be ashamed to return to the ancestors.[1] Combined with long-standing Igbo taboos—in Igboland, suicide was considered a bad death and a suicide's corpse was thrown into the bush to rot—this was intended to discourage Igbos from killing themselves. But not even these measures were enough to keep Igbos from suicide . . . and the expression *"Ibos pend cor a yo,"* "the Ibo hang themselves," can still be heard in Haiti.[2]

Today, the Ibo are among the nations honored in Vodou's Petwo rite. They are considered strong but proud, difficult to handle, and demanding. Gran Ibo is seen as grandmother to the Ibos, and Ibo Lele is one of the most powerful and well known of the Ibo spirits. Their service varies considerably among different houses: in some houses they are very important, whereas in others they are not served at all. But even houses that do not pay homage to the Ibo spirits perform ceremonies that show an Ibo influence.

After a house member dies, the société will perform the rite of desounin. In this ceremony, the departed person's soul and lwa are separated. The soul is sent on to heaven, and the spirits that person had will often possess someone present; those horses are said to "inherit" the lwa. After at least a year and a day has passed, the dead are "taken out of the water" through the ceremony called retire nan mo dlo. The dead person's spirit is called up from the ancestral waters and installed in a clay pot called a govi. The spirit is now said to occupy that govi; it watches over the temple and offers advice and counsel. At times, the spirit may even "speak" through the govi in deep, haunting tones. (I have heard a spirit speaking through the govi. It is an unsettling and powerful experience.)

Both these ceremonies have their roots in Ibo service to their ancestors. Like many African tribes, the Ibo believed that the living are watched and guarded by the ancestors. By honoring the ancestors, those on this side of the veil gain protection and assistance from those who have passed before them. In Igboland, the dead speak through the *udu* (pot), a clay drum shaped like a water vessel with a side hole. Like modern Vodouisants, the Ibo relied on their ancestors to protect them from malevolent forces; indeed, they spent more time honoring their departed relations with prayer, reverence, and sacrifice than they did calling upon the powerful but inaccessible Supreme Creator Chi-Ukwu.

The Ibo in America: Working with the Ibo

In mid-May 1803, the schooner *York* arrived at the bluff of Dunbar Creek on St. Simon's Island, Georgia. Two coastal plantation owners, Thomas Spalding and John Couper, had purchased seventy-five of the Igbo slaves carried on the boat. As the schooner reached its landing place, the Igbo rebelled. In the confusion, Couper's overseer and two sailors jumped overboard and drowned in their attempt to reach shore. Under the direction of a high Igbo official among them, the Igbo went ashore. Then, singing an Igbo hymn ("The water spirit brought. The water spirit will take us home. *Orimiri Omambala bu anyi bia. Orimiri*

Omambala ka anyi ga ejina."), they walked in unison into the creek. At least ten of them drowned rather than submit to slavery. The surviving Igbo carried their stories to the plantations, and the so-called Ibo landing became an important part of African American folklore.

Many of the Africans brought to the United States were Igbo; by some estimates, as many as 80 percent of the slaves who made the Middle Passage to American ports came from Igboland. If you are African American, it is likely that you have at least some Igbo ancestry. As such, you would do well to honor your ancestors who faced the horrors of slavery. Preparing them a stew of yams (a favored Igbo food) or okra sautéed in palm oil (another favorite) will help to ensure their continuing protection. Even if you are not African American, you may want to make an occasional offering to the Ibo who died as slaves and whose suffering helped build so much of Western culture. In Igbo culture, it is appropriate to make offerings of atonement for the dead you have wronged, or to whom you owe an ancestral debt. Offer them a bowl of clean water for drinking. Present them with palm wine (available in many African markets), or, if you can't find palm wine, cola. (The kola nut has long been eaten and stewed by Igbos.) Feed them on a red cloth, and burn a white candle on their behalf. Don't ask them to do favors for you; instead, make this offering as payment for services already rendered.

If you want their aid, you will probably be best advised to ask them for courage. The Igbo were famous for maintaining their honor in the face of brutal racism. They can give you that courage and teach you how to meet bigotry and ignorance with dignity. Light a candle for them and ask for their wisdom. The Ibo spirits can be proud and demanding, but if they are approached with reverence and humility, they can impart important lessons.

22
THE DJABS

There are leading men and character actors: there are rock stars and club favorites. Sometimes the most talented artists labor in relative obscurity, their skills known only to a handful of afficionados. The spirit world is no different than ours. There are the well-known lwa, the ones served in most sociétés, and then there are the djabs. They may not be as famous as some of the spirits served in the Reglamen Gineh, but many Vodouisants find their services indispensible.

Neither ancestor nor angel, neither African nor Catholic spirits, Djabs occupy a liminal place in the Vodou pantheon. They can be called upon to heal or to harm, and they are known to be strong, if at times unpredictable and difficult to control. Although they may not fit into the liturgy, Djabs are still powerful guards and working spirits. Vodou's worldview is a hierarchical one: a Vodouisant will often deal with "work lwa" on practical matters. Spirits who are less well known will frequently do faster and more effective work than their more popular brethren. Much as a local patrolman standing on the corner might be able to stop a crime more quickly than the chief of police, a Djab might be quicker to intercede on your behalf than lwa who have many followers and many petitions to which they must attend. The Djabs are essentially free agents. Accountable to no one, they serve those who serve them.

Like Greek *genii* (land spirits), some Djabs are connected to a particular locale. In Haiti, many caves are known to be home to individual Djabs. The Djabs can travel from their home caves, but they'll return after they've finished their task . . . and those who call on the Djabs' services must often travel there regularly to offer the appropriate sacrifices. Other Djabs are "house spirits," connected to a particular family or société. Often they are passed down from generation to generation, along with the instructions for their care and feeding. They may be well known and well respected in their region or among the members of that société, but not known at all outside a small circle. Indeed, many Vodouisants will not speak publicly at all about their Djabs. They know that if they talk some people will accuse them of being evil sorcerers who deal with devils . . . and others will try to steal their spirits.

Although the name Djab comes from the French *diable,* the Djabs are not necessarily diabolical or evil. As stated above, most are wild spirits who are untamed but not necessarily malevolent. However, there are some Djabs that are identified with demons and devils. French grimoires like the *Petit Albert* and *La Poule Noire* have also influenced Vodou. Some of the entities that are considered demons by Renaissance and medieval sorcerers are also called upon by houngans and mambos. Spirits like Le Roi Lecife (King Lucifer) are honored by some who "work with both hands." These "two-handed" magicians serve the lwa and beneficial spirits, but they are also willing to call upon the forces of darkness to get what they want or what their clients want. These spirits have a reputation for ferocity, dishonesty, and raging anger. Other Djabs should be approached with caution, but most houngans and mambos will advise that these diabolical Djabs should not be approached at all.

Working with Personal Spirits

Local and family spirits have been an important part of most traditions since before recorded history. House altars were erected to gain their protection and favor, and offerings were regularly left in their sacred places. As you continue working with the lwa, you are likely to encounter a few personal spirits of your own.

Vodouisants have different ways of handling different Djabs and personal spirits. Those that are fierce or rough will be "tied" with chains and other devices designed to control them and to force them to do the will of the Vodouisant. These practices are not only ethically questionable, but also dangerous. An enslaved spirit is an angry one, and if it gets loose it is likely to wreak havoc on the person who trapped it, and on everyone in the immediate vicinity. If a spirit can only be controlled by the use of chains or coercive magic, you're better off banishing it and purifying your space.

On the other hand, a family lwa or a benevolent work spirit might be treated with as much respect and reverence as any other lwa. They would be fed with their appropriate sacrifices, given gifts that pleased them, and consulted on matters in which they had particular expertise. Instead of being ordered around like a slave, the Vodouisant would ask for their assistance as though they were a friend or a relative. This model of interaction is much healthier for all concerned—and can be effective.

When you are walking around your area, be aware of your surroundings. Is there a particularly large and gnarled tree that seems to be staring at you every time you pass? Did you find a small, smooth, lovely stone that "jumped out at you" as you walked down the street? These may both be homes to spirits that could become valuable allies. Lakes, streams, lightning-struck stumps, boulders—all can provide homes for spirit entities. Look for these and follow your instincts.

If your grandmother told stories of the "pale woman" or "tall man" seen by her, and by her grandmother, at portentous times, that could be a family spirit. Imaginary friends that you had in childhood may not be so imaginary after all: they could be spirits that are following you and are still there, waiting to help you and your children. In my experience, these family guardians are far more common than family curses, and they have been honored in most cultures and time periods.

Working with these allies can help you to develop on the spiritual and material planes. They may well have been with your family for centuries, or they may have followed you through various incarnations. As such, they're happy to help you and likely to have your best interests in mind. As to how you work with these spirits . . . well, that's between you and them! House spirits will have their own personal likes and dislikes;

to discover those, you'll just have to ask. Pay careful attention to your dreams. If, for example, you dream repeatedly of a spirit at a nearby location, it could be that the Djab of that area is trying to contact you. If you find yourself repeating dreams from childhood, it could be a spirit contact. This is yet another reason why you need to keep a detailed dream diary. Like the lwa, Djabs and nature spirits will often contact you in dreams, providing you with useful information.

The Djabs can do powerful magic on their own. As a bonus, I have also found that some can help you work more effectively with the lwa. A warlike Djab honored with iron nails and rum might be close to Ogou; a sea spirit or water elemental might have a deep connection with Agwe and La Sirene. Much as the lwa and the saints intercede with God on our behalf, "house lwa" can speak with their more well known brethren and transmit messages between you and them. They can provide you with helpful hints on how to serve the lwa and ensure that your petitions and offerings are noticed.

You may already be working with spirits that are not part of the Vodou pantheon. Many people pay tribute to faeries or nature spirits connected to their local area. Although these spirits are not diabolical or evil, they can be extremely powerful—and they can bring you either joy or grief, depending on how you approach them. Giving them regular offerings of bread, milk, and honey or other sweet things will help you gain their blessings. I don't recommend trying to control or coerce the faeries, unless you want to find yourself starring in your very own Brothers Grimm tale. On the other hand, I've found they're wonderful allies and benevolent protectors if they're approached with love and respect. (One note of caution: In my experience, most faeries deeply resent being called Djabs. I suspect they are still offended over the Church's attempts to demonize them. Calling them "the good folk" instead will help you avoid their wrath.)

Many of the readers of this book have some experience working in other pantheons. Although I don't subscribe to the "all gods and goddesses are just masks for the One True God/dess" approach, I have found that certain deities respond well to being served with some of the techniques and practices found in Vodou. Aphrodite may not be Ezili Freda, but she certainly appreciates offerings of sweets and flowers just as much as her Haitian cousin. Ganesh may not be Papa Legba, but you'll find that he enjoys a good joke as much as his fellow guardian of the crossroads and opener of the gates. If you start treating these spirits like friends and allies, and get to know them as individuals rather than as abstractions or symbols, you are likely to be much more successful in working with them.

The Ghede Lwa

In Lucumí and the Afro-Cuban traditions, the dead are served before the orishas. In Haitian Vodou, the nachon Ghede (Nation of the Ghede) is served at the end of the evening, after the other lwa have been saluted. This does not mean that the dead are less important in Vodou. If you are working with the spirits of Haitian Vodou, you will need to honor the dead. Where we are, the dead have been. Where they are, we one day will be. They can provide us with valuable counsel and wisdom, helping us in this life and in the next.

In Vodou, the Ghede are the souls of the "forgotten dead" —those who did not receive proper funerals, those who have no one to mourn for them, or those who died in difficult circumstances. Ghede Nibo reclaims these dead and gives them a voice—and once they've got a voice, they're rarely silent. The Ghede always speak the truth, Vodouisants say. They may be crass, crude, and vulgar, but they'll never lie to you; and their practical, if foul-mouthed, advice is frequently sought on matters of health, love, money, and other details of daily life.

Not only do Vodouisants serve the forgotten dead, but they also pay tribute to their ancestors. African diaspora traditions developed among people who had been torn from their homes and their families. The family relationships they could form in their new, alien land were precarious ones. Slave auctions regularly separated mother from child, husband from wife, and brother from sister. It is not surprising that the slaves and children of slaves came to place particular emphasis on roots and ancestors. Our greatest appreciation is typically reserved for those things we have lost. Today, ancestral veneration continues to be an important part of African diaspora traditions. Vodouisants believe that dead ancestors who are propitiated will bless their descendants, whereas ancestors who are ignored may bring ill fortune and sickness.

23
THE GHEDE

Vévé for the Ghede, Bawon, and Brigitte

Some say that Papa Loko, the first houngan, pulled the first Ghede out of the waters of death; some credit Bawon Samedi, lord of the cemetery. (It could be that each is trying to blame the other.) Anthropologists are as divided on the issue as Vodouisants. A few scholars claim that the Ghede originated among the Arawak and Taino Indians, whereas others believe they come from the Gede-Vi, an African tribe wiped out during a war that took place before the slavers arrived. Whatever their origin, the Ghede have become popular and beloved spirits throughout Haiti, and, increasingly, among ceremonial magicians, Neopagans, and others who find these clowns from beyond the grave helpful, protective, and endlessly amusing.

When the Ghede arrive at a fet, they dance the banda. One performs the banda by keeping the back straight while swiveling the hips in a figure-eight motion . . . and yes, this does look a lot like dry humping the air. This dance is accompanied by the banda rhythm, a distinctive staccato drumbeat that supposedly mimics the bump and grind of sexual intercourse, and by songs that honor the Ghede. Some of the songs for the "root" Ghede, like Ghede Nibo and Brav Ghede, can be stately and solemn, almost like hymns. Most Ghede songs are neither stately nor solemn. They tend to focus on sexuality in all its messy and glorious details, with many colorful metaphors, graphic descriptions, and politically incorrect observations.

Upon coming back to the land of the living, the Ghede put on sunglasses to shield their eyes from the light. Some Ghede will punch out one of the lenses ("so I can keep an eye on my food," said one Ghede to Maya Deren[1]), whereas others will wear their sunglasses upside down, or wear several pairs at one time. The Ghede also favor battered black hats—particularly top hats—and worn black suits. (You can give a Ghede new clothes, and he will brag about them to anyone who will listen—but he will still wear his moth-eaten old clothing.) The Ghede also powder their face, so that their skin has the pallor of the grave. Many Ghede walk with a cane. Often this cane will be carved to resemble a large phallus. In case you miss the Freudian symbolism, the Ghede will happily stick it between their legs and wave it about until you get the joke.

The Ghede generally like their drinks spicy—really spicy. *Piman,* their beverage of choice, is raw rum in which twenty-one Scotch bonnet peppers are steeped. When the Ghede possess a person, they will often wash their face with this fiery mixture, or splash it on their armpits and genitals before drinking a healthy swig.* In Haiti, this is a sign that you have a true possession: anyone who was faking it would be in far too much pain to continue the charade after the piman hit their mucous membranes. The Ghede also like their food served with liberal amounts of pepper and hot sauce. In Haiti, the Ghede are often fed stewed goat and salted herring—but they are known to eat just about anything and then ask for seconds. Death is insatiably hungry, always ready to consume someone else, and so the Ghede are always hungry, too.

The Ghede's holiday, November 2 (All Soul's Day), is one of the biggest festivals in the Vodou calendar. People who have attended no other ceremonies will often show up at the Ghede's party, knowing that

*But not all of the Ghede drink piman. Some prefer cola, wine, or other beverages. Because the Ghede are the reclaimed spirits of the dead, there will be as much variation between individual Ghede as between individuals within any group of people.

they're in for a good time. This party is among the most raucous and high-spirited of ceremonies, a celebration that, like the Ghede, joins the spiritual with the carnal. The alcohol flows freely and the merriment continues until dawn, with multiple Ghedes showing up for fun and festivities. The Ghede are very proud of this fact, and they never let the other lwa forget that everyone wants to attend their party.

People die all over the world; thus, the Ghede come from all races. In Haiti, you will find Dominican Ghede who speak Spanish; among American practitioners, I have seen individual Ghede from various backgrounds. When the spirit of a deceased Italian from Brooklyn was asked why he didn't speak Kreyol, he replied, "Whaddya want, a waiter? 'Ah, bonjour, madame. My *coq* is very large for you today.'" Wherever they come from, all of the Ghede share a certain outlook on life that can charitably be described as irreverent. I know a Jewish Ghede who likes his food as *treyf* as possible. He's never happier than when he's eating ham and cheese and complaining about his second wife who wanted to keep kosher. ("And I said, 'Why? So you can have two kitchens you don't cook in?'")

There are female Ghede. Karen McCarthy Brown mentions "Ghedelia" in *Mama Lola,* and Houngan Aboudja of New Orleans knows a Ghede named "Famn Batis" (Baptist Woman), a churchgoing Protestant lady who can be anything but ladylike. Still, even though the Ghede can come from all races and backgrounds, the vast majority of them who appear at ceremonies are male. Perhaps in response to this, a few male Ghede wear dresses when they come—although they will protest strenuously if you infer from this that they are homosexual.

Excuse Me, I Don't Think You Were Invited . . .

A Vodou ceremony may look chaotic to an outside observer, but there is a strict reglamen that underlies the anarchy. Each nachon is saluted in its proper place; and within those nations, there is a set protocol for which lwa is saluted in which order. There will be variation in this reglamen between regions and houses—but within a house, that order will be kept in every ceremony. You will not see Ogou saluted before Agwe; nor will Freda arrive during a song honoring Zaka or Damballah. The Ghede are the only exception to this rule. The salutes and songs to the Ghede are only performed at the end of a ceremony, after the other spirits have been honored . . . but that doesn't mean you won't see the Ghede make an appearance before they've been called. They'll bum cigarettes during the Rada songs and interrupt the Petwo service to sing about their *zozo* (penis). Like death, they come whenever and wherever they wish.

Even the lwa are not spared the Ghede's irreverence. You never take Zaka's food: indeed, when you are cooking for Zaka you must be careful not to taste the food before it is served, lest Zaka think you are stealing his possessions. Yet I have seen the Ghede arrive at a party for Zaka, stroll over to the table set up in Zaka's honor, and walk away with a large plate of chaka. At a maryaj lwa (marriage to the spirits) I attended, the Ghede made an appearance after the bride had married Damballah, Ogou, and Zaka. The particular Ghede who arrived went on at some length about her husbands, asking, "How is Damballah going to #@%$ you? He doesn't have any legs!" and observing that Ogou had "more balls than $@%!."

Among the Arawak and Taino who inhabited the island now known as Haiti before the Europeans and slaves came, the dead were known for their obscene talk. In keeping with that tradition, the Ghede have become famous—or notorious—for foul language. The Ghede are quick to spew obscenities and comment at length about their sexual prowess and the prowess (or lack thereof) of others. It is difficult to appreciate just how vulgar the Ghede can be until you've spoken to one up close and personal . . . and even then you may have a hard time believing what you just heard.

Death and Sexuality, Haitian Style

The Ghede's loudly erotic behavior and preoccupation with genitalia and sexual affairs point to their dual role. They are connected not only to the graveyard but also to procreation. Women wishing to conceive will ask for the Ghede's assistance in becoming pregnant; while they're likely to provide a long and colorful commentary about "your man's limp $%!@," they're also known to provide potent aid to the childless. Worried parents with sick children will often seek the Ghede's aid. The Ghede are known to protect children, ensuring they grow up so they can make babies of their own. No matter how ill a child may be, they will not die if the Ghede refuse to dig the grave.

Some Vodouisants say that the Ghede helps dead spirits to reincarnate. Others say that this is a "modern" interpretation, or a "corruption" of "pure" Vodou by "New Age" practices. But, although reincarnation does not figure prominently in the traditional religions of West Africa, Vodou is not exclusively African. It has long incorporated imagery and ideas from Taino and Arawak practices, folk Catholicism, Freemasonry, and other traditions. In Cuba, reincarnation has been part of Lucumí and Espiritismo practices for over a century, thanks largely to the writings of nineteenth-century French Spiritualist Alain Kardec. Like these religions, Vodou is a growing and living tradition that's quick to incorporate other ideas into its melange. If the idea of reincarnation has been "introduced" by exposure to Neopagan or Spiritualistic ideals, this is a sign not of corruption but rather of Vodou's continuing vitality.

The Ghede as Divine Jesters

Kings and courtiers were bound by rigid codes of etiquette and propriety; their fools were under no such obligations. They could say what everyone else knew but dared not mention. The Ghede fulfill a similar function in Haitian Vodou. They speak truth—including truths you might not want to hear. Neither alive nor truly dead, they stand outside the social order and have no need to concern themselves with issues of propriety. (As a Ghede of my acquaintance says, "What the #@$% are you going to do, kill me?") Although they may use a few dirty words—okay, many dirty words—their advice is generally sought by those who appreciate their blunt honesty and earthy wisdom.

The Ghede take special glee in tweaking the noses of the uptight.

If they see their antics are making you uncomfortable, they will likely redouble their efforts. Although they can be insulting if they are treated rudely (or if you try to take their food), their humor is generally good natured. I've found that their vulgarity is often almost childlike. If you've ever seen an eight-year-old who has just learned a new dirty word and wants to share it with the world, you'll have some idea of how the average Ghede uses profanity.

For most of its history, Haiti has been ruled by one dictator or another. Dissent and open expression have typically been brutally suppressed. As a result, Haitians tend to be reticent about their feelings and not given to loud displays. And yet even the army is unable to suppress the Ghede's humor—or their appetite. During the height of one "antisuperstition" campaign, a group of Ghede gathered during the Fet Ghede celebration. Soon hundreds of Ghede were marching through the streets of Port-au-Prince. Finally, they came to the presidential palace, where they knocked at the door and demanded loudly to be fed. The president, despite his bold talk about "rooting out Vodou nonsense," promptly complied . . . and the Ghede marched away well fed and well satisfied with themselves.[2]

At one party I attended, conflict broke out over a song that calls Danto a *madavine* (lesbian). Some members of the house thought it inappropriate, but a few guests—lesbians devoted to Mama Danto—insisted on singing it in her honor. The argument was finally settled when a Ghede appeared. Taking his phallus-cane and placing it between his legs, he swung it like a conductor leading an orchestra. Soon everyone was laughing as this Ghede conducted the room in several choruses in honor of Danto the Lesbian, and a tense situation was defused by Ghede's irreverent humor.

Another Word of Warning

Anybody who has done any work with Spiritualism will tell you that there are few things nastier than the malevolent dead. Because they are so close to our plane of existence (hence the term *earthbound*), these spirits can do real damage if they become attached to you. When dealing with the Ghede, or with any other spirit connected with death or the grave, caution is in order. Before calling on the Ghede, be sure to take appropriate precautions. Cleanse yourself and your area by whatever means you use to create sacred space. If, after making contact, you or others notice any signs of negative infestation—unexplained fatigue, weight loss, changes in personality, or similar—banish this entity. If you find yourself unable to do this, consult a professional, preferably someone acquainted with Vodou or other African religions. Forewarned is forearmed.

Working with the Ghede

If you take those precautions, you should have little or no problem with the Ghede. The dead are all around us, and they can be contacted by just about anyone willing to make the effort. If you've been having dreams about foul-mouthed spirits in black hats, it could well be that they've already made the effort to contact you! The Ghede can be described using many adjectives, but *shy* is not among them. The Ghede are often among the first spirits to contact a person who is called to Vodou; their liminal position between life and death means they are particularly close to the world of the living and can intercede therein more easily than some of the other lwa.

If you have the space, you may want to set up an altar for the Ghede. A plain table will do, preferably a well-used and battered one. Put a black or purple cloth atop it—again, the more moth-eaten and tattered, the better. On this you can leave the items the Ghede like: a bottle of rum with hot peppers steeping inside, a pair of sunglasses with one eye poked out, a battered black hat, a cross, and cigarettes. You can burn purple and black seven-day candles on the altar, but you probably should keep them on a fireproof dish. Pyrex is good for this, as is a Teflon cookie sheet.

When arranging your altar, there are a few things you should keep in mind. In Haiti, the Ghede are typically set apart from the other spirits, placed in their own small room if at all possible. Other spirits find their presence a bit loud and distracting, particularly Ezili Freda. You should also avoid putting your Ghede altar—or any other Vodou altar—in your bedroom or any place where you are going to be having sex. Vodouisants generally believe that this will "heat your spirits" too much, or cause them to disturb your dreams. If you can't provide your Ghede with a space of their own (even a small closet will do), or if you must put them in your sleeping area, you should put some kind of screen around their altar. This will shield you (and your other spirits) from their constant presence.

In Haiti, the images of various saints are used for the Ghede. Among the most common are St. Expedite and St. Yves. (St. Gerard Majella is often used to represent the Bawon.) However, you do not have to use saint images. I have seen cheap plastic laughing skeletons purchased at a post-Halloween clearance sale used to represent the Ghede. Others have used comic book drawings of the Joker from Batman, or Grant Morrison's Jim Crow, as symbols of the Ghede. If you get the feeling that a certain image, drawing, or statue would be an ideal representation of your Ghede, then use it.

Although most Ghede appreciate spicy drinks, sunglasses, and dirty jokes, some have different tastes. Your Ghede may well want, or not want, certain other items. Remember, these are the spirits of dead people, and they vary as much as people vary. Some Ghede prefer Coca-Cola to piman, and some prefer stars of David to crosses or Qur'ans to Bibles. You'll do better trying to please your individual spirits than by slavishly adhering to someone else's list of things you Must Do. Learn to talk with your spirits and determine what they want. (You can be sure that the Ghede will make their desires known.)

The Ghede's realm is the graveyard, and this is a good place to commune with them. But if you do this, be sure not to leave any personal effects there. If you do a work that involves candles or herbs, put them in a bag and dispose of them outside the cemetery, preferably at a crossroads or in a forest. Vodouisants believe that leaving things in a cemetery may cause a mort (malevolent dead spirit) to attach to you. You can bring back some graveyard dirt for your Ghede altar, but if you do, be sure to ask permission first, and leave some change and a sprinkling of rum or cola for the deceased. Similarly, anytime you do work in a graveyard, you should leave something outside the gates and ask for Bawon's permission and help. It doesn't need to be elaborate—a few pennies will do—but the act of asking for his permission is important. Like any other authority figure, the Bawon demands that you respect his rank.

Although they are spirits of death, the Ghede are also great healers. If you're feeling ill, you can ask them to help you out. (You should also see a professional for any serious medical condition. The spirits will often help you by putting you in touch with a good doctor. As in the physical world, the spirits typically follow the path of least resistance.) They are also good for issues dealing with fertility and childbirth, and they can assist you in finding lovers—long-term and short-term. If any spirits are sex-positive, it's the Ghede: they've got no qualms about a mutually enjoyable one-night stand and will gladly aid you in finding the same. (Your ethical code may proscribe "one-night-stand magic" as an unethical control over the will of another. If so, don't ask your Ghede for assistance in this arena . . . but don't be surprised if he offers to help you, frequently and graphically.)

Burn a black or purple candle in your Ghede's honor, make a nice dish of his favorite food, and then talk to him about your wants and needs. If he does something really nice for you, you should return the favor. In exchange for my Ghede's help in various matters, I've bought him things like a Tibetan skull kapala, a Haitian dwapo, and a large collection of *Playboys*.

The Ghede aren't what you might expect from the living dead. They are more Beavis and Butthead than *Pet Sematery*—more likely to make you laugh than to scare you. They're often rude, crude, and socially unacceptable. But when it comes to deflating windbags, tweaking the pompous, and telling the emperor his wrinkled ass is flapping in the breeze, they can't be beat. Working with the Ghede may be many things, but it will never be boring.

24
THE BAWON AND BRIGITTE

Vévé for the Ghede, Bawon, and Brigitte

According to Haitian belief, the first man and first woman buried in any cemetery automatically become the Bawon (in English, Baron) and Brigitte of that place. The Bawons are more or less the authority figure of the Ghede world—inasmuch as any of the Ghede answer to authority, which is to say, not much.

One of the most well known of the Bawons, Bawon La Kwa (Baron La Croix), arrives like a corpse. A person possessed by La Kwa will lie on the floor, while others prepare him as you would prepare a corpse in Haiti. The horse's jaw is tied shut and the nostrils stuffed with cotton; others powder the face and wrap the body in a funeral shroud. Thus prepared, Bawon La Kwa lies on the ground while others stand over him and shake his hands. Another, Bawon Kriminel, is a cannibal and a headhunter. He carries a sack in which he keeps the souls he has stolen, and he wears a belt made of the severed heads of his enemies. Bawon Samedi is perhaps the most well known of the Bawons outside of Haiti. He is particularly popular in New Orleans.

The Ghede are given to mocking authority figures of any stripe, but the Bawons are far more serious. In Haiti, political leaders and important types are most often treated with a mixture of respect and fear, and the Bawons are treated in much the same way. François "Papa Doc" Duvalier counted Bawon Samedi among his entourage. He would frequently ask Samedi for counsel; often he would call the Bawon down during meetings with his advisors. In a country with notoriously unstable politics, Papa Doc was able to hold on to his office for almost three decades, until he finally went to meet his friend face-to-face.

Generally, the Bawons are more solemn and businesslike than the Gede. Often they will wear Masonic aprons, hats, and items connected with Masonic burial rites. (The Bawons are known to be powerful Freemasons.) Those Bawons who talk speak with the Ghede's nasal whine, but generally they are not as given to profanity. Some people say that the Ghede are the spirits of the dead, but the Bawons are death itself.

Maman Brigitte is the Bawon's wife. A tough-talking woman in black, she takes no guff from anyone and can cuss up a storm that would make a Ghede take pause. Brigitte does not come in possession as frequently as the Ghede and the Bawons, but she is still an important part of Haitian culture. Maman Brigitte is considered the consummate judge, and those who have been wronged will often go to her cairn of stones seeking justice. She is also feared as a powerful sorceress. Because she is strong and open about her sexuality, some mambos and houngans claim she is the patroness of prostitutes and sex workers. (Others give this office to Gran Ezili, the "old Ezili" who is the grandmother of Ezili Freda.)

One Vodou song claims that Maman Brigitte "comes from England." Because of this, some have claimed that Brigitte is really the Celtic fire goddess Brigit (or Brigid), brought to Haiti by indentured Irish servants. It may be a pleasant story, but this attribution raises more questions than answers. Why do we not find Brigitte on other Caribbean islands that had a far larger Irish population, and why do we not find Maman Brigitte in Ireland, Brittany, or other areas where St. Brigit was worshipped? The truth is that we do not know Maman Brigitte's origins—but we do know that she is a powerful no-nonsense lwa.

Brigitte takes many of the same things that are given to Bawon: she favors black and purple, and she will often take sweets in those colors.

Sallie Ann Glassman has said that her Brigitte likes gauze bandages; others will give Brigitte banana peppers. (In Haiti, women possessed by Brigitte will often rub their genitals with these hot peppers. When not possessed, I strongly advise against trying this!) Some Brigittes are fond of flashy, revealing purple-and-black clothing; others favor a more refined, Victorian, or "antiquity" look. As with other dead spirits, there will be considerable variation among individuals. Many Vodouisants use the image of Mary Magdalene lying prostrate at the foot of the cross with skull in hand to symbolize Maman Brigitte. You can use this lithograph, or any image of a skeletal woman you can find.

The *Envoi Mort:* The Malevolent Dead

With the Bawon's assistance, a Vodouisant can use the *envoi mort* (sending of the dead) to wreak havoc against an enemy. The details of this operation are generally taught only by a trained professional to a student who is sworn to keep them secret. This is how I learned of the operation. I must also admit that I have never performed this ceremony, although I have spoken to others who have and who have reported that it is frighteningly effective. I will not give here the specific details of how this is performed, and I strongly advise against experimenting with it on your own. Doing so, without proper protections, will most likely result in you becoming infested with the spirit you wished to send.

The basic operation involves going to a cemetery, to the grave of a person who died young or by violence. After petitioning the Bawon for his aid, the Vodouisant then "sends" that dead person's spirit against the target. If this spell is successful, the cursed person will begin to manifest the symptoms of whatever killed the mort. If the mort died of AIDS or cancer, the target will begin losing weight despite the best efforts of doctors. If the mort was shot, the target will suffer from intense pains in the area of the wounds, and so on. Needless to say, this wanga raises several ethical concerns. Not only are you doing serious harm to another (indeed, if the mort is not released or driven away, the target will eventually die), you are enslaving a troubled soul and using it for your own ends. It is not something that should be undertaken lightly, if at all. In my experience, magicians who work extensively with malevolent dead spirits are among the most damaged and unpleasant people I have ever encountered.

Just as I recommend against sending the dead after an enemy, I also advise that you be aware of the effects of a mort infestation. Troubled dead spirits can attach themselves to you in any number of ways; they don't have to be sent. Staying in a haunted house, visiting the site of a crime, next-door neighbors who enjoy playing with Ouija boards—there are any number of ways by which a sensitive individual can attract unwanted attention from negative dead spirits.

You've probably met people who gave you bad vibes—people who left you feeling like you needed a shower. You've probably been in areas that left you nervous or edgy; rooms where you felt someone was staring at you or where you felt cold or tired. What you were sensing may well have been a spiritual infestation—which could be contagious. Unless you have extensive experience as a psychotherapist *and* as a magician, you probably don't want to play exorcist. Distinguishing between mental disorders and spiritual oppression is challenging at best . . . and incompetent or unprepared exorcists run a very real danger of becoming infested by the entity they're trying to banish. Much as you would leave open-heart surgery or bankruptcy law to professionals, you probably should leave these matters to people with the proper training and experience.

As you become more sensitive, you should wear some form of holy amulet or other protective item. You don't have to display this; keeping it discreetly tucked in your shirt is fine. Just because it's not plainly visible doesn't mean that wandering spiritual nasties can't sense it, and won't give it a wide berth. Keeping a holy symbol of your choice displayed in your home will also help to keep them out of your living area. Crosses, mezuzahs, "Hands of Fatimah," pentagrams, crystals—all serve as focal points for spiritual light and will cause discomfort to beings that are more comfortable amidst darkness.

Should you find that you've attracted the attention of the malevolent dead, quick and decisive action is in order. Prepare a bath with the herb rue *(Ruta graveolens)*. You should be able to find rue in most botanicas, in many garden shops, or online. Steep a few healthy pinches of dried rue, or a few stems of fresh rue, in hot (not boiling) water for five to ten minutes. Add it to some spring water and soak in it or pour it over your head. This will drive away bad or unwanted dead spirits while strengthening positive dead (like ancestors or spirit guides). After you are done bathing with it, place some rue in some house-cleaning soap and cleanse your home. (If you have wall-to-wall carpeting, you can sprinkled crushed dried rue about the place, and then vacuum it up. Placing a pinch of salt and camphor at each corner of your bed may also prove helpful. The dead do not like salt or camphor and placing them where you sleep will ensure that they cannot disturb your dreams. If this proves ineffective, and you continue to be troubled, seek outside assistance immediately.

Avoid séances performed by or with people who are silly, chemically impaired, or mentally unstable. There are innumerable anecdotes about bored teenagers who wind up inviting something they couldn't control, many of which have some basis in truth. If you wish to contact the dead, or any spiritual entity, be certain you have purified the space beforehand—and make sure you approach the whole operation with a reverent and respectful spirit. In the spiritual world, like attracts like: reverence and respect will draw more evolved and intelligent spirits, whereas a frivolous, sneering approach will attract trickster spirits and the bored dead.

Ultimately, an ounce of prevention will be more useful than several pounds of cure. Make sure your living quarters are clean, physically and spiritually. Negative entities prefer clutter and chaos to cleanliness and order. You may also want to make regular offerings to the Bawon and Brigitte, at the cemetery or at a table you have set up for this purpose. A negative dead spirit may not take orders from you, but it will not want to offend the Bawon. If he tells it to leave, or refuses it entry, it will be unable to harm you.

25

THE ANCESTORS

In Haiti, most Vodouisants will regularly visit the graves of their departed loved ones. But this may not be possible for Haitians who have left the country. Hence, many Vodouisants in the diaspora will set up a "white table" for their deceased ancestors. This is essentially identical to the white table of Kardecian spiritualism. A table is draped in a clean white cloth. Photos of deceased loved ones and/or items that belonged to them are placed atop that table. You should also place glasses filled with clean water on the table, and holy symbols that represent your ancestral religion. You may no longer identify as Christian, Muslim, Jewish, and so forth—but that doesn't mean that your ancestors over on the other side have rejected their religion. Providing them with tefillin or a Bible is just good manners. Instead of forcing your religious beliefs on your ancestors, you're showing respect for their feelings and their faith.

The white table is a personal shrine, and each white table will differ. If your departed uncle loved horse racing, you can provide him with a copy of the latest racing form. If he kept up on current events, you can give him the Sunday paper. An ancestor who smoked may want a pack of his favorite cigarettes; an ancestor who wore a particular brand of perfume will be delighted if you get her a small bottle. You can even give your ancestors some of their favorite foods, although you should not use any salt when preparing their meals. Although the Ghede don't object to salted food, many ancestral spirits find salt unpleasant or caustic.

As with all other altars, you should not put this table in your bedroom or in any place where you will be having sexual intercourse. If this cannot be avoided because of space restrictions, make sure you have some way of placing a screen around this table so that you and your ancestors both can have some privacy. This does not have to be elaborate or expensive: a simple clean white sheet, placed over the table when the need arises, will be sufficient.

The Definition of "Relatives"

Vodou recognizes that you can have spiritual ancestors as well as blood relations. One of the perks of initiation is that you gain a linkage to the spiritual ancestry of your house, and become a "child" of the houngans and mambos who have gone before you. This is in keeping with the African traditions where Vodou developed. The proverb "It takes a village to raise a child" may have been made famous by Hilary Clinton, but it originated, among others, with the Igbo and Yoruba peoples of Nigeria.

Some people will tell you that you should only put blood relatives on a white table. I believe that anyone who earned your love and who was important in your life can be honored there. Adoptive parents, stepparents, beloved teachers—they may not have provided your genetic material, but they certainly helped you become who you are and have earned a place in your family. I use the word *ancestors* to include loved ones: relatives, family friends, and those who guided you during your formative years. I even know people who have included beloved pets on their white table. Some may scoff at this, but I think it is completely appropriate. Many people who have had near-death experiences have reported seeing childhood pets on the other side; and spirits that manifest as animals appear in cultures around the world. Who is to say that your deceased dog wasn't a spirit sent to teach you valuable lessons about unconditional love, or that your cat's affection was less important than a human being's?

Acknowledging Your Roots

When you have set up a white table, you are acknowledging that you didn't arrive at this place in your life alone. You can begin your work with your ancestors by examining yourself. Determine what you have acquired from your parents, your family, and those who have come before you. Take an honest inventory of your strengths and weaknesses. Ask yourself what positive things you gained from your family. Did you inherit your father's musical talent, or your mother's skill at baking? Do you have your aunt's bull-headed drive for success, you great-grandmother's love of gardening, your grandfather's outgoing nature? Thank your deceased relatives for the strengths they've passed on to you . . . and in the process you may want to say thank you to your relatives who are still living.

Respecting your ancestors doesn't mean believing that your family is perfect. Knowing your roots means knowing both the good and the bad. None of us grew up in a Norman Rockwell painting. You can honor your relatives while at the same time recognizing their faults. Respecting your uncle's heroism in World War II doesn't mean you have to buy into his less-than-enlightened ideas about black people. Admiring your grandmother's struggles and quiet heroism during the Depression doesn't mean you have to pretend her drinking problem didn't exist. Once you have acknowledged their weaknesses, explore how those weaknesses have manifested in your own life. Do you reenact your mother's screaming temper tantrums with your loved ones? Have you transformed your uncle's compulsive gambling into "compulsive dating," riding an endless merry-go-round of relationships in a quest for excitement and novelty?

Working with our ancestors can be an empowering experience—but it can also be painful. Many of us were not as close to our families as we might like. Others escaped nightmarish childhoods in dysfunctional homes and have no desire to speak with our parents and grandparents, let alone honor them. For these people, all this emphasis on roots and ancestors just serves to increase their feelings of alienation and discomfort. It's as if they have to deal with odes to family holidays 365 days a year, complete with the assumption that if you don't get into the family spirit there's something wrong with you.

Adult children of healthy families had realistic role models of family behavior, and they are able to understand the difference between real families and the idealized versions we see on television. Children of abusive families, however, do not have these role models. As a result, they frequently assume other "healthy" families behave like those we see on TV. These unrealistic expectations often leave them feeling like there is something wrong with them because they didn't have this kind of idyllic childhood, and because they cannot provide it for their own families.

Not all abuse is physical or sexual. Many people grew up in emotionally abusive homes, where they were constantly belittled and humiliated. These people may believe they were never abused, because they were never molested, neglected, or assaulted. Yet they can carry those emotional scars throughout their lives—and repeat these destructive behaviors with their own partners and children. Emotional abuse can be overt, with threats and insults, or covert—a subtle, long-standing pattern of negative feedback that rips apart the target's self-esteem. Recognizing your father's unrealistic expectations, or your mother's pattern of hurtful remarks, is a first step toward rebuilding your self-esteem . . . and toward breaking the cycle of abuse. Acknowledging that your parents are human and fallible can help you understand that you are human and worthy of respect.

The Question of Forgiveness

In some situations, recognizing and acknowledging abusive behavior may be enough to heal old wounds. In other cases, parents and family have behaved so badly that they no longer deserve your honor or your respect. You don't have to reestablish contact with abusive family members to honor the lwa or the orisha. Nor do you have to tolerate abuse in the name of "respecting your parents." Respect is earned, not given—and there is such a thing as unforgivable behavior.

Many believe that forgiveness is the first step in the healing process.

In reality, it is one of the last stages of recovery from childhood abuse. Many abuse victims have been raised in an environment of denial and repression. Telling them they should forgive and forget is just another way of saying "don't tell anyone about this" or "you are to blame for your feelings"—sentiments with which many victims are all too familiar. People abused as children have a right to be angry at their abusers—and acknowledging this anger is also an important part of the healing process, one that must come before "letting go" and "forgiving." Some never reach the stage where they forgive their abusers—and yet they are still able to get on with their lives and function as survivors, not as victims. What they have achieved in the place of forgiveness is resolution. They have acknowledged their abuse, and their anger, and they have come to terms with their feelings.

In her book *Jambalaya,* Luisa Teish recommends that you light a candle for deceased abusers and give them your best wishes that they may someday find the light . . . while making clear that they are not welcome in your domain and that you want nothing further to do with them.[1] This is excellent advice. There is no reason for you to offer rent-free space in your head to someone who has passed on. You do not have to let the abuse go—but you are well advised to let the abuser go. In freeing them, you free yourself. They need no place on your ancestral altar, nor do you owe them any assistance in their quest for peace. (Indeed, you don't even owe them your best wishes. If it is more therapeutic for you to confront these spirits and tell them how much they hurt you and how much anger you still hold toward them, do it—and then send them off to where they can no longer hurt you.)

Working with Difficult Ancestors

Some spirits regret the bad things they did in life and wish to make amends for their misdeeds. If you feel like one of your "toxic" ancestors might fall into this category, *and* if you wish to help them, you can light a simple white candle for them. You may also wish to follow the lead of Mexican spiritists, who make altars for the "souls in purgatory," which they keep separate from their ancestral altars. These souls receive "positive vibrations" in the form of prayers, clean water, and white candles, but they are not intermingled with the "blessed dead." This provides them with material and energy they can use to work out their karma and ascend to a higher level, while keeping them from interfering with your daily life.

Many people have problems with the phrase "working with spirits." For them, this evokes images of enslaving your kindly grandmother and making her do tricks for you on command. In actuality, working with a spirit is a two-way street. Most practitioners of African traditional religions believe that sooner or later, every spirit will find its way to the light—and that by working with departed spirits and offering them positive energy, you are helping their evolution. Just as we learn during our lifetime and grow from our good deeds, so too can a deceased spirit grow and advance by doing good things. By healing the sick, helping the poor, and doing positive things they may have neglected in life, the dead benefit as much as the people they have helped.

(This is yet another reason why you should not use the troubled dead for negative magic. Taking spirits who were violent in life and using them as attack dogs will only hinder their enlightenment. Instead of helping those spirits to grow and to conquer their problems, you will be encouraging them to wallow in their weakness and become more, not less, flawed.)

White Table Meditations

As with your other shrines, you can meditate before your white table when you wish to talk to your departed loved ones. Begin by cleansing the space through whatever means you normally use. You may also want to honor your family's religious beliefs by saying a few of their favorite prayers: a psalm you grandmother particularly loved, or a recitation of the Kaddish. If you are not allergic to incense, you may want to burn a tiny bit of copal resin: it has traditionally been used to honor and strengthen the dead in Mexico and Central America, and in my experience the dead are quite fond of its smell. If you can't find copal, you can burn myrrh instead. Myrrh is also connected with funeral rites and strengthens the benevolent dead while driving away negative spirits. And if one of your ancestors was particularly fond of a particular type of incense, feel free to burn that as well as, or instead of, copal or myrrh.

When you have cleansed and purified the space, you can ask your ancestors for their advice, if you're having a problem, or offer them your thanks if things are going well. This is another personal area: think of your white table as a telephone with which you can chat with your friends and relatives on the other side. You may feel a bit awkward or self-conscious at first. But with practice, you will find chatting with your ancestors as natural and easy as calling a faraway friend. Whether you come to share good news or because you need a shoulder to cry on, you can be sure your ancestors will hear you.

Remember that your ancestors may retain many of the prejudices and misconceptions they carried in life. Although they now have a different view of the world, and they may well recognize their mistakes and failings, they are neither perfect nor infallible. Your dear Auntie Edna may still be wondering when you're going to meet a nice girl and settle down, even after you tell her you're gay. Your loving grandfather may advise you to quit art school and get your MBA, even though you have no interest in the business world and would rather paint. As with living relatives and loved ones, at times you may have to agree to disagree. Like they say in Alcoholics Anonymous, "Take what you need and leave the rest behind."

Those who loved you in life still love you even after they have passed on. They want to help you and see that you succeed. Not only are they willing to provide you with advice, but they can also help you in material matters. If you are having monetary difficulties, health problems, or romantic woes, your ancestors can help you overcome these difficulties. (Indeed, in material matters, many Spiritualists prefer working with the dead to calling on more "advanced" spirits. Because they once lived on this plane, and because they are still close to it, they can act quickly and effectively.) They won't do everything for you—you still should consult a doctor, watch your spending, and so on—but they can definitely "grease the wheels of fortune" and help you find opportunities.

Working with the dead can have many other profound and lasting benefits. We may have heard that death is just a passage into the afterlife; talking with and working with the dead can help us understand this on a visceral level. If you think of death as terrifying, the Ghede's antics can help you overcome those fears; and although Bawon and Brigitte may be stern, they hold the keys not only to death but to the life that comes after death.

Perhaps most important, studying and honoring your roots can help you know yourself. None of us is self-created; each of us bears the marks of our environment and of the people who raised us, for good or ill. Honoring our biological and spiritual ancestors means more than just paying them lip service. It means understanding where we came from, and where we are going. Finishing the work our forebears began is the best tribute we can offer, to ourselves and to them.

Part Four

CEREMONIES AND WANGA

Like other religions, Haitian Vodou has specific ceremonies by which it interacts with the Divine and calls upon its power for protection and healing. These are found in most Vodou houses. The specifics may differ, but the general outline remains the same. There are also wangas—magical spells. Each individual houngan or mambo will have different ways of performing wangas, based on what they learned from their teachers and from the lwa.

You may not be an initiate; you may not even be a member of a house. But that doesn't mean you can't learn from other Vodouisants, initiated and noninitiated. Nor does it mean you can't take lessons from the spirits. By studying some of the techniques used in Vodou, you can incorporate these powerful and well-tested methods into your own practice and reap some of their benefits.

Please keep in mind that these are *not* the actual ceremonies of Haitian Vodou, as practiced by trained initiates. After reading this chapter, you will know how to create a spiritual doll or a cleansing bath. You will not know how to give someone a garde (a guard) or how to perform a lave tet (head washing). These secrets are not something you can learn in a book. If you want to experience these ceremonies, you will have to find a working house of Vodou and have people skilled in the art perform them for you. And if you wish to learn how to perform them for others, you will have to find someone who will accept you as a student. I offer some pointers on how to do this in the conclusion.

26
ILLUMINATIONS

Thousands of years before Sigmund Freud smoked his first cigar, analysts struggled with dreams. The biblical Joseph's skill at dream interpretation won him release from an Egyptian jail, and a job at Pharaoh's court. The Greeks believed the *Oneiroi* (bringers of dreams) who came via the Gate of Horn brought truthful messages, whereas those who came via the Gate of Ivory brought phantasms and lies. John the Evangelist catalogued his dreams for the book of Revelation; the emperor Constantine dreamed of a cross in the sky and made Christianity Rome's official religion.

Today, dreams remain one of the major ways by which the lwa communicate with their servants. Vodouisants believe that in dreams, the *ti bon ange* ("little good angel," the part of the human soul that represents us in the human world) leaves the body and goes wandering in the heavenly realms. There it can commune with the lwa and receive blessings, warnings, and advice. As one Haitian explains, "[T]he Divine Source created several worlds connected with each other. From our human perspective there is the visible world, where Humans consciously dwell and the invisible world, where Ancestors and Spirits dwell, as well as to where Humans make frequent incursions, usually unconsciously."[1]

Many noted Haitian artists, like painter Hector Hippolyte, flag maker Antoine Oleyant, and sculptor Pierrot Barra, claim to receive inspiration from the spirits in their dreams. Houngenikons regularly hear chante lwa in their dreams, and then transmit them to the waking world at the next fet. Still others, Haitian and non-Haitian, have decided to undergo the maryaj lwa, or the kanzo, after a dream that told them they needed to do so. (I am one of these people. I began my training with Société la Belle Venus #2 after a dream wherein a lwa dragged me into the djevo.)

Vodouisants pay careful attention to their dreams. When they are in particular need of guidance, they will prepare an *iluminasyon* (illumination) to encourage nocturnal visits from the lwa. This practice can be easily adapted for the needs of solitary servants of the lwa, and it offers an excellent way to get in touch with your spirits.

To prepare for an illumination, put clean white sheets on your bed. You should also clean your bedroom thoroughly and create a sacred space. Fill a basin (preferably white enamelware; if that is unavailable, a white ceramic bowl or other white and fireproof container will do) with clean, pure water. Place a seven-day candle in the basin, in a color appropriate to the spirit with whom you wish to commune. Use a dark blue or red candle for Danto, a dark green or dark blue candle for Zaka, pink for Freda, purple for the Ghede, and so on. If you are just seeking general guidance, use a white candle. You can also include some items connected to the lwa in the basin. A dash of Florida water for Danto, some wormwood for Zaka, a touch of orgeat syrup for Damballah, some leaves from the forest for Gran Bwa, or some rum and iron nails for Papa Ogou. Use your imagination and creativity. Go with your gut feelings and follow your instinct. Don't hesitate to add something if you feel the spirit wants it.

Wrap your head in a white cloth. Vodouisants believe this will shield you against negative influences while allowing positive energy to pass through. A pure white head wrap will serve as a barrier against negative or frivolous spirits, but it will not cause any difficulties for the lwa if they choose to come and visit you. Say a few prayers of your choice, and then light the candle and get into bed.

You can focus on the flickering candlelight, allowing it to lull you into sleep. You may also find it helpful to meditate about the spirit or spirits as you are drifting off. You don't have to concentrate or focus;

just think about the spirit as you are nodding off. If you are trying to contact Ogou, for example, imagine him standing before you. Talk to him as you fall asleep: give him any messages you may have for him, along with any requests. As you are doing so, imagine his responses. Try to imagine with more than one sense. You don't just hear him speaking; you can smell rum and gunpowder, and feel his rough, unshaven skin as he presses his face to yours. Don't force this, and don't strain yourself; that would be counterproductive. Do this as you relax, and keep doing it as you fall asleep. In time, you will find yourself much more likely to dream of the lwa.

When you awaken, write down any dreams you had. Be sure to put down everything that you remember. Don't neglect to write things because you think they are too trivial; and don't try to censor your dreams or embellish them for dramatic effect. (This is a particular problem for those of us who are writers; we often have to stop ourselves from "improving" on messages and facts.)

If you do not yet do so, start keeping a dream diary. Purchase a book specifically for this purpose. It doesn't have to be fancy—a simple notebook will do—but like any other magical tool, it should be dedicated specifically to its purpose, in this case, recording dreams. Keep this by your bedside, along with a pen or pencil used only to record your dreams. Place them where you will be able to grab them immediately upon awakening, not in a drawer or across the room.

When you awaken, open your dream diary and record your dreams. Do not wait: do it immediately. With every minute you wait, you will forget more and more details. Record the location, the people or spirits involved. Even if you can only recall vague feelings and emotions, write them down. By doing this each morning, you will establish a link in your mind between the diary and your dreams. This will improve your recall and allow you to note more details.

You may find that awakening a bit earlier than usual helps you to remember your dreams. You may also find that setting your alarm for the middle of the night, then writing down all the dream information you can remember, is useful. Some practitioners have reported that putting a "dream pillow" filled with mugwort beneath their pillows helps them have more vivid dreams; others recommend a mug of warm milk before sleep. But it's difficult to tell anyone how to dream. This is a personal process, and everyone will find their own way to slumberland.

Like everything else, practice makes perfect. In time, you will discover patterns in your dreams; places, images, and people will recur, and themes will pop up over and over. You will become more familiar with your dreamscape—and with the lwa who speak with you there. By meditating upon these images, places, and people before you go to sleep, you will have a better chance of visiting them again in your dreams. You may even master the techniques of lucid dreaming. This means you will be able to enter your dreams with full waking consciousness and gain some measure of control over your interactions with those spirits who live in the land beyond the gates of sleep.

27

ACTIONS DE GRACE

You've probably met a few people in your lifetime who only talk to you when they want something—and who never bother to thank you after you give it to them. I'm sure you find this kind of behavior rude and annoying. So do the lwa. Like people on this side, the lwa and those who have passed on appreciate a heartfelt thanks when they do something nice. Vodouisants will frequently respond to favors received with an action de grace (action of grace), a ceremony of thanksgiving for favors performed by the lwa.

To perform an action de grace, a table is prepared. Statues and images connected with the various lwa are brought out and placed there, along with some of their favored items (Ogou's machete, Zaka's straw bag, etc.). Food is placed there, as well as bottles containing their libations. A lamp will also be "mounted" or lit. This is made by floating a cotton wick in a bowl of olive oil that contains other ingredients. Vodouisants believe it will serve to "heat" the spirit and draw it near.

Catholic prayers and the priye Gineh begin the ceremony, and then prayers are given in honor of the various spirits. Typically these ceremonies do not involve drums; instead, they feature quiet prayers. Frequently one or more lwa will arrive through possession, so they can give their personal thanks and offer the appropriate counsel and warnings. Basically, the action de grace is a low-key, low-profile version of more public ceremonies. If a fet is a neighborhood party, an action de grace is a quiet dinner with friends in honor of a special event.

Vodouisants who have moved into a new house may hold an action de grace to welcome their spirits, and to thank them for their assistance in getting the mortgage. Graduation from school, a raise, a new child—all these events may be honored with an action de grace. An action de grace may also be performed when a member of the house is ill or suffering from financial problems or bad luck. Vodouisants believe that these intimate services for the lwa will show devotion and make the lwa more favorably disposed toward the suffering member. It also helps to build a sense of community, and a closer personal relationship with the spirits.

There are certain ways initiates prepare a table for an action de grace. The specific making of lamps, and the specific foods provided, are secrets of the djevo. However, there is nothing stopping an uninitiated person from saying thank you to the spirits—or from spending some quiet time with them as a friend.

The late Mambo Orleanna, a student of Mambo Samantha Kaye, created a lwa "cocktail hour." This is a great way of getting in touch with the spirits in a close and personal setting. Many noninitiates have performed this ritual, with excellent results. As the name would suggest, the lwa cocktail hour involves preparing drinks for the particular spirits, and then sitting back and mingling with them. I am indebted to Mambo Orleanna and to Mambo Kaye for sharing this ceremony with me, and I am grateful for their generosity in allowing me to reproduce it here.

Whatever lwa you are inviting over, make sure you prepare a rum cocktail for Papa Legba, so that he will open the gate and let the other spirits in. Also prepare a couple of drinks for the other spirits you are asking down. A champagne flute for Freda and/or La Sirene, a hefty drink of rum for Ogou, some rum and hot peppers for the Ghede—follow the likes and dislikes listed in this book, but feel free to add your own personal twists. Just as there's no one right way to hold a dinner party, there's no one right way to hold a lwa cocktail hour. Your personal touches will only make the lwa more excited about showing up at your house.

If you'd like to have a party for one particular lwa, that's fine. You may also want to have a small affair with only a couple of spirits. You shouldn't invite Freda and Danto to the same party; and you should probably give the Ghede their own cocktail hour, because their raucous behavior may be off-putting to more sedate lwa. However, it would be perfectly fine to hold a cocktail hour with Agwe and La Sirene, for example, or Freda and Ogou or Freda and Damballah. (In the latter case, the party should be alcohol-free, to honor Papa Damballah's dislike for alcohol. Orgeat or other sweet drinks can be prepared for all in place of rum.) As I said, whoever you invite, make sure that you ask Legba to open the gate first, so the other lwa can come down.

When you have everything ready, light a white candle. Then pick up Legba's highball glass. Say, "This is for you, Papa." Now say aloud: "Hey, Legba! Let my words carry to the other side. Open the gate, please, Alegba. Let the helpers pass over. [Pause] Thank you!"

Next clap your hands three times and say aloud: "[Name of lwa], please come join me for cocktail hour." Pick up the drink you have prepared for the lwa, hold it out and to your left, and say, "This is for you." Then place the glass back down on the table you have prepared for the spirits. If you have a house altar or shrine, you can use that; otherwise you can prepare a temporary table with a simple white cloth.

Light the white candle. As you light it, say, "[Name of lwa], thank you for joining me for cocktail hour. I appreciate your spending time with me!"

After you light the candle, pick up one of the glasses and clink it with the other in a toast, saying, "*A sante, mes amis,*" or, "To your health, my friends." You can mix yourself a drink along with the spirits—or you can have soda or some other nonalcoholic beverage if you're a recovering alcoholic, a nondrinker, or otherwise unable to consume alcoholic drinks. Whatever you do, be sure to clink glasses with Legba and your other guests. After all, this *is* a toast. And if you want to bring them some of their favorite food, or surprise them with a nice present, you can do that as well. Just imagine this is a small dinner gathering with a friend.

When you're ready to end cocktail hour (which doesn't have to be an hour—do it for however long you want), extinguish the candle by pinching it with your fingers or using a spoon or a candle snuffer. Don't blow it out. Then say, "Thank you, [name of lwa]. If it pleases you, you may depart now," and, "Thank you, Papa Legba. If it pleases you, you may close the gates now." Later, take the drink offerings outside. Pour the rum at the foot of any tree, near the corner of any intersection, or at a wooden fencepost, telephone pole, or lamppost.

You can do this whenever you want to be close and speak to the lwa. Anytime you have a joyful event and would like to share it with a friend, or when you need a loving shoulder to cry on, it's a good time to hold a lwa cocktail hour. Remember, the lwa aren't genies in a bottle; nor are they trained animals that you call to do tricks. They are loving companions and stalwart friends. If you only call on the lwa when you want them to do something for you, you'll quickly find yourself ignored. If, on the other hand, you develop a close personal relationship with your spirits—one where you reward their help and good advice with gratitude and praise—you'll find that your work with the lwa is extremely beneficial and gratifying.

28

THE LAVE TET

The lave tet (literally "head washing"; also known as the *sevis tet* or "service for the head") is a cleansing that feeds the spirits. It strengthens the particular lwa who guards the Vodouisant, and it sends away any negative spirits or bad energy that may have become attached to the person. The lave tet also "cools" the head, making the recipient calmer and more balanced. A person who is hotheaded—easily angered, prone to emotional outbursts, and easily distracted—may get particular benefit from a lave tet. So too might a person who is suffering from violent, uncontrollable possessions or who has been feeling tired, depressed, or otherwise emotionally drained.* Often people who are considering membership in a house will have a lave tet performed as their introduction to the société and its lwa.

The specific actions and items required for a lave tet are generally house secrets, taught only to initiates. But without violating any of my oaths, I can provide a basic outline of the ceremony I was taught, as well as some of the differences I have seen in the ways the lave tet can be performed. As always, there is no one right way to perform a lave tet. If your house gets beneficial results, you are doing it correctly.

*Of course, depression or anger management difficulties can be caused by spiritual oppression, by chemical or emotional issues, or by some combination thereof. These problems may well require medication or therapy. If you are in doubt, seek the aid of a competent physician or counselor. A lave tet (or any other Vodou service) should not be used as a substitute for professional help.

A lave tet involves water in which various herbs and other items have been steeped. (The specific herbs, and the amounts used, will vary from house to house.) The recipient's head is washed with this water, and then the head is "fed" with either an herbal paste or with the blood of a chicken or dove. The recipient is then dressed in white and lies down in the badji (the sacred room where candidates are also laid down for initiation and where many of the house's holy items are kept) for several hours or several days, depending on various factors and house traditions. Afterward, the recipient must avoid sexual intercourse or other situations that might cause "contamination" (like entering a jail or cemetery) for a period that can range from a day or two to as long as a week.

In some lineages of Vodou, a head washing serves as an initiation in itself. In Dominican Vodou, the three grades of initiation are *refrescamiento, aplasamiento,* and *bautiso* (refreshment, settlement, and baptism). Each of these involves as their centerpiece a mixture of seven *refrescas* (soft drinks) of various colors, along with water, herbs, and fruits being placed on the initiate's head to "feed" and "set" the spirits. In Cuban Vodou, the initiates are "baptized" with a head washing and seclusion along with the tools connected to their "saints"; later an egg is cracked on their head to feed their spirits.[1] Other houses consider the lave tet to be an introduction to the spirits and the société—not an initiation per se, but a first step on the path toward initiation.

Although the lave tet ceremony can only be performed by someone with the proper training, uninitiated practitioners can do many things to keep their heads cool and feed their spirits. Baths are frequently used as magical and spiritual tools throughout the African diaspora, and there's no reason why you can't use this powerful technique yourself. You will find that cleansing baths will clear you of negative energy, cooling baths will help you to feel more calm and focused, and power baths will help strengthen your connection with the spirits and make you better able to overcome the obstacles life throws at you.

Cleansing Baths

It's difficult to avoid coming into contact with other people's negativity. A day spent among tense coworkers, stressed-out commuters, and angry customers can leave us with a residue of psychic "sludge." Much as we clean the grime and dirt off our skin after a hard day's work, or take a shower before we go out on the town, we can use cleansing baths to rid ourselves of this spiritual detritus.

When making a cleansing bath (or any other kind of spiritual bath), you should use clean spring water. Put a quart or so in a clear, wide-mouthed bottle. Now add a healthy pinch of salt: sea salt is ideal, but regular salt will do just fine. If you'd like, you may bless the salt beforehand using whatever blessing you prefer. To this salt water, add some hyssop (*Hyssopus* spp.) and rue *(Ruta graveolens);* these can be found in many botanicas or online. Salt, hyssop, and rue have been used to remove negativity for millennia, and each is widely used by Vodouisants in Haiti and the diaspora. If you wish, you can also add some clear quartz crystals to the bottom of the bottle. Crystals are not often used in Haiti, but they can be a powerful tool for focusing positive energy. Say a few prayers over this bottle. As you do, concentrate on sending healing energy and white light through the liquid.

Before you prepare any kind of spiritual bath, you should make sure your body is clean. Shower or bathe so that you're thoroughly clean. When you're ready, take the spiritual bath. Concentrate on cleansing white light as you pour the contents over yourself, starting at your head and working your way downward. As the cleansing water rolls off your body and down the drain, imagine it's stripping away nastiness and negative energy. After the bath has poured off your body, you can step under the shower again for a moment or two, to remove the last traces of bad energy. Now towel off and dress in clean white clothing. You can use this bath whenever you've been around negative people, or when you want to prepare yourself for spiritual activities.

Cooling Baths

When we're forced to deal with stress (and who isn't?), we can become irritable and depressed. This can even lead to physical illness if it continues too long. This stress doesn't always come from bad people or bad situations. Being a parent, for example, is a great joy but also a great burden; and, although most small business owners would welcome a big contract, they might not welcome the long hours required to fill that contract. A cleansing bath will help get rid of negative things you may have picked up from outside. A cooling bath is subtly different: it will help you attain peace of mind and calm, allowing you to deal with the pressures of daily life. It will also help you to become more attuned to the Divine and Transcendent, and less focused on petty concerns.

The cooling bath calls on the help of the coolest, most peaceful lwa of them all: Papa Damballah. Like the cleansing bath, the cooling bath is prepared using a quart or so of spring water. To that you add a tiny bit of orgeat syrup, a pinch of sugar, a few ounces of condensed milk, and some white flower petals. Light a white candle for Papa Damballah; show him the bath and ask him to make you clean and pure like he is. (If you have an altar for Papa Damballah, you can do this in front of the shrine; otherwise you can just light a candle on a clean surface and call on him.) After you have presented the bath to Papa Damballah, you can get undressed and step in the shower. After you've cleaned yourself off thoroughly, pour this cooling bath over your head. As it pours over your body, feel Papa Damballah's peaceful, ancient, benevolent presence. He can take care of all your problems; he can give you the strength you need to handle the challenges of daily life.

Now step out of the shower and let your skin air-dry; without toweling off, put on some clean white clothing. (White sweat pants and a white T-shirt will do.) Prepare your bed with clean white sheets if you can, and sleep alone for the night. At the very least, do not have sexual intercourse on the night when you do this. Sexual intercourse "heats" you and raises your energy; after doing this you want to stay cool for at least a day. You should also avoid alcohol and other mind-altering substances; instead of stimulants like coffee, you may want to drink warm milk (soy milk if you're lactose-intolerant or vegan) or lots of fresh water. Meditate or engage in other calm, peaceful activities, and try to get some sleep.

If you can, try to do this bath on a Thursday (Damballah's day) or a Sunday. It's probably best to do it after sundown or at night, given that you're going to be sleeping in white clothing for the night. This is a good way to keep yourself grounded and focused. You may want to take a cooling bath before making a major life decision, or when you feel like you're not up to handling all the demands life is throwing at you.

Power Baths

Not only can baths be used to take away stress or negativity; they can also be used to strengthen you and your spirits. Vodouisants regularly use baths to "bring up" their luck and make them more successful. Any competent houngan or mambo will have dozens of recipes for baths designed to bring good fortune, improve health, attract the attention of a love interest, and so forth. Most of these baths will be closely guarded professional secrets, known only to the priest and sold at a premium price. Although I cannot reveal some of the baths I was taught without incurring my mambo's wrath, I can give you some pointers on creating baths of your own.

You create a power bath for a particular lwa based on that lwa's likes and needs. A power bath for Freda, for example, would include pink rose petals, nice perfume, a liberal amount of sugar, and some champagne; you could also add some rose quartz to the bottom of the jar. For La Sirene, you might do something similar, only with white rose petals, sea salt, and some clear quartz crystals. You would prepare this on a Thursday and leave it to soak throughout the day. As you prepared it, you would tell Freda how beautiful she was, and how you wish she could help you to be more beautiful and more wealthy.

A power bath for Ogou, on the other hand, would be made by adding a few shots of rum to the bath, along with some tobacco. Instead of quartz crystals, you would include some pieces of iron—iron spikes from train tracks, perhaps, or iron nails. This would be prepared on a Wednesday. For Ezili Danto, you would add a sprinkle of cinnamon, red rose petals, a liberal dose of Florida water, and some basil, and prepare it on a Tuesday. You can do something like this for any of the spirits; use your imagination and your creativity, along with the information I've given on each spirit's particular tastes.

Before using the bath, clean yourself thoroughly with a new bar of soap. When you are thoroughly clean, pour the bath over your body, making sure your whole body is soaked with the bath liquid. Do *not* pour this over your head: these baths will make your head too "hot" and it may cause you to become too excitable. After you have poured the bath over your body, you can sit in the bath for a while if you have a tub. Otherwise, you can rub the bath into your skin with a clean washcloth or loofah. Start at your feet and work your way up, drawing the lwa's power into your body. (But stop at your shoulders; if you get a little bit on your head or neck that's fine, but try to avoid getting too much on your noggin.) When you are finished, don't use a towel, but let yourself air-dry. Put on clean clothes (either white or the color favored by the spirit) and spend some time in quiet reflection and meditation. If you do this before going to sleep, you can combine it with an illumination.

29

THE GARDE (GAD)

Like most clichés, "pinpricked Vodou dolls" owe more to wild imagination than reality. There is indeed a long history of magicians using effigies in baneful magic; but it is a history from Europe, not Africa or the Caribbean. Allegations of malefic magic performed with dolls were common in seventeenth-century Britain, and "hex figures" have been found in the ruins of seventeenth- and eighteenth-century homes in New England. This practice survives even today among the folk witches of the Ozarks and Appalachians. But in Vodou, most practitioners spend far less time casting curses than they do defending against them. Vodou is not an aggressive tradition so much as a defensive one. For most Vodouisants, the best offense is a good defense.

One of the ways Vodouisants protect themselves is through receiving a garde (in English, a guard; in Kreyol, a *gad*). In the most common garde, the Vodouisant receives ceremonial cuts on his or arm (typically the upper left arm). Before cutting, the arm is doused with rum; after the cuts are made, certain herbs are rubbed into the cut; a cloth is then tied around the wound. Most often this cloth is red, because gardes are typically made "on the point of," or using, a Petwo spirit. It is believed that this ceremony "seals" a spirit into the Vodouisant's body. In exchange for an occasional drink of rum (which the Vodouisant takes in his or her hand and then splashes on the healed scar), the spirit offers protection.

Garde spirits are notoriously short-tempered and aggressive, and those who tamper with them may find themselves facing the spiritual equivalent of a pit bull. The owner of the garde need not make any conscious effort to resolve the situation. The garde does what is required to neutralize any danger—much to the discomfort of anyone foolish enough to trigger them. The garde protects against physical threats—muggers, drunk drivers, and the like—and spiritual threats like malevolent ghosts, negative spirits, and other baneful beings.

Another garde is a gad migan (a stomach guard). One of the most famous of these is prepared by Ezili Danto after she kills a pig. She places the pig's blood in a basin, and then adds some Florida water and a few other ingredients. Those present will each drink three teaspoons of this nauseating mixture. Afteward, it is believed that the gad migan will cause them to vomit up any poison, spiritual or physical, that they consume. Many Haitians have a great fear of being poisoned. Cautionary tales abound of people who died after taking food from strangers, or who were poisoned by jealous neighbors or relatives. The gad migan is widely sought as protection against the evil intent of others. Much as they might take repulsive-tasting medicine, Vodouisants will overcome their gag reflex in exchange for the benefit it provides.

Vodouisants see both the spiritual and the material world as potentially dangerous places. They believe that not every person wishes you well, and not every spirit has your best interests at heart. The evidence suggests they are on to something. Positive affirmations and visualizations of white light have their place, but they may not be particularly effective when you're faced with a hopped-up crackhead or when you move to a house that's suffering from a demonic infestation. A little bit of prevention, and a few simple techniques, can help make your world a safer place.

Psychic Self-Defense

Many people have done little to train their will, which means it can be manipulated easily by those who have. Many of us are couch potatoes and television junkies, open to whatever stimulus crosses our minds. I'm not saying that it is ethical to manipulate people like pawns on a chessboard—but I will say that those who have a bit of training and self-discipline will often find it easy to do so. (Those who are drawn to occultism and magic—like those reading this book—can be among the easiest to control. They are often more sensitive, and more impressionable, than the average person.)

I recommend that anyone who is working with the lwa, or with any other powerful spiritual entities, read Dion Fortune's excellent book *Psychic Self-Defense.** Fortune was a gifted sensitive who had to learn psychic self-defense in the trenches after numerous attacks by malicious people and entities. (Among her attackers was Aleister Crowley, the self-proclaimed "Great Beast of the Revelation"—no slouch as a magician despite his lack of interpersonal skills and ethics.) Fortune's work can teach you how to shield yourself against corporeal and noncorporeal attackers.

The techniques of cleansing and creating sacred space that I mentioned in chapter 4 will also prove useful—and they should be mastered before you do anything else. The Hermetic Order of the Golden Dawn, one of Victorian England's most famous and influential magical societies, made all prospective students spend one year doing nothing but the lesser banishing ritual of the pentagram. Once they had mastered that banishing technique, they had a potent weapon by which they could dispel negativity, ground and center themselves, and create sacred space on short notice.

In addition to all these techniques, I would recommend an elementary book or course on logic, one that covers the major logical fallacies. If you understand the ways people can manipulate words and images to "pull your strings," you will be much more able to avoid being turned into a puppet. Psychic attacks and oppression are real, but they are comparatively rare. Pushy salesmen, sleazy politicians, and people trying to take advantage of you are far more common—and they can be a

*A revised edition was released by Weiser Publications, York Beach, Maine, in 2001. Please try to forgive her unenlightened comments about "primitive Negro magic." Fortune was a brilliant psychic, magician, and writer; but she was also a child of her class, place, and time (upper-class Great Britain during the early to middle twentieth century).

far bigger drain on your energy and resources. A healthy BFMD (bovine fecal material detector) will prove invaluable in matters spiritual and otherwise—and it may well be a magician's most useful and powerful tool.

Amulets and Holy Symbols

Many Vodouisants wear crucifixes, rosaries, or other holy items that have been blessed by a priest or other Catholic official. They wear these not only to show their faith (remember that most Haitian Vodouisants also identify as Roman Catholic) but for protection. Often they will also have blessed items in their home: crosses, images of the Virgin, pictures of the pope, and similar items. They believe that these symbols will help them to overcome evil and will protect them from both spiritual and material dangers.

You don't have to be Catholic to wear or display a holy symbol. Amulets and talismans for protection are found in many cultures. A pentagram, hand of Fatima, Om symbol, thangka, or star of David can also function effectively as a shield and as a magnet for positive influences. Despite contrary (and conflicting) claims, the Divine is not sectarian. She or he has given us numerous symbols that can protect us from evil. If these symbols are blessed by a cleric of their faith, so much the better. Clerics can function as a conduit by which divine energy is brought down to Earth. Their blessing can transform an object into a container for heavenly power. If this is not possible, you can bless the item yourself. A simple statement of intent will suffice—for example, "I present this pentagram to the Horned God and the Mother Goddess, that it may become an instrument of their will and a container of their power." If you are sincere, you can rest assured that the Divine will hear you.

Some people have had the vévés of one lwa or another tattooed on their bodies so that they may receive that spirit's protection. I would think long and hard before doing this. A tattoo is permanent, of course—and you may not be ready to handle the sheer influx of energy that may arise from having a spirit's vévé on your skin. If you sincerely feel the need to do this—if you have been asked to do so in a dream, for example, or if you were advised to do so after a reading—then you can use the appropriate vévé or image and find a competent tattoo artist. (If you can find one who is also a Vodouisant, you will be particularly blessed; but outside of New Orleans, that may be difficult to impossible to do.) Once your tattoo is healed, you may want to feed it occasionally with things connected to the spirit. Sprinkling a little perfume on Freda's image, or wetting Damballah's vévé with orgeat syrup, will serve to empower the tattoo and ensure your continued success and protection.

Dolls

Poppets and pins may be largely the stuff of pulp fantasies, but Vodouisants do use dolls for protection and aid. In Haiti, Vodouisants will use dolls to house protective spirits, much as dolls are used in Cuban Espiritismo. Dolls are also widely used for this purpose in New Orleans Voodoo and in hoodoo, practices that have been strongly influenced by European folk magic traditions. These dolls are not mutilated, damaged, or tortured. On the contrary, they are fed and pampered. Vodouisants talk to their dolls, asking for their aid and protection. Sometimes they will even take a doll into the djevo with them and "initiate" it as a houngan or mambo. These dolls can be powerful protectors, and creating them is not particularly difficult.

Children are natural magicians, and psychic sensitives will frequently note that well-loved toys are "staring at them" or otherwise seem "alive." This is because to children, the toys *are* alive: they treat them as beloved friends and provide them with lots of attention. But although children typically have excellent powers of imagination and visualization, they generally lack the discipline and willpower required to direct those powers toward an intended target or goal. The difference between a poppet and a greatly beloved GI Joe action figure is that magicians have focused their will, thereby using their doll to effect changes in the world. Like the child with a stuffed animal, magicians treat their dolls like living beings.

When you are creating your own protection doll, you should first decide which lwa you will place it on the point of, or use. If your doll is going to call on the energies of Bossou, you might want to use a stuffed bull; for Ogou, you might use that well-loved GI Joe mentioned above. (If you still have some of your toys from childhood, they will be particularly good tools for this purpose, because they're already well along the way to "awakening.") You can also use a standard doll, clothed in the appropriate colors (blue or red gingham for Danto, blue denim for Zaka, etc.).

The witches of Christian Europe would frequently "baptize" their poppets, thereby giving them a name and, by extension, a spirit. You should baptize your poppet, or hold a naming ceremony of your own design. When you give it a name, keep it a secret. Anyone who knows the name can gain power over the doll, and over you. (You can give it a "true name" and another name by which you will introduce it to other people. This is quite common in Vodou.) Once your doll is named, you can ask it to help you.

Talk to your doll regularly. Provide it with food and drink; pamper it and give it lots of attention. You should also keep a record of how things are working—an honest record that includes both your successes and your failures. I have seen negative entities attracted by spirit dolls. Be sure to keep track of any unusual manifestations that take place around this doll. If you start noticing cold spots in your home, or a persistent feeling of fatigue, you may want to destroy the poppet and do a cleansing and banishing on your residence. You should begin the ritual of creating your doll by making a sacred space. You may also want to fumigate your poppet with sweet herbs and frankincense regularly to keep a positive vibe going.

30

THE MARYAJ LWA

Within the various African tribes whose members came in chains to the New World, there were many different conjugal relationships. Some tribes were polygamous; others were monogamous. Cross-cousin marriages, slave marriages, secondary marriages, and ritual marriages could all be found in central and western Africa. But few of these customs had meaning in the harsh conditions of St. Domingue. Family relationships were regularly torn apart at auctions, and plantation owners who wanted to sleep with an attractive slave woman rarely considered their own marital vows, never mind those of their "property." Slave owners forbade anything that smacked of African "heathenism" and "voodooism," and brutally punished any slaves who were caught preserving their native traditions. Nor would the customs of any one tribe necessarily be reflected in the customs of another. To minimize the risk of organized uprisings, it was common practice to keep slaves from different groups together on a plantation; Africans separated by language and by ethnic identity were considered less likely to band together than Africans from the same region or tribe.

Flung together in this hellhole, the slaves were forced to re-create their ancestral religious traditions with whatever was at hand. Africans had never been afraid to incorporate the deities of neighboring tribes. Obviously the French gods were powerful: they kept the whites in wealth and gave them mastery over the black slaves. And so the slaves appropriated many of the symbols and practices of Catholicism into their own religious melange, including the sacrament of marriage, though a religious marriage was by no means considered necessary. On November 25, 1820, the *Niles' Weekly Register* of Baltimore reported that, "The sacred obligations of marriage are but little regarded in [Haiti]; the two sexes live in a state of concubinage; and, according to M. de la Croix, many irregular unions have taken place."

For most Haitians, a civil or religious marriage is a luxury. The most common relationship among peasants and the urban lower class is *plasaj* or common-law marriage. Haitians typically refer to any woman who lives with a man, keeps house for him, and bears his children as a wife. The husband and wife often make explicit agreements about their economic relationship at the beginning of a plasaj. These agreements typically require the husband to cultivate at least one plot of land for the wife and to provide her with a house. Women perform most household tasks, although men often do heavy chores like gathering firewood. These unions are distinguished from *vivavek* or *tizammi* relationships, sexual affairs that carry less responsibility and are less stable than a plasaj.

Among the Haitian elite, civil and religious marriages are the norm. The "best" families can trace legally married ancestors back to the nineteenth century. Legal marriages are seen as more prestigious than plasaj, but they are not necessarily more stable or productive, nor are they always monogamous. In fact, legally married men are often more economically stable than men in plasaj relationships, and so it is easier for them to separate from their wives or to enter into extramarital relationships. Although Haitian women are expected to maintain sexual fidelity to their husbands, whether they are legally married or in a plasaj relationship, Haitian men are more free to pursue polygamous relationships. Polygamy among Haitian men is not so much a sign of virility as of social and economic success: few Haitian men can afford to keep more than one family. Because the lwa are wealthy and powerful, they can pursue as many relationships as they want—and so they have taken to marrying many of their followers.

When the lwa possess Vodouisants at a ceremony, they will frequently offer advice and blessings—and make demands in return. Often their demands will include a request for marriage. The coquettish Ezili Freda often proposes to several men when she arrives at a ceremony, and the rum-swilling warrior Ogou is known for his love of the ladies and often asks for their hands in marriage when he comes. Frequently these proposals are met with reluctance. A maryaj lwa is at least as expensive as a civil or religious marriage, and it may eat up several years of savings. In lieu of a marriage, a Vodouisant might offer to buy the proposing lwa a gift or to make some sacrifice that is less costly and onerous. Sometimes the lwa will be satisfied with these counteroffers; as spirits residing in an impoverished land, they have long since learned to accept what is available to them. At other times they will insist on the maryaj. Vodouisants who continue to ignore these demands will often discover their luck turning for the worse, as the spurned lwa brings them misfortune and sickness. Sometimes the lwa will even punish the Vodouisant's partner, making him or her ill until such time as the marriage demands are met.

When the Vodouisant decides (or is persuaded) to marry the lwa, a ceremony is held. The space is prepared by the priye Gineh. A table is set up for the spirits who are going to be married. Cakes are prepared in their favorite colors (pink for Freda, red and blue for Danto, etc.). Their favorite offerings are placed on the table, alongside offerings for other lwa who might show up at the ceremony to give their blessings. The ceremonial clothing or objects of the brides or grooms will be close at hand. The human bride or groom, meanwhile, will be dressed in his or her finest clothing, as befits such a solemn ceremony.

After the priye, the houngan or mambo in charge will begin calling the various lwa. At the appropriate time, the bride/groom spirits will possess one of the participants. That *chwal* (horse, that is, the participant) will be dressed in the clothing of the lwa—a straw hat and bag for the agricultural lwa Zaka, a denim dress for Ezili Danto, and so on. Then the participant will be seated before the table beside the Vodouisant being married. A prêt savann (bush priest) will recite the Catholic marriage ceremony; the lwa and the Vodouisant then pledge fidelity to each other. The Vodouisant's ring or rings are "passed through fire"—incense smoke, really—and then the lwa places the ring on the Vodouisant's finger.

This ritual is repeated for each lwa the Vodouisant is going to marry. Only rarely does one marry a single lwa: usually it is necessary to marry two or three so that their energies will be balanced. A woman who marries Ogou will also marry Damballah, the Great White Serpent, and Zaka: it is believed that Damballah will cool Ogou's hot, intense energy while Zaka will help to ground it. And any man who marries Freda must marry her hardworking peasant sister Ezili Danto, and vice versa: the acrimony between these two women is legendary in Vodou and it is believed that marrying only one will cause the other to become enraged with jealousy. (Polygamy is also the rule among the lwa themselves: Ezili Freda is wife to Damballah, Ogou, and the sea king Met Agwe, and even Ogou has to wear the rings of both Freda and Ezili Danto.)

The Vodouisant is now married to the lwa. The newly married will be expected to set aside at least one night per month, and perhaps as many as three nights a week, during which there are no sexual relations with anyone else. During that time, many spouses of the lwa will sleep alone in a bed that they have specially prepared for the occasion. They may wrap their heads with a cloth in their spouse's color, and they will almost certainly wear their wedding ring. On that evening, they are frequently visited by their husbands/wives in dreams that may have sexual content or that may involve more platonic counsel and advice.

Although most wealthy plantation owners in St. Domingue had sexual relations with one or more of their slaves, few would admit to this publicly. They might grant favored status to those women and their offspring, but always in private. The whole process became an open secret, one of those things that everyone knew but no one discussed. Among Haiti's wealthy, the same could be said of Vodou. Rather than holding public fets, or attending ceremonies, wealthy Haitians might honor the lwa privately through a maryaj lwa performed in their homes. This allows them to serve the lwa discreetly. By setting aside days for the lwa and maintaining an inconspicuous shrine, they can gain the spirit's continued protection and blessings without incurring the social stigma that open service to the lwa would bring. If it could be said that poor Haitians *marry* the lwa, then rich Haitians take them as concubines.

The maryaj lwa ceremony not only is costly, but it also involves considerable responsibility. Violating your wedding vows is seen as extremely dangerous. Edeline St.-Amand, a Haitian mambo living in Brooklyn (and my initiatory mother), tells the story of a man who married Ezili Freda, and then had relations with another woman on the day he had promised to set aside for the lwa. Freda decided to ensure that this wouldn't happen again—and so she rendered her errant husband impotent.

"I try to call Freda for him so he can say he's sorry. For three hours I try to call Freda, but Freda won't come," Mambo Edeline says. "Finally I call Brav Ghede. Brav come and he say [to the scorned man], 'Freda don't want to talk to you.' He beg Brav, tell her I'm sorry, tell her I'm sorry. Finally Brav tells him, 'Okay. Freda say you got to go to Mass every day for twenty-one days, then you need to throw a big party for Freda. Then maybe she think about forgiving you.'"[1]

Whether rich or poor, Vodouisants see the maryaj lwa as both a sign of devotion and a guarantee of success. The Vodouisant throws a party for the lwa and sets aside special days for the spirit's honor. In exchange, the lwa is expected to provide support and protection. The maryaj lwa, like marriage and conjugal relationships, is as much a promise of mutual support as a sign of undying love.

The maryaj lwa is another one of those things you cannot do on your own. You will need to find a houngan or mambo to perform this ceremony for you. Any reputable priest or priestess will want to have a long, hard talk with you about why you wish to marry the lwa. They will explain the responsibilities to you and make sure that you are serious and committed. (Getting a quickie maryaj lwa is a singularly bad idea. There is no quickie divorce lwa—or, for that matter, any other kind of divorce lwa.) Ideally, they will insist that you attend a couple of ceremonies, where you will get a chance to speak to your prospective spouse and let him or her be the final arbiter on the question.

31

KANZO

Whereas many Vodouisants in Haiti serve the lwa all their lives, and may even do magical work for clients, others choose to take the next step and become initiates—or, more precisely, the lwa choose them. Haitian Vodouisants will often do everything they can to avoid the rigors and expense of the kanzo ceremony, the one by which they become houngans and mambos. Anyone who serves the lwa is a Vodouisant—but not every Vodouisant is an initiate. Sometimes only a persistent illness or a streak of bad luck will force them to listen to the spirit and commit to a kanzo ceremony. The kanzo is a major commitment, requiring a large expenditure of money, weeks of time, and a lifelong pledge to serve the lwa.

Most houses of Vodou recognize three grades of initiation. The first is hounsi kanzo, also known as *kanzo semp* or simple kanzo. This is where most people begin their journey to Gineh, and for many it is the only initiation they will receive. Hounsis—as those who have completed this initiation are known—will regularly attend services and learn the prayers, dances, songs, vévés, salutations, order of greetings, and other information that they'll need to function as a houngan or mambo. Vodouisants believe that by becoming a hounsi kanzo they will gain better control over possessions and be more able to relate to their spirits. If they choose to go further, they may initiate at the sipwen grade. A *houngan sipwen* or *mambo sipwen* has been initiated "on the point of" (*sur point,* or, in Kreyol, *sipwen*) his or her met tet—the lwa who rules their head. They can assist in most Vodou ceremonies, and they learn how to serve the lwa and the dead. Often they will lead songs and salutes and assist the houngan or mambo in performing work or in holding a ceremony—or they may prepare wangas for clients on their own. Those who take the highest grade, asogwe, will undergo the kanzo ceremony, but they will also be taken to the demambwe (the sacred ground) and there given an asson by Papa Loko. They will receive langaj that they can use to call the spirits, and special pwens (magical objects) that will allow them to work as full priests and priestesses of the religion. As a houngan sipwen I have not yet met Papa Loko. If I had, I could say no more about the demambwe or about the ceremony by which the asogwe rank is conferred. It is a closely guarded and oathbound secret.

In each of these grades, candidates receive passwords and gestures that can be used to "prove" their status. In practice, this sort of proof is mostly ceremonial. Haitian Vodou tends to be a community event: the congregation knows who has or has not been initiated, and most visitors will be tested via the *teledjol* or "tele-jawbone." ("My uncle knows the houngan who made him in Cap Haitien," or, "She says she was made by Mambo Y in Jacmel—but I work with Mambo Y's cousin, and he says Mambo Y never put her in the djevo.")

The kanzo is also known as a *kouche* from the French word "to lie down"; this is because it involves a period of seclusion when the initiate is "put to sleep" in the djevo. (Most of the details of the kanzo are secret. Several authors have written descriptions of the ceremony, but their accounts contain numerous errors and omissions.) The period of seclusion is literally seen as a death and a rebirth. The initiates are sent into the djevo with funeral songs; they are greeted upon their return to the world of the living with a baptism, and given a new *nom vayan*—a "valiant name"—which expresses their lineage. (When I am asked for mine, I reply, "I am Houngan Coquille du Mer, ti Mambo Azan Taye and Houngan Si Gan Temp, ti-ti Houngan Jou Mah Longe"—that is, the child of Mambo Azan Taye and Houngan Si Gan Temp, the grandchild of Houngan Jou Mah Longe. These are the magical names of my Mama Kanzo, Papa Kanzo and their Papa Kanzo, respectively.)

After exiting the djevo, new initiates must observe a period of abstinence. They must refrain from sexual activity and from eating certain foods; they also need to keep their heads covered when they are outdoors. They will also wear *kolyes* (collars), sacred necklaces that help to "tie" the energy of the spirit to their own energy. After forty-one days, the period of abstinence ends; they are able to remove their kolyes and are fully initiated. They still have a lot of learning ahead of them—initiation is a beginning, not an end—but they are now prepared for the spiritual challenges that lie ahead.

Initiation also makes the new member part of an extended family. Vodouisants speak of initiatory "parents" and refer to other members of their société as brothers and sisters. Like churches, synagogues, and mosques, peristyles function as community centers where members of the Vodou family seek medical help, psychological counseling, legal advice, commercial assistance, and other services. In return, members are expected to contribute to the well-being of the house by looking out for one another. An unemployed member is likely to receive several job leads from working members; a member who is having day care issues may get an offer of temporary baby-sitting assistance until an opening comes up at her local child care center. As with any family, there will occasionally be disagreements among members of a société. However, these will generally be treated like family disputes. The société will try to intervene and work out the difficulties between the feuding members. Failing that, the arguing parties will be expected to remain at least civil to each other at société functions. This is not "groupthink"; heated arguments at société meetings are not at all uncommon. However, the emphasis is on resolving them, not on stirring them up. A member who is constantly at the center of these arguments, or who is unwilling to pitch in toward helping other members in need, may become an ex-member, if all else fails.

Kanzo for Noninitiates

Simply put, there is no self-initiation into Vodou. You can only kanzo with the assistance of a société that has accepted you as a student and member. This does not mean, however, that you must be initiated to work with the spirits—or that initiation is a one-way street. I have seen people who were not initiated, who were not trained by initiates, and who had little knowledge of "real Vodou" (save what they gathered from books) get solid, undeniable results. I have also met initiates who showed little spiritual or magical ability—while other initiates within the same house became fine and productive houngans and mambos. I've seen people who benefited from "phony" rituals, and people who got nothing out of "authentic and correct" ceremonies. The ceremonies of Haitian Vodou can be powerful and life-changing experiences—but only if you are ready for them. As in most things, the secrets protect themselves from the profane and reveal themselves to those who are worthy.

I have never heard the phrase *authentic Haitian Vodou* used by Haitians. Most often I've heard *serve the lwa* or *serve Gineh*. Haitians who serve the lwa *know* what the words *Vodou* and *Vodouisant* mean, but they don't often use them among themselves. This is something a lot of people miss in the endless debates about "authentic Haitian Vodou." The simple fact that you have to call your practices "authentic Haitian Vodou" is a huge sign that you are *not* practicing A.H.V. It's as if I said I was practicing "authentic Yemenite Mohammedanism" or "real Irish Papism." (Indeed, those of a postmodern bent might say that your need to assert your "authenticity" suggests you are an outsider. "Real" insiders don't have to prove themselves: they know what they are already.)

That being said, there are offices, gestures, and signs that have a particular meaning within that culture, and that belong to that culture. Declaring ourselves houngans and mambos, and stringing our own assons, is cultural theft and disrespect. Most people wouldn't think of reading a couple of books and then proclaiming themselves rabbis, or archbishops—yet they see nothing wrong with appropriating the titles and symbols of the Vodou priesthood. Anybody has the right to worship Jesus, but not everybody has the right to declare himself a Roman Catholic priest, or a Mormon bishop. Although you can honor and serve the lwa as an individual or even as part of a group, you should leave the offices of the priesthood for those who have earned the right to those titles. Haitian Vodouisants may not "own" the lwa . . . but they do own some of the ways the lwa are served.

The Responsibilities of Initiation

Although many speak of the privileges, benefits, and powers you can get after becoming initiated in Haitian Vodou, few make clear the requirements that accrue upon entering the djevo and after taking on the title "mambo" or "houngan." This is a serious mistake. Going into the djevo is (or should be) a major commitment, not something you undertake lightly. Kanzo is a joyful, amazing experience—but it is also grueling and labor intensive.

Here are some of the responsibilities you will be expected to uphold after leaving the djevo.

Respect

You will be oathbound to respect your Mama Kanzo (your initiatory mother), your Papa Kanzo (your initiatory father), and your brothers and sisters in your société. This doesn't mean you must serve them with mindless loyalty and overlook their misdeeds, but it does mean you will behave toward them as you would behave toward your closest friends, or members of your family. Accordingly, you should make sure you know the people to whom you are making these commitments. If their behavior, character, and knowledge aren't worthy of your respect, then you should not swear that you will treat them with respect. Respect is not given: it is earned. Before you go in their djevo, before you take this oath, they should have earned your trust and admiration. Otherwise, you should seek another société.

Some houngans or mambos get caught up in the guru syndrome, and expect unquestioning obedience from their "underlings." Others exploit their followers financially or sexually. This behavior is deplorable and should not be condoned or excused. If you find yourself on the receiving end of this treatment, run, don't walk away from this house as quickly as your legs can carry you. Because a société is like a family, use this rule of thumb: Don't tolerate any behavior that you wouldn't tolerate from a parent or close family relative. There is never an excuse for exploitation, emotional bullying, and sexual misconduct.

Secrecy

Secrecy has become unfashionable in many quarters of late. With the advent of the Internet, many of the "secret rituals" of various traditions have become available to anyone with a computer and a Web browser. If you are initiated in Vodou, you are going to be bound by oaths of secrecy not to reveal what you have experienced in the djevo. This is a very serious and very profound commitment. If you cannot agree to this, then you should seek another spiritual path. It is fine to believe that "information must be free"; but it's not fine to lie about your intentions, or to receive information under false pretenses and then disseminate it.

Knowledge

If you're going to claim the title "houngan" or "mambo" for yourself, you should know enough to act in that capacity. You should at least be familiar with the ceremonial reglamen and with the colors and offerings used to honor the major lwa. You should have at least a basic idea of how to set up a lamp, what goes on a table, and so on. If you're going to call yourself "asogwe," you should have more than a basic idea: you should be able to lead most ceremonies. Nobody expects you to learn all this overnight, but you should have at least a solid foundation upon which to build. Obviously you will grow into a position and learn as you go along, but if you have no experience at all, you might well find yourself in over your head. You might be able to learn what it takes to be a proper hounsi kanzo within a few days' time. But you almost certainly will not be able to grasp the basics of being sipwen or asogwe without months or years of work.

Humility

When you first arrive at your new house, you are a rank beginner. You may be high priestess of a coven, you may be initiated in Palo or Ocha, you may be a longtime scholar of ceremonial magick and the occult—but that doesn't mean you are an expert in Haitian Vodou. Put aside your ego and recognize your own limitations. No Catholic priest would presume that his ordination made him an expert on Judaism or Islam, and you shouldn't assume that your attainments in other disciplines translate into knowledge of Vodou. You are always going to be junior to your initiatory parents and to those who went into the djevo before you. Those who come from traditions where "everyone is a priest" and "everyone is equal" may have a hard time with this.

Duty

To be a mambo or a houngan is to be a priest or priestess of Vodou, with all the burdens that entails. You're not just a servant of the lwa; you're a servant of the Vodou community, and you should expect to dedicate a good bit of your time to meeting those obligations. Priesthood is not a solitary practice. It gains its meaning only within the context of an organized community. If you aren't ready to take on that mantle of responsibility, you may want to think about whether or not you need to take on the title of houngan or mambo.

All this is not intended to discourage you from seeking initiation. The kanzo is definitely a profound experience, one that can confer numerous benefits. However, it confers obligations along with those benefits. Before you kanzo, you should ask yourself why it is you feel the need to go in the djevo. Idle curiosity is not enough; neither is the desire for power. I might go so far as to say that you should only go in the djevo if you have no choice but to go in. If you don't feel that strongly about initiation, you should wait until you do. I say this not out of a sense of elitism. I don't wish to exclude sincere seekers, but neither do I wish to mislead. The decision to kanzo is one of the most important you will ever make. Don't sign up for the lifetime-plus plan until you're sure this is what you want to be doing for the rest of your life and afterward.

32
WANGA

Some claim that using magic to improve your material condition is morally suspect. Most Vodouisants would find this ridiculous. Service to the lwa involves responsibilities and expectations; the costs are real and tangible, and so are the rewards the Vodouisants expect in return. Bad luck and monetary woes are seen as signs that the lwa are displeased with you, whereas wealth and good luck are tokens of power and of favor with the lwa. Not all wealthy people are automatically viewed as good or moral. Indeed, unusually successful people are often accused of "working with the left hand" or making pacts with evil spirits. However, there is no moral virtue attached to poverty, nor any particular stigma attached to prosperity. Again, we should remember that renunciation is typically seen as a virtue by those who have something to renounce; and that those who claim that money isn't everything usually have at least enough to meet their basic needs of food, clothing, and shelter.

Houngans and mambos certainly preside at various public and semipublic functions, but they also do a great deal of work with and for individuals. Vodou is a religion of the miraculous. Vodouisants not only believe in divine intervention in earthly affairs—they expect it! Through various wangas (magical spells), they seek to call on spiritual entities to improve their health, cure their romantic woes, and bring financial success. Unlike many Western magical practices, Vodou is results oriented. Vodouisants do wanga not to alter their consciousness, but to alter their world. Houngans and mambos who cannot improve their clients' physical condition will soon find themselves without clients. Should this condition persist, they will seek assistance themselves, so they can find out why their spirits have deserted them and what they can do to make amends.

Clients often seek personal consultations with the lwa. Vodouisants who have a powerful lwa will call that spirit, invoking a possession by whatever means they find most effective. Houngans or mambos asogwe will use the langaj they received during initiation; others might sing a song that draws their spirit or do something that causes it to "come into their head and possess them." When the lwa arrives, it can give information and advice. If you are not already skilled with possession states, I do not recommend trying this, for the reasons I listed in chapter 6. However, there are many magical techniques used by Vodouisants that you can use safely and effectively in your own service to the spirits.

Readings: Foretelling the Future, Clarifying the Present

There is less emphasis on divination in Vodou than in Lucumí or Ifá. The obí (reading by casting coconut pieces), diloggún (cowrie reading), or table of Ifá did not become part of Haitian culture the way they did in Cuba. I've heard Vodouisants comment, with good-natured humor, that Santeros "throw coconuts for everything, except when they're throwing cowrie shells." That does not mean that Vodouisants aren't curious about what the future has in store for them. Houngans and mambos regularly do readings for clients, using a number of different divination methods.

A client who seeks advice may hire a houngan or mambo to do a card reading. In Haiti, playing cards are typically used; most of the American houngans and mambos I know use Tarot cards instead. These readings are generally very much like card readings performed by other professionals. However, rather than focusing on the future, a reading from a houngan or mambo will often focus on the lwa: which lwa is working in your life right now, what do your lwa desire, what should you do. For example, a Vodouisant might interpret the Queen of Swords as Ezili Danto. A crossing Queen of Swords might mean "Danto is upset with you" or "Danto doesn't want you to do this," whereas a Queen of Swords near the Two of Cups (love) might mean "Danto wants you to marry her." They might see the Rider-Waite Nine of Wands (featuring a bandaged gentleman leaning on his staff) as representing Papa Legba, or, if inverted, Carrefour. There are no hard-and-fast rules for these attributions; most Vodouisant readers will use a great deal of "free association" and let the cards speak rather than trying to impose some textbook meaning on them.

Teaching you how to read the Tarot is beyond the scope of this book, but there are a number of excellent books available for beginners. I particularly like Arthur Edward Waite's *Key to the Tarot.* I know others who swear by Louis Martinie and Sallie Ann Glassman's New Orleans Voodoo Tarot set. If you are already familiar with the Tarot or with other systems of card reading, you can ask the spirits to sharpen your sight and help you to be more accurate in your readings. Before doing a reading, I always drop some rum on the floor and ask Papa Legba to "open the door for me" and "show me what lies ahead on the path." After I began doing this, I found that my ability to read cards improved dramatically. As you learn more about the lwa, and get to know them personally, you may also find yourself recognizing them in your readings. This is another thing you can't force, but that will come with practice.

Some Vodouisants find scrying a more effective technique for divination. They will stare into a mirror or a basin of water. Typically they will do this in a dark room, with a single white candle burning; they believe the candle both illuminates the area and drives away negative entities. As they concentrate on the blank surface in the flickering light, images will arise. The Vodouisant will then interpret those images. This technique is found throughout the world. It may well be inspired by French ceremonial magic. (Eliphas Levi wrote about scrying at some length, and it was also well known to Rosicrucian magicians in France and throughout Europe.)

If you want to try scrying yourself, you should be sure to create sacred space beforehand. If you have given La Sirene a mirror, you may use it for this exercise (make sure, of course, that you get La Sirene's permission and that you provide her an appropriate offering—a few white candies or a nice white flower, for example). Otherwise, you should use a bowl or mirror that you use for no other purpose. When you've established sacred space, stare into the bowl or mirror—and *relax*. Many people find this last step difficult. They struggle heroically to "see images" and then get disappointed when their efforts don't bear fruit. Instead of trying to see, you should just focus on a space inside the bowl or mirror, and then clear your mind. Don't concentrate on anything: imagine that your mind is as clear and placid as the water or glass. After a time you may notice that the surface appears foggy or misty. Don't try to stare through the mist or concentrate on it. Just let the mist form as it will.

You may not get great results at first. Learning how to clear your mind and let images arise can be challenging, particularly coming from a control- and ownership-obsessed culture like ours. However, as you keep trying, you will learn how to "let go" and watch the images. You may find techniques like chanting a mantra or praying the rosary help to quiet your conscious mind. You may also want to try some yogic breathing exercises like the fourfold breath: count four as you inhale, count four as you hold the breath, count four as you exhale, and count four as you wait to inhale again. Many people experience success like a lightning flash. They struggle for days or weeks, and then suddenly they attain the desired mental state and start seeing images.

Whether you use cards or scrying, be sure to keep a record of your results. Record your images honestly; be sure to record your failures as well as your successes. This will help you determine how well you have improved. It will also teach you how to better interpret the images that arise.

Candle Magic

Candles have always been more than just a source of light. Magicians have used them to call on the heavenly hosts and to light a way for the infernal legions. They have burned candles for spells to heal and harm, to bless and to curse. In Vodou, candles can be used to call on the lwa. By burning a seven-day candle in the appropriate color (and decorated with a fitting image or vévé), you can create a link between your space and the world of spirit. If you can't set up a permanent shrine to your spirits, you can call on them by burning a candle, and then snuffing it out when you are done speaking with them. Candles are an inexpensive offering that are easy to find and will be appreciated by any spirit.

When you light a candle for the spirit, you also create a focal point. You can speak to the burning candle as if you were speaking to the spirit face-to-face—because you are. The candle's light and heat provide energy for the spirit to manifest. When the candle is aflame, the spirit is present. This means that once you light the candle, you should be on good behavior. Basically, don't do anything in front of the candle that you wouldn't do in front of a beloved elder. You should also want to prepare for your meeting with the spirit by taking a bath and putting on clean clothing, and by cleaning the space in which you will be holding the ritual. If you treat your conversations with the spirits like a game, they're not likely to respond favorably. If, on the other hand, you treat the spirits with respect, you'll find they return your respect.

A Candle Love Wanga

Although I generally advise against working love magic against a specific target, I see nothing wrong with asking the universe to send you a lover. Often we don't know what we need in a lover; many of us make repeated bad choices in the arena of relationships. When we tell the lwa, "You know the kind of love I really need in my life—please bring that love to me," we're far more likely to find success. Love spells against a specific target are inherently coercive: you're trying to force another to do your bidding. A general love spell is like calling on a Cosmic Dating

Service. You are trusting the spirits to find you a love that is beneficial to all concerned, one that helps lover and beloved alike.

To create a love wanga candle, start with a white seven-day "pull-out" candle—one that can be removed from its glass chimney This is going to be a "dressed" candle—anointed with ingredients designed to make this spell more powerful. Remove the candle from the chimney and place some magnetic sand in the bottom. (Magnetic sand is merely magnetized iron filings. If you can't find magnetic sand, you can make your own with a magnet, file or rasp, and an iron nail.) This magnetic sand will serve to "draw" love toward you. Now anoint the candle with honey, cane syrup, and rose water: this sweetness will serve to attract your love to you. Tie three ribbons around the chimney: a white one (for the highest love), a pink one (for affection), and a red one (for sexual attraction). Create sacred space, and then light a white Sabbath candle. As you do this, ask for healing, positive energy, and white light. Now use the Sabbath candle to light the seven-day candle. When that candle is lit, you may extinguish the Sabbath candle.

Now talk to your candle. Pour your heart out; express your loneliness, your heartbreak, your sorrow. Don't be afraid to cry (in fact, you may want to have a box of tissues handy, just in case you need them). Explain that you need love in your life. Tell the candle some of the things you want in a lover. If you're pining for a specific person, it may be tempting to say, "Make X love me." What I would advise instead is that you make a list of things that you find appealing about X. Now ask the spirits to send you someone who has all those qualities. If you can let the candle burn to the end, do so. Otherwise, snuff it out when you are finished. Repeat your petition each day for seven days. When you are finished, take the candle and leave it at a crossroads, so that Papa Legba can deliver your petition.

Not Just Candles—Chimneys

If you burn a lot of seven-day candles to the lwa, you're soon going to find yourself with lots of empty candle chimneys. You can dispose of these in the usual manner—or you can use them in creating other wangas. When you use a candle to call on the lwa, you bring that lwa's energy into your home, and into the candle. The candle chimney that remains still holds some of that spirit's energy. You can use those chimneys, and that energy, to create powerful wanga items. I've included instructions for three magical pakets (packets) that use candle chimneys and that are constructed in a manner influenced by the pakets Kongo made by Vodouisants. They will serve as powerful protectors and guardians. You can create others, using the model I've provided here.

Damballah Paket for Peace

Take the chimney from a candle that was offered to Damballah. Wash it thoroughly with Pompeii lotion and rose water. Do this until it is sparkling clean. Make sure *every* trace of black soot has been removed; Damballah doesn't like black things. Now fill this chimney with white or clear stones (small quartz crystals will be ideal for this) and insert a white ostrich plume (you can find these at florists, craft shops, or online). Wrap a white satin moushwa or a piece of white satin cloth around this, and tie it shut with white ribbons, so that the plume is sticking out the top but nothing else is visible. Pin the ribbons to the cloth using stick pins with white heads.

Present this to Papa Damballah. Ask him to look after you and to bring peace and tranquility to your home. If you have a Damballah shrine in your home, you may place it there. Otherwise, you can place it on a high shelf where it will not be disturbed. (If you are going to be naked in front of it or will be engaging in sexual activity near it, be sure to surround it with a screen or otherwise block it from view. Also, avoid drinking or smoking in the room where this paket is kept.) You will find this paket very helpful in creating a peaceful, tranquil vibration throughout your home.

Met Agwe Paket for Financial Success

Clean Met Agwe's candle chimney thoroughly with Pompeii lotion, and then wash it again with sea water (or, at the very least, with water in which some sea salt has been dissolved). Add sea sand, some sea salt, and some blue and green sea glass to the chimney. If you'd like, you can even add a tiny piece of driftwood, one or more loose sea pearls, or some loose aquamarine stones. Place a white ostrich plume or a piece of fan coral in the chimney so that it's sticking out. Now wrap the paket in a light blue or light green cloth and tie it with white ribbons. Pin the ribbons to the cloth using light blue, light green, or white-headed stickpins. Leave the fan or plume visible.

Present the paket to Met Agwe. He is one of the wealthiest of the lwa, because all the ocean's treasures are his. Ask him to help you with your money problems. If you ask politely, you'll find that he is as generous as he is wealthy.

Danto Paket for Protection

After you have finished burning a candle for Mama Danto, wipe the chimney thoroughly with Florida water. Now place a small, sharp knife in that chimney—a paring knife will do. Add lots of cinnamon and hot pepper, because Mama Danto likes heat. Place a red or blue ostrich plume in the chimney; wrap the chimney in denim and tie it with red and blue ribbons, which you attach using red- or blue-headed stickpins.

When you are finished, present the paket to Ezili Danto. Ask her to look after you and keep evildoers and bad spirits away from your door. Now place this paket near your door, or near a window. This will help to protect your home and your family, especially your children. If this paket ever falls and breaks, it is a sign that Danto has taken out some major misfortune that was intended for your family. Dispose of the paket by a crossroads, and then make an offering to Mama Danto in thanksgiving. (You can use the candle chimney from that offering to create another paket for protection.)

Wanga and Your Spirits

Most houngans and mambos keep their wanga as closely guarded secrets, passed down only to their students. That is because they receive many of their wangas from their spirits. You may well get a strong feeling that Kalfou wants you to do something that will help you with a problem, for example. Take notes on what he wants, and then do it. (Within reason, of course. If any lwa requests an animal sacrifice or demands that you violate civil laws or your ethical code, you can and should refuse. This probably is a trickster spirit looking to get you in trouble. Even if it isn't, you certainly are free to bargain with a lwa or refuse an unreasonable request. Vodouisants serve the lwa. They are not enslaved by them.)

Take notes on the process, and on its results. If it works, you've got a wanga you received from the spirit and that you can use in the future. Be discreet about sharing this information, and if the lwa tell you to keep it secret, keep it secret. Power shared may be power lost—and one of the four deeds of the magician is "to keep silent."

This is an interactive tradition and a Gnostic one. No book can make you a Vodouisant. Only the lwa can do that—and they will only do that if you interact with them and directly experience their presence and their power. I have provided various wangas as guidelines. It's up to you to take these passive words from the page and transform them into living magic.

Purchasing Wanga

Many Vodouisants who need serious assistance for their problems will call on the services of a professional: a houngan or mambo, or someone who is known to have a powerful lwa. This professional will provide advice in exchange for a fee. This may seem unnerving to those who come to these traditions from a Western magical background. Many Wiccans and Neopagans believe it is wrong to charge money for work, teaching, or initiations. They think that accepting money for doing work somehow detracts from the "spiritual" aspects of our calling, turning it into a mere business. This idea does not exist in Haitian Vodou. There is no more social stigma in a Vodou priest or priestess charging for services than in a lawyer or doctor charging for their time and efforts.

Unlike many Western traditions, initiation into Vodou has a price, typically a steep one. In Vodou, paying for an initiation is like paying for a college education—and it can have similar benefits. Becoming a houngan or mambo isn't just a spiritual choice, but also a career move. A houngan or mambo known to do good work can become an important person in the community. Admittedly, this has led to many houngans and mambos selling initiation ceremonies to the highest bidder. Sometimes these ceremonies are completely fraudulent; at other times, they are "authentic"—but they do not include the training required for the participant to actually function as a priest or priestess. Although this might suggest that Gerald Gardner, the father of modern Wicca, was on to something when he prohibited charging for initiations, we should also keep in mind the complexity and rigor of a Vodou initiation. The ceremony of initiation into Haitian Vodou takes approximately two weeks. Drummers must be hired; food must be prepared for the candidates and for the houngans and mambos assisting in the kanzo. Many items are required, some quite costly. Even a less complicated ceremony—a fet in honor of a particular spirit, or a maryaj lwa, for example—involves a considerable expenditure of time, energy, and resources.

If you consult a Vodouisant for work, you can expect to be charged money. This does not, in and of itself, mean that you are being ripped off or taken advantage of. However, it does mean that a bit of caution and some healthy skepticism are in order. Although you should trust your instincts, you should also be aware that successful con artists don't act or seem like con artists. Many scam victims say, "But he [or she] seemed like such a nice and caring person!" No houngan or mambo can guarantee 100 percent success—nor can they tell, upon one meeting, that you are suffering from an "ancient family curse" that will require a prolonged and expensive ceremony. If you feel like you're being played for a sucker, then you probably are. If you think you're being pressured, bullied, or exploited, then you probably are. In any event, it's not likely that you'll be able to work well with that particular person. Like any other counseling relationship, it's important that you feel comfortable with your priest or priestess.

There are advantages to consulting another person for work. A good diviner or spiritual professional is able to examine your situation without any prejudices or preconceptions, and an initiated Vodouisant will usually be capable of creating a more powerful wanga than an enthusiastic but inexperienced newcomer. Many of the houngans and mambos I have listed in the online resources section do readings and other work for clients. If you find your efforts are not working, you may want to call on their services. A little guidance from a professional can go a long way.

CONCLUSION: THE NEXT STEP— SEEKING A TEACHER

Men anpil, chay pa lou
(With many hands, the load is not heavy)

As you continue in your studies and get to know the lwa better, you may want to join a société. Vodou is a religion that requires group rituals. You cannot do even a simple lave tet or a garde for yourself. Vodou is also an initiatory religion: there is no book (not even this one!) that can make you a Vodouisant. The gestures, the passwords, the ceremonial order, and many other things are oathbound secrets, to be taught only in the djevo. Any book or Web site that claims they can show you these without requiring similar oaths from you is the work of either a liar or an oathbreaker, and in either case it is not to be trusted. To progress in Vodou, you will need to find a teacher.

Alas, this can be easier said than done. Unless you live in an area with a substantial Haitian population, you're going to have a hard time finding a société. Even in a city with many Haitians, like New York or Miami, it may be difficult for an outsider to gain admission, even to public events. Centuries of oppression drove Vodou deep underground. Although things have improved somewhat, the "bunker mentality" persists. Many Vodouisants view interested outsiders with skepticism . . . and some, sadly enough, view them as suckers ripe for exploitation. A healthy respect for the culture can help to open doors for you; a bit of healthy caution can ensure you pass through the right doors.

Some Words of Caution

In Haiti, most initiates know their housemates before they become affiliated with a société. They are well aware of the reputation and status of their Mama Kanzo and Papa Kanzo—the mambo and houngan who will be responsible for their initiation. Frequently they are related to one or both by blood or marriage. Having attended dozens if not hundreds of services and ceremonies, they know what to expect and can easily spot an imposter. As such, they need not worry about "authentic Vodou." Those who grew up outside this culture are not so fortunate.

When seeking a teacher, you'll find no shortage of people who have read a few books, and then set themselves up as houngans or mambos. Beads, string, and gourds are cheap: library cards are free. Just because somebody can present something that looks like an asson is no guarantee of authenticity. Even claims of "lineage" are difficult to prove. How can someone in Peoria or Phoenix contact Mambo Clutterbuck in the Artibonne to ascertain whether or not Houngan Blowhard is really an initiate of Société Fictitious—or if this société even exists?

There will always be con artists, and there will always be sincere but deceived people. With the growing interest in Vodou has come a growing industry in "initiations for sale." Enterprising tour guides target people who have never attended a Vodou ceremony and who know nothing about the religion. In exchange for a check, they show these "initiates" a few dance steps and gestures, and then put them in a room that resembles a djevo and provide them with an impressive-looking ceremony that they call a kanzo. At the end of all this, the candidates are told they are now houngans sipwen or mambos asogwe. Lacking any frame of reference, these instant priests and microwave-ready priestesses have no way of knowing they have been bilked—until they meet a real houngan or mambo and discover the "initiation" they purchased is as valid as a matchbook diploma. And even a valid asson and extensive knowledge of Vodou is no guarantee of moral rectitude or mental stability. By all accounts, Papa Doc Duvalier was validly initiated, as were many of the Tonton Macoutes who terrorized Haiti during his reign.

Before you throw up your hands in despair, let me reassure you that the vast majority of Vodouisants are sincere and dedicated people. It may take you time to find them, but they are out there, and, if the lwa so choose, you will find them when the time is right. In the meantime, here are a few things that should raise warning flags.

Be leery of "ancient family curses" that require complex and expensive remedies. Treat statements that you must be initiated immediately, or that you must purchase some other ceremony, with healthy skepticism. In Haiti, Vodouisants regularly barter with the lwa. If Zaka says you need to marry him next week, you are perfectly within your rights to say, "I'm sorry, Cousin Zaka, I can't do that right now. If you want me to make a maryaj, you're going to have to help me get the money." The lwa are generally amenable to this, and they will work with you if you work with them. (One note of caution: Be *sure* you follow through when the lwa help you. If you suddenly receive an unexpected windfall that happens to be just enough to pay for your wedding to Zaka, don't use it for anything else!)

Some houngans and mambos initiate their romantic partners; société members often form deep friendships that sometimes blossom into love affairs. In each case, these love affairs happen *outside* the context of a ceremony. This is a very important point. If you believed the old pulp novels and B-movies, you'd think that most Vodouisants divided their time between making zombies and engaging in primitive lust-befogged orgies. In reality, sexual magic and sex rituals are not part of Haitian Vodou. Still, as in the Pagan community, there are those who will try using their priesthood to seduce people. People who try to coerce you into sex as part of a "Vodou ritual" are liars; people who tell you that you must sleep with them to be an "authentic initiate" are authentic sleazeballs. If someone's advances make you uncomfortable, you should feel free to decline politely. If the advances continue, you should find another teacher. The relationship between teacher and student should never involve exploitation or coercion.

Be skeptical of people who tell you there is "one true way" of doing Vodou. Invariably they mean *their* way, soon to be followed with long rants about how everyone else is doing Vodou "incorrectly" or "inauthentically." Some people try to present Vodou as a monolithic orthodoxy. It's actually closer to chili. Some people make their chili with chicken; others make theirs with beef, and others swear go vegetarian. Some include green pepper; some prefer red pepper. All of these are valid recipes; which one is best is a matter of individual taste. There are things that almost every chili will include; and some ingredients you'll only find in certain types of chili or in certain places (if you see cinnamon and cocoa in the pot, you know you're in Cincinnati). And if you try passing off a cheddar cheese soufflé as "French chili," everyone at the cook-off is going to laugh at you. Vodou is an oral tradition; there are variations from region to region and from house to house. There's no "one true chili" . . . and there's no "one true Vodou."

In my experience, the phrase "authentic, correct Vodou" is most often used as a marketing tool or to attack competitors. Even in Haiti, not everyone who serves the lwa is initiated . . . and what we call "Vodou" actually encompasses a number of practices that may differ to a greater or lesser degree. Much as advertising executives will try to present sugar water as "the real thing" or caution you against the dangers of "settling for less than a Genuine [insert here]," some self-proclaimed Vodou experts will try to sell you "the real secrets of Haitian Vodou" or warn you against "phony baloney" clerics who offer the same services.

Initiatory parents are as mortal as the rest of us, and it can be difficult to reach people living in Haiti. But if your prospective teacher cannot put you in contact with his Mama or Papa Kanzo, and cannot provide anyone else who can vouch for her credibility, there is something very wrong. Even if your prospective teacher's initiator is deceased or cannot be reached by telephone or e-mail, there should be someone else with whom you can speak, and who can attest to the truth of what your teacher says. Vodou is a social religion. If you are calling yourself a houngan or a mambo and claiming you are an initiate of Haitian Vodou, yet know nobody within the Haitian community who will stand up for you, you are a dupe at best and a liar at worst.

You can also judge your prospective house by its current and former members. Almost every société will have people who drift away or who leave because of personal clashes; but in a legitimate house, most people will stick around after their initiation and will speak proudly of their affiliation. If your prospective teacher is hesitant to introduce you to former students, you may want to think twice about signing on at that house. If your teacher's former students are not recognized as initiates by others in the community, or if others have recurring complaints about this teacher's teaching style, character, and so forth, then you should think long and hard before you decide to sign on.

It would be nice to say that the Vodou community is free of the gossip, backbiting, power tripping, and so on that characterize the Neopagan community at its worst. Alas, that's not the case. There are egos aplenty in Vodou, along with the corresponding ego clashes. Avoid houngans and mambos who seem to have a disproportionate number of enemies. If your own house is in order, there's no reason for you to be concerned about all the mistakes everyone else is making. Many of these ego trippers justify their behavior in the name of "protecting Vodou." They would have you believe that a religion that survived two hundred years of slavery and four hundred years of eradication efforts is in mortal danger because their competitors are Bad People Who Are Threatening The Tradition. You should always remember that, protests of religious fervor notwithstanding, crusaders have historically had ulterior motives for their attacks.

That being said, where there is smoke there is often fire. If one person has something bad to say about Mambo X, it may well be the result of jealousy, malice, or some other personal conflict between them. But if five people, or ten people, are saying the same thing, then there may be something to it. There are no absolutes here: the Vodou community is no more immune to gossip than any other group, and malicious lies often spread faster than honest praise. But if you can find few people who have anything good to say about your prospective teacher, and lots of people with complaints, you're probably wisest to steer clear.

By the time you're seeking a teacher, you should have made some contact with your spirits and be working with them and seeking their guidance. Listen to their input and ask them to help you find a suitable teacher. Your intuition and your instinct (*konesans* to Vodouisants) are good guides, although not infallible. You must learn the difference between wishful thinking and the real "voice of the spirit." This can be a tough distinction. If you desperately want to become part of a Vodou community, you're likely to jump at the first available opportunity. You'll also probably feel overwhelmed and intimidated by the strange new world in which you now find yourself. It's easy to mistake those desires, or those fears, for spiritual communication. Like everything else, your ability to communicate with your spirits and your gift of discernment will improve with practice.

It is important that you feel comfortable with your house—and that they feel comfortable with you. Take your time and choose wisely. Attend a few services. If you feel interested in going further, get a lave tet or a garde from them. This will give you a chance to learn more about your prospective initiatory parents, and about their past and present students. It will also give you a chance to learn more about what being a member of a Vodou société entails, and to decide if you are able to make the required commitment of time, energy, and resources. You may decide this isn't something you can handle at the present time, or that you really aren't called to join a société. That's perfectly valid: better you should figure this out now than that after you've already made a substantial investment, or have become oathbound to serving the lwa as a priest/ess.

You should choose your teacher carefully, and they should show the same care when choosing students. Beware of any houngan or mambo who would offer you an initiation after one meeting—or worse, one e-mail. The best houngans and mambos don't advertise for clients because they don't need to: they have more than enough work and more than enough prospective students. What's more, they know that the community is going to judge them by the quality of their initiates.

Ill-behaved, ill-prepared, and unimpressive hounsis and houngans don't just bring shame on themselves: they reflect poorly on their initiatory parents. Membership in a société should be a badge of honor, not something available to anybody who can afford it.

Many people come to Vodou with the idea that they need to be houngans or mambos. Most of them are mistaken. You don't need an asson to serve your spirits; for most people, going in the djevo as a hounsi kanzo will be sufficient. That will ground you, introduce you to your lwa, and give you the benefits of an initiation without the burdens of a priesthood. (I'm indebted to Houngan Aboudja for this observation. Based on my experience, it is a very sound one.)

Authority in Vodou

Someone coming from a loosely organized tradition like Neopaganism may find the Afro-Caribbean traditions to be rigid and authoritarian. The elders (those who have more experience than you, which at this juncture means just about everyone in your house) receive considerable respect, and sometimes they will make no bones about telling you "this is wrong" without regard for your feelings or your freedom to "honor the spirits as you understand them."

This being said, keep in mind that respect for one's elders does not mean that you have to check your common sense at the door. A société is not a cult; there is a difference between expecting respect and expecting you to sign over your checkbook and your ego. If you find that your encounters with your teacher leave you feeling resentful, or exploited, you may want to put things on hold until you can find another teacher whose style is more suited to your personality. And, as I said before, beware of people who insist that they know the One True Way of Doing Vodou—particularly if no one else in the community seems to agree with that One True Way.

The Question of Race

Some will tell you that race plays no role at all in Haitian Vodou, and that every real Vodouisant will welcome sincere seekers, be they white, black, or yellow. People who claim otherwise, they say, are nasty and immoral and are just using Vodou to justify their own shortcomings, just as some Christians use the Bible to justify racism and oppression.

Others who will tell you that Vodou is only for Haitians. They will swear that no non-Haitian has ever received a valid initiation into Vodou, and that those who claim otherwise are either liars or dupes who received bogus ceremonies for their money. Still others will say that only those of African ancestry can serve African spirits, and that white people cannot and should not serve the lwa.

The truth, as truth tends to be, is somewhat more complicated than either of these claims.

Haitian culture has never been a racially diverse utopia. Soon after the first European colonists arrived, rigid class and social lines were drawn between blacks and whites—and, not long after that, between blacks, whites, and those of mixed race. White people had the money and owned the land, and the black people who worked on it. The free mulattoes were second-class citizens at best; most were little better off than the slaves. These social lines were rigidly enforced. The whites kept their position at the top of the heap by terror. Those who challenged the order of things were dispatched in the messiest and most painful ways, to serve as an example for those who would attempt to rise above their station.

When the revolution erupted, the slaves killed every white person they could lay hands on. Thousands died and thousands more were driven out of the country. The mulattoes who had been shopkeepers or artisans now found themselves at the top of the social heap; and, like the poor whites of the southern United States, they fought bitterly for every scrap of privilege they had been able to acquire. They did not want to overthrow the established order of things. Rather, they wanted to take their place as rulers over the majority. To this day, most wealthy Haitians are light-skinned mulattoes, and light skin is associated with social privilege. As one Haitian proverb says, "A rich black man is a mulatto, a poor mulatto is black." The word *blan* literally means "white person," but in Haiti, it is frequently used to describe any wealthy non-Haitian, regardless of race. (If you have the money to vacation in a foreign country, you are wealthy by Haitian standards.)

Once they found themselves in power, light-skinned, prosperous Haitians typically spoke of Vodou as superstitious nonsense, something practiced only by poor, uneducated, and ignorant blacks. This does not mean that they did not consult mambos or houngans when they had a problem; many did, though they would never admit it publicly. Still, they resented outsiders who assumed that all Haitians sacrificed chickens in their basements and cast curses on those they disliked. For them, Vodou was an embarrassment at best. They were not interested in exploring their "African roots" but rather in following European social customs—including, sadly, the custom of rule by force.

Dark-skinned, poor Vodouisants frequently found themselves targeted by church and state alike. The Catholic Church (and, later, evangelical missionaries) railed against "folly and superstition." Haiti's rulers saw Vodou as a threat to their position: they were well aware of the social influence a houngan or mambo could wield, and that frightened them as much as any magic. For over a hundred years, Vodou was under constant attack, and those who served the lwa risked jail and worse. Vodou became a very insular and secretive tradition, and those who practiced were unlikely to admit their beliefs to strangers.

Later, people realized that there was a market for Vodou—and so "Vodou dances" and "ceremonies" were arranged for tourists seeking "real Voodoo." These events typically bore little resemblance to actual Vodou ceremonies, but featured writhing, scantily clad women, spectacular "possessions," and other titillating spectacles designed to entertain wealthy and predominantly white vacationers. Other enterprising Haitians found that some of these tourists didn't just want to watch; they wanted to become Vodou priests themselves. In exchange for large sums of money, they taught them the "real secrets of Haitian Vodou," and then sent them on their way, poorer if not wiser.

Knowing what has gone before will help you to understand the way things are. Many non-Haitians have come to Vodou seeking the sensational and spectacular. They haven't shown any love for the lwa or any desire to understand the culture in which Vodou arose. Instead, they've wanted to know how to make zombis and how to cast curses on their enemies. Like it or not, you may well be judged by their ignorant example. Until you prove that you are sincere and trustworthy, you may be seen as yet another Spooky Kid Who Wants to be a Vodou Priest or Priestess.

Still others have assumed that every Haitian practices Vodou, much as some assume every Italian is in the Mafia, every Irishman is a drunkard, and every Jew cheats on taxes. Most Haitians in the diaspora have heard at least a few stupid jokes about "voodoo dolls"; some have lost jobs or been assaulted when people decided they were "working black magic on them." If they react defensively to questions about Vodou, it could be because they've had bad experiences, or because they're tired of dealing with the superstitious or the idly curious. You may have the best of intentions—but a stereotype is still a stereotype.

Old resentments die hard. Some Haitians see their history as proof that non-Haitians are not to be trusted. Others view it as proof that everybody is out to exploit them, and they see nothing wrong with returning the favor. It would be naïve to say that there are no Haitians who dislike Americans, or white people, or non-Haitians. On the other hand, it would be a gross overstatement to say that *every* Haitian feels this way. Misconceptions and misunderstandings can only be corrected with time and positive examples. Provide those positive examples, and you'll do fine. If you're meant to travel to Gineh, you'll get there in due course. In the meantime, learning what it feels like to be shut out because of your skin will go a long way toward helping you understand the African experience in the New World.

From Haiti to the New World

Almost every Haitian Vodou société in the United States has a sister peristyle in Haiti. Members go to their sister peristyle regularly for services and initiations, or merely to be in the place where Vodou began. Much as Roman Catholics view Vatican City or Orthodox Jews view Jerusalem, many Vodouisants see Haiti as a holy place, a land where the lwa are closer to their followers and a place where miracles happen more frequently than they do in the diaspora.

Most Vodouisants go to Haiti to be initiated for many reasons. A good number of the herbs used in the djevo are easier to find in Haiti, as are many of the supplies. (But this is not always true: after the 1994 overthrow of Aristide and the subsequent U.S. embargo, the glass beads used in making kolyes and assons became nearly impossible to find in Haiti, although they were readily available in most craft stores outside the island.) The kanzo is also labor intensive, requiring two weeks of undivided attention from a number of houngans and mambos. Their fees tend to be lower in Haiti than in the diaspora—much as Lucumí initiations in Cuba typically cost around 50 percent of what they do in the United States.

Some have claimed that you can be initiated only in Haiti. This is an exaggeration, and one that neglects both Vodou's history and its present-day situation. Haitian Vodou developed amidst people who had been uprooted from their homes and their sacred places. Unable to worship at their village shrines, they found ways to serve the spirits in the New World, and to pass on the priesthood they had received in Africa. The spirits heard their call and came; they did not insist that their priests could only be made in Africa. Why then would they insist now that their priests must be made in Haiti?

Many Haitians living in the diaspora are exiles. They cannot return to Haiti, for initiation or for any other reason. Not all of them have become Protestants, or decided that they cannot take the asson (be initiated into Vodou). Since at least the 1970s, initiations into Vodou have been performed outside Haiti. If these initiations are done properly, they are recognized by other houngans and mambos (including those initiated in Haiti) and by the lwa.

The decision on whether to be initiated in Haiti or at home is personal. There are definitely advantages and disadvantages to both. Vodou

Initiation Tours to Haiti may be a pleasant vacation, but they will do little to prepare you for the responsibilities of being a priest or priestess. If you choose to be initiated in Haiti, you should make sure that your initiatory house also has a presence in your area back home. This will allow you to continue learning after you get out of the djevo, and to participate in ceremonies as an initiated priest or priestess. Initiation is an intensely individual process, but it is also a communal one. When you are initiated, you are welcomed into the community as a servant of the lwa and their children. If you do not take your place as part of that community, then you are no initiate at all.

Finding a Teacher and a Société

Admission into a Vodou société typically requires an introduction. Someone who is already a member will vouch for you, and then you will be invited to a public ceremony or to a private meeting with the houngan or mambo who heads the house. This may seem like an insurmountable obstacle: How can you meet people involved in Vodou if you must first know people who are involved in Vodou?

Remember that Vodou is not something isolated and discrete, but is instead an integral part of Haitian culture. If you go blundering about looking for "real Vodou," you're not likely to find much. If, on the other hand, you show a sincere interest in the culture from which Vodou has grown, you will have far greater success.

Here are a few possibilities.

Botanicas and Haitian Stores

One way to spot a Haitian botanica (as opposed to a botanica specializing in Espiritismo, Lucumí, or Palo Mayombe) is the name: most Haitian botanicas have French or Kreyol names. You may also want to check out Haitian general stores. Although these aren't specifically "spiritual supply stores," they will often sell *plates Gineh* (dried gourd plates used to feed certain lwa), *zins* (clay pots used in the initiation ceremony), moushwa, Florida water, lithographs, herbs, and other things you need to serve the lwa. If you become a regular customer, you may find yourself chatting with the staff. (They're likely to be as curious about the blan who comes in to buy herbs such as *zodevan* and *fey kapab* as you are about Vodou.) They might offer you a few pointers for serving the lwa, or some suggestions as to what you might find useful. After a while, when they have established that you are serious and stable, they might be able to put you in touch with a practitioner or a house. These stores will appear in most cities with a good-sized Haitian community.

Art Galleries

Haitian art is considered among the finest in the Caribbean, and much of it is Vodou related. The brightly sequined drapos and beautiful paintings are wonderful decorations and can be a great offering to your lwa in appreciation, or a centerpiece to a niche. Keep an eye out for Haitian and Caribbean exhibits; watch for galleries specializing in Caribbean artists. This is an excellent place to meet others who share your interests, and to acquire some objects of art that are generally both beautiful and reasonably priced.

Afro-Caribbean Drum and Dance Classes

Rhythm and dance are at the heart of Haitian Vodou; there are specific drumbeats for each family of lwa, and particular steps and movements for each part of a ceremony. Unlike gestures and passwords, these can be taught to noninitiates. (The drummers at a Vodou ceremony frequently are not initiates; in New York, for example, many of the drummers who work at ceremonies are Rastas from Jamaica, who know the beats but do not otherwise serve the lwa.) In many cities, and even in smaller towns, you can find classes in Afro-Caribbean drumming and dance. Learning the drums and dance steps will help immeasurably in your future studies in Vodou. It will also help you meet other people interested in the tradition, including some who may be able to introduce you to a house and a teacher.

Community Centers

Is there a Haitian community center in your city? If so, you may want to volunteer some time working there. If not, you may want to support some of the Haitian relief organizations and charities listed in the resources section. You may not get an immediate introduction to Vodou but you will get a chance to work with Haitians and learn something firsthand about their culture. What's more, you will also be giving back something to the community. Many outsiders come to Vodou, and to other religions, with a sense of entitlement. They feel they can use any religion and co-opt any deity or practice in their quest for self-enlightenment. If you want to work with Vodou, Haiti's greatest creation, it behooves you to give something back in exchange.

Kreyol Lessons

Kreyol, Haiti's native language, combines French, English, and Spanish words with an African grammatical structure. As the number of Haitians in the United States has grown, so too has the need for Kreyol speakers. Look for Kreyol speakers and Kreyol tutors in your area. If you can understand even a little bit of Kreyol, you'll find it much easier to meet Haitians. Even those Haitians who speak English will appreciate the efforts you took to learn their language. A little Kreyol knowledge will go a long way toward understanding the songs that are such an important part of any Vodou ceremony—and they will make any future trip to Haiti much more pleasant.

The Internet

As cartoonist Scott Adams once said, "On the Internet no one knows you're a dog." Anyone with a computer and an ISP account can build a free Web page and go into business as Gwo Mambo Spamsalot or Houngan Asogwe Fraudulent—and quite a few have. Beware of anyone peddling initiations over the Internet, be skeptical of any self-proclaimed houngans or mambos who aggressively market their services, and run away from those who make grandiose claims yet refuse to provide proof.

That being said, there are a few Web sites that offer some interesting information on Vodou and mailing lists where you can correspond with others of a like mind. Several of these are run by initiated houngans and mambos. Although they are no substitute for face-to-face teaching or attendance at ceremonies, they can help you on your journey and possibly put you in touch with other Vodouisants in your area.

And, At Last, the Conclusion's Conclusion

Ultimately, all this boils down to a question of trust. Has your prospective teacher shown honesty and good character when dealing with you? If so, then you can probably trust your new teacher. If not, the question is irrelevant. You cannot and should not do the work with someone you do not trust. Trust is something you earn, over a period of time. The time you invest in building a relationship with your future house will be nothing compared to the time, and money, you will waste with fakes, flakes, and frauds.

Whatever else you do, *listen to the spirits*. Vodou is not a religion you can learn by studying. Of course study is important—but the most important part of Vodou is developing a personal relationship with your spirits. As I've said, the road to Gineh is a long one. There's no need to begin your journey with a sprint. You've already made your first steps. Now let go and let God (with assistance from the saints, ancestors, and lwa) and rest assured that they will lead you to where you need to be.

RESOURCES

Books

When speaking of Haiti, it is often difficult to draw distinct lines between the history, culture, religion, and art. Accordingly, I have made no effort to separate these books into categories. Each has important lessons to teach about Vodou and about the culture in which it developed.

Aristide, Jean-Bertrand. *In the Parish of the Poor: Writings from Haiti.* Amy Wilentz, trans. Maryknoll, N.Y.: Orbis Books, 1990.

Bell, Beverly, and Edwidge Dandicat, eds. *Walking on Fire: Haitian Women's Stories of Survival and Resistance.* Ithaca, N.Y.: Cornell University Press, 2001.

Brown, Karen McCarthy. *Mama Lola: A Vodou Priestess in Brooklyn.* Berkeley: University of California Press, 1991.

Cadet, Jean-Robert. *Restavec: From Haitian Slave Child to Middle-Class American.* Austin: University of Texas Press, 1998.

Cosentino, Donald J., ed. *Sacred Arts of Haitian Vodou.* Los Angeles: UCLA Fowler Museum of Cultural History, 1995.

Dandicat, Edwidge. *After the Dance: A Walk Through Carnival in Jacmel, Haiti.* New York: Crown, 2002.

———. *The Dew Breaker.* New York: Knopf, 2004.

———. *The Farming of Bones.* New York: Penguin USA, 1999.

———. *Krik? Krak!* New York: Vintage, 1996.

Dandicat, Edwidge, ed. *The Butterfly's Way: Voices from the Haitian Dyaspora in the United States.* New York: Soho Press, 2001.

Davis, Wade. *The Serpent and the Rainbow.* New York: Touchstone, 1997.

Dayan, Joan. *Haiti, History, and the Gods*. Berkeley: University of California Press, 1998.

Deren, Maya. *Divine Horsemen: The Living Gods of Haiti*. New York: McPherson, 1985.

Desmangles, Leslie G. *The Faces of the Gods: Vodou and Roman Catholicism in Haiti*. Chapel Hill: University of North Carolina Press, 1992.

Dubois, Laurent. *Avengers of the New World: The Story of the Haitian Revolution*. Cambridge, Mass.: Belknap Press, 2004.

Farmer, Paul. *The Uses of Haiti*. Revised edition. Monroe, Me.: Common Courage Press, 2003.

Galembo, Phyllis. *Vodou: Visions and Voices of Haiti*. Berkeley, Calif.: Ten Speed Press, 1998.

Glassman, Sallie Ann. *Vodou Visions*. New York: Villard Books, 2000.

Greene, Graham. *The Comedians*. New York: Penguin USA, 1991.

Heaven, Ross. *Vodou Shaman*. Rochester, Vt.: Inner Traditions, 2003.

Hurston, Zora Neale. *Tell My Horse: Voodoo and Life in Haiti and Jamaica*. New York: Harper Perennial, 1990. (Orig. pub. 1937.)

James, C. L. R. *The Black Jacobíns: Toussaint L'Ouverture and the San Domingo Revolution*. New York: Vintage, 1989.

Métraux, Alfred. *Voodoo in Haiti*. Hugo Charteris, trans. New York: Random House, 1989.

Nicholls, David. *From Dessalines to Duvalier: Race, Colour, and National Independence in Haiti*. New Brunswick, N.J.: Rutgers University Press, 1995.

Rigaud, Milo. *Secrets of Voodoo*. Robert B. Cross, trans. San Francisco: City Lights Books, 1985.

Schmidt, Hans. *The United States Occupation of Haiti 1915–1934*. New Brunswick, N.J.: Rutgers University Press, 1995.

Trouillot, Michel-Rolph. *Silencing the Past*. Boston: Beacon Press, 1997.

Turlington, Shannon. *The Complete Idiot's Guide to Voodoo*. New York: Alpha Books, 2001.

Wilcken, Lois. *The Drums of Vodou*. Tempe, Ariz.: White Cliffs Media Company, 1993.

Online Resources

The Internet resources dedicated to Vodou are a mixed bag. Innumerable sites offer Powerful Magic Voodoo Love Spells and the like. Other sites seek to "warn" you away from "sorcery and heathenism" or to "expose" Vodou as "devil worship." That being said, other sites contain a wealth of useful information and offer products that might not be available in your area.

The Art of Haiti: www.medalia.net

Haitian Art: www.haitianart.com

Two superb sources for Haitian art, offering works to fit just about every budget.

The Crossroads Vodou Products and Services: www.tearsofisis.com/vodou.htm

Services and supplies from Tamara Siuda (Mambo Kouwone Andezo Daginen), a Chicago-area mambo and a Kemetic (Egyptian) priestess of the house of Netjer Kemetic Orthodox Temple.

Haiti Action Committee: www.haitiaction.net

San Francisco Bay Area–based activists supporting Haiti's struggle for democracy.

The History of the Republic of Haiti: www.hartford-hwp.com/archives/43a/index.html

Fantastic resource for information about Haitian culture, religion, history, and economics. Highly recommended.

Houngan Gate sa Daginen: houngangatesa.tripod.com/vodou/index.html

Hector Salva (Houngan Gate sa Daginen) is a houngan living in southern New Jersey who offers seminars, wanga, kanzos, and other services.

Island of Salvation Botanica: www.feyvodou.com

New Orleans botanica run by Mambo Sallie Ann Glassman. It features her artwork along with other supplies.

Rev. Samantha Kaye: www.spellmaker.com

Rev. Samantha Kaye learned New Orleans Voodoo from her family. Later, she was initiated into Haitian Vodou in Jacmel. She also runs a very active mailing list that can be accessed at groups.yahoo.com/group/spellmaker.

Lucky Mojo Curio Company: www.luckymojo.com

Cat Yronwode, the proprietor, is one of the Internet's foremost experts on hoodoo and African American folk magic. Most of Lucky Mojo's products draw from Yronwode's hoodoo expertise, but she also stocks many items that are used in Haitian Vodou.

New Orleans Mistic: www.neworleansmistic.com

Located in the Big Easy, New Orleans Mistic is run by several hougans and mambos, and it has many herbs and supplies that cannot be found anywhere else online.

Sosyete du Marche: www.sosyetedumarche.com

Pat Scheu (Mambo Vye Zo Komande la Menfo Daginen), an artist and student of Wicca and Ceremonial Magic, leads this southern Pennsylvania house.

Temple of Yehwe: www.vodou.org

Connected to Le Peristyle de Mariani founded in 1974 in Mariani, Haiti, by Houngan Max-G. Beauvoir. This site includes much information about Caribbean herbology, as well as upcoming events and seminars, photos, and a discussion forum.

Tristatevodou: groups.yahoo.com/group/Tristatevodou

A mailing list run by my partner Kathy Latzoni and myself. Although the site is dedicated to the practice of Vodou in the NY/NJ/CT tristate area, all servants of God, Gineh, and the Lwa, as well as those who would like to learn more about the religion, are welcome.

Troupe Makandal: www.makandal.org

Haitian drum, dance, and performance troupe led by master drummer Frisner Augustin. The troupe offer CDs that provide an excellent introduction to the complexities of the chante lwa—and they are well worth seeing live if you get a chance.

Vodoun Culture: www.geocities.com/Athens/Delphi/5319/tableofcontents.htm

Densely packed with information, this page by Estelle Manuel, one of Max Beauvoir's children, contains material on vévés, rhythms, and langaj that is not available anywhere else online or in print. Maybe a bit intimidating for beginners, but well worth the effort.

Music

Rhythm, dance, and music are an integral part of praising the spirits in Vodou. Here are a few bands and compilations that will give you a taste of Vodou music.

Compilations

The following are some compilations of Haitian folk music and rhythms heard at Vodou ceremonies.

Angels in the Mirror: Vodou Music of Haiti (Ellipsis Arts, 1997)
Caribbean Revels: Haitian Rara & Dominican Gaga (Smithsonian Folkways, 1992)
Peasant Music from Haiti (Budamusique, 1997)
Rhythms of Rapture: Sacred Musics of Haitian Vodou (Smithsonian Folkways, 1995)
Rough Guide to the Music of Haiti (World Music Network, 2002)
Vodou: Ritual Possession of the Dead (Enterra, 1997)

Boukman Experyans

This band's blend of rock music with Haitian folk rhythms and Vodou lyrics has garnered them international attention. Some critics have compared their fiery brand of mysticism to Bob Marley's Rastafarian reggae. Below is a list of their albums.

Vodou Adjae (1991)
Kalfou Danjere (1992)
Liberte (Pran Pou Pran'l!) (1995)
Boukman Experyans—Live at Red Rocks (1998)
Revolisyon (1998)
Kanaval Rasin—Vodou Adja (2000)

Bonnie Devlin

Bonnie Devlin is a gifted teacher, an initiate, and one of the few female drummers in Haitian Vodou. She has released the following album.

Action of Grace: The Soul of Haitian Vodou (1999)

La Troupe Makandal

This Brooklyn combo, led by master drummer and Houngan Frisner Augustin, has been profiled in numerous publications. Their CDs, listed below, are available at their Web site: www.makandal.org.

Prepare (2004)
The Drums of Vodou CD (1992)
Erzili (1986)

RAM

One of the most famous Haitian "roots" bands, RAM combines Vodou drumming and Haitian folklore with electric guitars and excellent vocals. Bandleader Robert Morse is part owner of the legendary Olofsson Hotel, site of Graham Greene's *The Comedians*. Their albums are as follows.

Aibobo (1996)
Puritan Vodou (1997)
Kite Yo Pale (2001)
RAM: the Greatest Hits (2003)

Charities

If you are inspired by the lwa, and you find yourself feeling indebted to Haiti and its culture, here are some ways to pay that debt back. Even if you can't give a lot, every little bit helps. Each of these charitable organizations works in Haiti; many do good work around the world. Although some are run by religious organizations, they do not seek to convert those they assist.

ACCION International
56 Roland Street, Suite 300
Boston, MA 02129 USA
Phone: (617) 625-7080
Fax: (617) 625-7020
www.accion.org

Aid to Artisans—Haiti Project
331 Wethersfield Avenue
Hartford, CT 06114
Phone: (860) 947-3344
Fax: (860) 947-3350
www.ata-haiti.org

Alternative Chance/Chans Alternativ
c/o Lynx Air International
PO Box 407139
Ft. Lauderdale, FL 33340
Attn. Michelle Karshan,
Executive Director
Phone: +011 (509) 404-1546
Answering Service:
(212) 613-6033
www.alternativechance.org

American Friends Service Committee
1501 Cherry Street
Philadelphia, PA 19102
Phone: (215) 241-7000
Fax: (215) 241-7275
www.afsc.org

AmeriCares Foundation
88 Hamilton Avenue
Stamford, CT 06902
Phone: (800) 486-HELP
www.americares.org

AMHE—Association of Haitian Physicians Abroad/Association des Médecins Haitiens a l'Etranger
1166 Eastern Parkway
Brooklyn, NY 11213
Phone: (718) 245-1015
Fax: (718) 735-8015

Amnesty International
5 Penn Plaza—14th floor
New York, NY 10001
Phone: (212) 807-8400
Fax: (212) 463-9193
www.amnestyusa.org

CARE USA
151 Ellis Street
Atlanta, GA 30303
Phone: (404) 681-2552
Fax: (404) 589-2651
E-mail: info@care.org
www.careusa.org

Dwafanm
P.O. Box 23505
Brooklyn , NY 11202
Phone: (718) 230-4027
www.dwafanm.org

FINCA International.
1101 14th Street NW, 11th floor
Washington, DC 20005
Fax: (202) 682-1535
www.villagebanking.org/

Fonkoze USA
P.O. Box 53144
Washington, DC 20009
Phone: (202) 667-1277
Fax: (202) 667-1277
www.fonkoze.org

Friends of the Children of Haiti
Rue FOTCOH #1
Cyvadier, Haiti
Phone: +011 (509) 451-3358
www.fotcoh.org

Haitian Health Foundation
97 Sherman Street
Norwich, CT 06360
Phone: (860) 886-4357
Fax: (860) 859-9887
www.haitianhealthfoundation.org

Hôpital Albert Schweitzer
P.O. Box 81046
Pittsburgh, PA 15217
Phone: (412) 361-5200
Fax: (412) 361-5400
www.hashaiti.org

Light for All Corporation
3308 Stony Brook Drive
Jeffersontown, KY 40299
Phone: (502) 499-5624
www.itdg.net/lifco/index.htm

National Coalition for Haitian Rights
275 7th Avenue, 17th Floor
New York, NY 10001
Phone: (212) 337-0005
Fax: (212) 741-8749
www.nchr.org

Operation Green Leaves
P.O. Box 5254
Coral Gables, FL 33114
Phone: (305) 644-9000
Fax: (305) 642-8805
www.oglhaiti.com/

Unicef USA
333 East 38th Street
New York, NY 10016
Phone: (800) 4UNICEF
www.unicefusa.org

NOTES

Chapter 1

1. C. S. Lewis, *The Lion, The Witch and the Wardrobe* (New York: Collier Books, 1970), 76.
2. Jean-Jacques Rousseau. "A Dissertation On the Origin and Foundation of The Inequality of Mankind and is it Authorised by Natural Law?" (1754), Marxists.org, www.marxists.org/reference/subject/economics/rousseau/inequality/ch01.htm.

Chapter 2

1. Quoted in Noam Chomsky, "Democracy Enhancement Part II: The Case of Haiti." *Z Magazine*, July/August 1994. Z Magazine Online, www.zmag.org/zmag/articles/chomdemenh2.htm.
2. "The Lord's Prayer According to Francois (Papa Doc) Duvalier." Bob Corbett's Haiti Pages, www.webster.edu/~corbetre/haiti/history/duvaliers/lordsprayer.htm.

Chapter 3

1. Karen McCarthy Brown, *Mama Lola: A Vodou Priestess in Brooklyn* (Berkeley: University of California Press, 1991), 241.

Chapter 5

1. Lee Anderson, "Legends in Sand: The Evolution of Modern Navajo Sandpainting," Anderson's Americana Indian & Western Shows, www.americana.net/sandptest.html.
2. Sallie Ann Glassman, *Vodou Visions* (New York: Villard Books, 2000), 17.

3. Houngan Aboudja, "The Story of the Ason in Vodou," http://groups.yahoo.com/group/VodouSpirit/message/4776.
4. Quoted and translated by Joseph J. Williams, in *Vodous and Obeahs: Phases of West Indian Witchcraft* (New York: Dial Press, 1932). Available at The Internet Sacred Texts Archive at www.sacred-texts.com/afr/vao/vao05.htm.
5. Dave, "Idolatry! The Catholic Veneration of Icons and Relics," DeOmnisGloria.com, February 7, 2004, www.deoomnisgloria.com/archives/2004/02/idolatry_the_ca.html.
6. Phil Hine, "On the Magical Egregore: All About Egregores," available at Chaosmagic.com, www.chaosmagic.com/archives/chaosmagicktheory/on-the-magical-egregore.shtml. Posted July 27, 2004.

Chapter 6

1. Steve Mizrach, "Neurophysiological and Psychological Approaches to Spirit Possession in Haiti," www.fiu.edu/~mizrachs/spiritpos.html.
2. Brown, *Mama Lola,* 198–201.

Chapter 7

1. Leslie G. Desmangles, *The Faces of the Gods: Vodou and Roman Catholicism in Haiti* (Chapel Hill: University of North Carolina Press, 1992), 142.

Chapter 8

1. Rachael Ndi, "The Material Culture of Twins in Western Africa," Cameroonian Twin Studies, www2.sfu.ca/archaeology/museum/ndi/mystudy.html.

Chapter 9

1. "Maya Deren," www.picpal.com/maya.html.
2. "Ayizan Velekete," submitted by Houngan Max Beauvoir on www.haitianinternet.com/resources.php/10.
3. Alfred Métraux, *Voodoo in Haiti*, Hugo Charteris, trans. (New York: Random House, 1989), 362.

Chapter 11

1. Maya Deren, *Divine Horsemen: The Living Gods of Haiti* (New York: McPherson & Company, 1985), 122–30.

2. William Shakespeare, *A Midsummer Night's Dream,* 2.1, The Complete Works of William Shakespeare on the Web, www.tech.mit.edu/Shakespeare/midsummer/midsummer.2.1.html.
3. Jonathan Zilberg, "Shona Sculpture and Shona Culture: the Water Spirit," available at Leonardo/OLATS—Observetaire Leonardo des artes et des technosciences, www.olats.org/africa/projets/gpEau/genie/contrib/contrib_zilberg.shtml.

Chapter 12

1. Desmangles, *Faces of the Gods,* 143–44.
2. Brown, *Mama Lola,* 247.

Chapter 13

1. Métraux, *Voodoo in Haiti,* 321.
2. "Saint Philomena, Powerful with God as revealed to Mother Mary Louisa of Jesus," available at Saint Philomena Patroness of the Children of Mary, www.philomena.org/ULRA/philomena2.html.
3. "St. Clare," Catholic Online, www.catholic.org/saints/saint.php?saint_id=215.

Chapter 14

1. Deren, *Divine Horsemen,* 280–81.
2. Houngan Aboudja, "Alaso Kouzen Zaka!—All About Azaka Mede," http://groups.yahoo.com/group/VodouSpirit/message/5323.

Chapter 15

1. Center for Electronic Resources in African Studies, University of Iowa, "Iron: Master of Them All," http://sdrc.lib.uiowa.edu/ceras/iron/.
2. "Met Special Topics: The Age of Iron," www.metmuseum.org/toah/hd/iron/hd_iron.htm.
3. Dion Fortune, *The Mystical Qabalah* (York Beach, Maine: Red Wheel/Weiser, 2000), 164–69.

Chapter 17

1. Brown, *Mama Lola,* 232.

Chapter 20

1. "Haiti: For the Visitors to the St. Louis World's Fair," www.webster.edu/~corbetre/haiti/misctopic/texts/stlouis.htm.

Chapter 21

1. Joan Dayan. *Haiti, History, and Gods* (Berkeley: University of California Press, 1998), 247–248.
2. M. J. Herskovits, *The Myth of the Negro Past* (Boston: Beacon Press, 1941), 36.

Chapter 23

1. Deren, *Divine Horsemen*, 108.
2. Ibid., 107.

Chapter 25

1. Luisa Teish, *Jambalaya: The Natural Woman's Book of Personal Charms and Practical Rituals* (San Francisco: HarperSanFrancisco, 1988), 88.

Chapter 26

1. Djalòki Ntjitjagagi Jean Luc Dessables, "Western Debt: The Invisible External Debt of the Western World," Haiti Travels, www.haititravels.org/westerndebt.htm.

Chapter 28

1. Joel James, Jose Millet, and Alexis Alarcon, *El Vodu En Cuba* (Santiago de Cuba, Cuba: Editorial Oriente, 1998), 123–26.

Chapter 30

1. Edeline St.-Amand, personal communication with the author, February 15, 2003.

GLOSSARY

action de grace: Thanksgiving for favors performed by lwa.

affranchis: In *St.-Domingue*, free people of mixed race. (See also *gens de coleur.*)

Agwe, Met Agwe: Master of the sea; king of the ocean.

Aristide, Jean-Bertrand (1953–): Former Salesian priest, president of Haiti 1994–1996, 2001–2004.

asogwe, houngan asogwe, mambo asogwe: The highest rank in Haitian Vodou.

asson: A sacred rattle wielded by *houngans* and *mambos*.

Ayida Wedo: Wife of *Damballah*, symbolized by the rainbow.

Ayizan: Wife of *Loko*, connected to the marketplace and the *kanzo* (initiation) ceremony.

badji: The room in which candidates are secluded during the *kanzo* ceremony. (Also called *djevo.*)

baka: An evil spirit.

Bakalou Baka: A fierce, "hot" spirit; best approached with caution, or not approached at all.

banda: A drum beat.

Bawons: From the French "Barons"; stern, menacing rulers over the cemetery. Some well-known Bawons include Bawon Kriminel, Bawon La Kwa (Baron of the Cross), and Bawon Samedi.

bokor: A sorcerer.

Bondye: God (from the French *Bon Dieu*).

Bossou: Strong bull spirits with roots in the Daome (Old Dahomey) region of western Africa in what is present day Benin. Some Bossous include Bossou Towo, Bossou Twa Kon (Bossou Trois-Connes or Three-Horns), Djobolo Bossou, and Kadja Bossou.

bougies: Rolled papers dipped in wax, burned when saluting the *Petwo* and *Ghede lwa*.

Boukman, Dutty (17??–1791): Led the *Bwa Kayman* ceremony that incited the Haitian Revolution.

boula: A ceremonial drum.

Boyer, Jean Pierre (1776–1850): President of Haiti 1822–1843.

Brigitte, Maman Brigitte: The queen of the cemetery.

Bwa Kayman: Literally "Alligator Forest"; site of the ceremony that launched the Haitian Revolution (1791–1804).

Carrefour: See *Kalfou*.

chaka: A bean, cornmeal, and tripe stew favored by *Zaka*.

chante lwa: Songs for the *lwa*.

chimés: Literally "monsters"; used to refer to pro-Aristide militias.

Christophe, Henri (1767–1820): President of Haiti 1807–1811, Emperor of Haiti 1811–1820.

chwal: A possessed person, from the French *cheval* (horse).

Damballah, Damballah Wedo: The great white serpent who lies between heaven and earth.

dechoukaj: Literally, "uprooting"; the riots that took place after Baby Doc Duvalier was ousted from power in 1986.

demambwe: A sacred place to which candidates for the *asogwe* initiation are taken.

Deren, Maya (1917–1961): Dancer and avant-garde filmmaker, author of *Divine Horsemen: the Living Gods of Haiti*.

desounin: Also known as "retire nan mo dlo" or "drawing out of the water"; a ceremony performed for deceased members of a *société*.

Dessalines, Jean-Jacques (1758–1806): Hero of the Haitian Revolution, Emperor of Haiti 1804–1806.

Djabs: "Wild spirits"; individual spirits not recognized in the regleman but honored by individuals or families.

djevo: The room in which candidates are secluded during the *kanzo* ceremony. (Also called *badji.*)

dwapo: Decorated and sequined flags used in Vodou ceremonies.

Djouba nachon: Agricultural spirits. (See also *Zaka.*)

Dunham, Katherine (1909–2006): Dancer, activist, mambo, author of *Island Possessed.*

Duvalier, François "Papa Doc" (1907–1971): President of Haiti 1957–1971.

Duvalier, Jean-Claude "Baby Doc" (1951–): President of Haiti 1971–1986.

Ezili Danto, Danto: Stuttering, scar-faced warrior woman who carries a dagger.

Ezili Freda, Freda: Light-skinned spirit of love, luxury, and beauty.

fet: A Vodou ceremony, from the French *féte* (festival, party).

garde: A ceremony performed to protect against illness, injury, bad luck, and malevolent enemies.

gens de coleur: Free persons of color; a term used for mulattos in *St.-Domingue.*

Ghede: Foul-mouthed jesters from beyond the grave. Along with the *Bawons* and *Brigittes*, they are saluted as the "Ghede *nachon.*"

Gineh: Ancestral Africa.

govis: Clay pots.

Gran Bwa: Master of the forest; a *Petwo* spirit.

Gran Ezili: Grandmother of *Ezili Freda.*

houngan: A priest of Haitian Vodou.

houngenikon: A song leader.

hounsi kanzo: The first degree of Vodou initiation.

Ibo nachon: Spirits originally honored by the Ibo (also known as Igbo) people of Nigeria. Gran Ibo and Ibo Lele are two of the more well-known Ibo.

iluminasyon: A ceremony used to seek guidance in a dream.

Jan Danto, Ti-Jan Danto: Son of *Ezili Danto* (and some say her lover).

Jan Petwo: Husband of *Ezili Danto.*

Jan Zombi: Powerful spirit served by members of the *sanpwel* and other secret societies.

Kalfou, Met Kalfou: Master of the crossroads, powerful *Petwo* spirit.

kanzo: The ceremony of initiation as a *hounsi kanzo, mambo/houngan sipwen* or *houngan/mambo asogwe.*

Klemezin: A young beautiful spirit represented by images of the Catholic St. Clare.

kleren: An alcoholic drink made from sugarcane.

kolyes: Necklaces worn by candidates during their initiation and for forty-one days afterward.

kouche tambour: A ceremony of "putting the drums to bed."

Kouzenn: See *Zaka.*

Kouzenne: Wife of *Zaka.*

La Sirene: Mermaid queen of the ocean; wife of *Agwe.*

langaj: Ceremonial language that preserves various African words and expressions.

laplas: Guardian of the *peristyle.*

lave tet: Literally "head washing"; a ceremony that can cleanse negativity and serve as an introduction to a *société.*

Legba, Papa Legba: The "old man at the crossroads" who opens the door so the other spirits can enter.

Linglessou Basin-Sang (Linglessou Bucket-of-Blood): Fierce spirit who often eats glass when he takes possession of a *chwal.*

Loko, Papa Loko: Ruler over the *kanzo* ceremony.

L'Overture, Toussaint (c.1743–1803): Leader of the Haitian Revolution, considered one of the fathers of the Haitian nation.

lwa: The spirits of Haitian Vodou.

Makandal (d. 1758): One-armed slave who led a bloody slave rebellion in St. Domingue from 1752–1758.

makoute: A sack. (See also *Tonton Macoutes.*)

maman: A type of ceremonial drum.

mambo: A female priestess of Haitian Vodou.

Marassa: Sacred twins; child spirits served with candy and sweet things.

maryaj lwa: A ceremony by which a Vodouisant is married to one or more spirits.

met tet: The *lwa* who is "master of the head" or who "owns the head" of an initiatory candidate.

mort: A malevolent dead spirit.

moushwa: A head scarf, from the French "mouchoir."

nachons: The "nations" to which *lwa* belong. For example, Legba and Damballah are part of the *Rada* nachon, while Ezili Danto is part of the *Petwo* nachon.

Nago nachon: Spirits originally served by the Yoruba peoples of West Africa. (See also *Ogou.*)

ogan: A piece of metal struck with a stick during ceremonies.

Ogou, Papa Ogou, Ogun: Spirits of war and iron; some of the most well known include Ogou Badagri, Ogou Balindjo, and Ogou Ferraille. They are members of the *Nago nachon.*

peristyle: A Vodou temple. (Also called a "houmfour" or "hounfo.")

Petwo nachon: Fierce but protective spirits served with pepper, gunpowder, and whip cracks.

Pétion, Alexandre (1770–1818): Mulatto leader of the Haitian Revolution, leader of the Southern Republic of Haiti 1806–1818.

plasaj: Common-law marriage.

poteau-mitan: A ceremonial pole in the center of a *peristyle;* seen as the passageway between Heaven and Earth.

priye Gineh: A lengthy prayer that combines salutations to the *lwa* and Catholic saints and which opens a *fet.*

pwens: Magical objects or "points" that are believed to concentrate spiritual energy.

Rada nachon: The name Rada comes from "Arara," a slave port in modern-day Benin. The Rada nachon consists of popular spirits like *Legba, Damballah,* and *Ezili Freda.* Rada *lwa* are generally considered "cooler" and more benevolent than the hot-tempered Petwo *lwa.*

reglamen: The order in which *lwa* are saluted.

reine dwapo: Flag bearers.

Sam, Guillaume (18??–1915): President of Haiti March 4–July 27, 1915. His assassination was the pretext for the American invasion and occupation of Haiti (1915–1934).

segon: A type of ceremonial drum.

sevis lwa: Service to the *lwa*. (Also called "sevis Gineh"—service to *Gineh,* or ancestral Africa).

Simbi: Mysterious snakelike spirits from the Kongo region of Africa. Among the most commonly served are Simbi Andezo and Simbi Makaya.

sipwen, houngan sipwen, mambo sipwen: The second grade of Vodou initiation.

société: A society of Vodouisants; typically led by a *houngan* and *mambo*.

St. Domingue: The French colony that became the Republic of Haiti.

tambouye: A drummer.

ti bon ange: "Little good angel" part of the human soul.

Tonton Macoutes: The pro-Duvalier militia responsible for many atrocities during the Papa Doc and Baby Doc years.

vévé: A ceremonial drawing used to symbolize and to call upon a *lwa*.

vire: A salute that consists of turning three times.

Vodouisants: People who practice Vodou. (Also known as "serviteurs lwa"—servants of the *lwa*.)

wanga: The act of performing magic ("doing wanga"), or a specific magical operation.

yanvalou: A drum beat, also a dance.

Zaka: Rough-hewn hard-working peasant spirit.

zepol: A drum beat.

INDEX

BOOKS OF RELATED INTEREST

The New Orleans Voodoo Handbook
by Kenaz Filan

Vodou Money Magic
The Way to Prosperity through the Blessings of the Lwa
by Kenaz Filan

Vodou Love Magic
A Practical Guide to Love, Sex, and Relationships
by Kenaz Filan

Drawing Down the Spirits
The Traditions and Techniques of Spirit Possession
by Kenaz Filan and Raven Kaldera

Vodou Shaman
The Haitian Way of Healing and Power
by Ross Heaven

Diloggún Tales of the Natural World
How the Moon Fooled the Sun and Other Santería Stories
by Ócha'ni Lele

Teachings of the Santería Gods
The Spirit of the Odu
by Ócha'ni Lele

The Diloggún
The Orishas, Proverbs, Sacrifices,
and Prohibitions of Cuban Santería
by Ócha'ni Lele

Inner Traditions • Bear & Company
P.O. Box 388
Rochester, VT 05767
1-800-246-8648
www.InnerTraditions.com

Or contact your local bookseller